Critical Muslim

Muslim Atlantic

Editor: Ziauddin Sardar

Deputy Editors: Samia Rahman, C Scott Jordan

Senior Editors: Aamer Hussein, Hassan Mahamdallie, Ehsan Masood

Publisher: Michael Dwyer

Managing Editor (Hurst Publishers): Daisy Leitch

Cover Design: Rob Pinney based on an original design by Fatima Jamadar

Associate Editors: Tahir Abbas, Alev Adil, Merryl Wyn Davies, Abdelwahab El-Affendi, Naomi Foyle, Marilyn Hacker, Nader Hashemi, Jeremy Henzell-Thomas, Leyla Jagiella, Vinay Lal, Iftikhar Malik, Shanon Shah, Boyd Tonkin

International Advisory Board: Karen Armstrong, Christopher de Bellaigue, William Dalrymple, Syed Nomanul Haq, Anwar Ibrahim, Robert Irwin, Bruce Lawrence, Ebrahim Moosa, Ashis Nandy, Ruth Padel, Bhikhu Parekh, Barnaby Rogerson, Malise Ruthven

Critical Muslim is published quarterly by C. Hurst & Co. (Publishers) Ltd. on behalf of and in conjunction with Critical Muslim Ltd. and the Muslim Institute, London.

All editorial correspondence to Muslim Institute, CAN Mezzanine, 49–51 East Road, London N1 6AH, United Kingdom.
E-mail: editorial@criticalmuslim.com

The editors do not necessarily agree with the opinions expressed by the contributors. We reserve the right to make such editorial changes as may be necessary to make submissions to *Critical Muslim* suitable for publication.

© Copyright 2020 *Critical Muslim* and the individual contributors.

All rights reserved.

C. Hurst & Co (Publishers) Ltd., 41 Great Russell Street, London WC1B 3PL

ISBN: 978-1-78738-333-3 ISSN: 2048-8475

To subscribe or place an order by credit/debit card or cheque (pounds sterling only) please contact Kathleen May at the Hurst address above or e-mail kathleen@hurstpub.co.uk

Tel: 020 7255 2201

A one-year subscription, inclusive of postage (four issues), costs £50 (UK), £65 (Europe) and £75 (rest of the world), this includes full access to the *Critical Muslim* series and archive online. Digital only subscription is £3.30 per month.

The right of Ziauddin Sardar and the Contributors to be identified as the authors of this publication is asserted by them in accordance with the Copyright, Designs and Patents Act, 1988.

A Cataloguing-in-Publication data record for this book is available from the British Library

IIIT BOOKS-IN-BRIEF

Concise Summaries of Key IIIT Publications

The IIIT Books-in-Brief Series is a collection of the Institute's key publications produced as short, easy-to-read, time-saving editions, to act as companion synopses to the original.

Books-in-Brief Boxed Set Contains 24 of IIIT's recent and most popular publications as condensed book summaries.

ISBN 978-1-56564-993-4

Contact:
Marketing Manager IIIT (USA)
500 Grove Street, Herndon,
VA 20170-4735, USA
Tel: 703 471 1133 ext. 108
• E-mail: sales@iiit.org
• Website: www.iiit.org

Critical Muslim

Subscribe to Critical Muslim

Now in its ninth year in print, *Critical Muslim* is also available online. Users can access the site for just £3.30 per month – or for those with a print subscription it is included as part of the package. In return, you'll get access to everything in the series (including our entire archive), and a clean, accessible reading experience for desktop computers and handheld devices — entirely free of advertising.

Full subscription

The print edition of *Critical Muslim* is published quarterly in January, April, July and October. As a subscriber to the print edition, you'll receive new issues directly to your door, as well as full access to our digital archive.

United Kingdom £50/year
Europe £65/year
Rest of the World £75/year

Digital Only

Immediate online access to *Critical Muslim*

Browse the full *Critical Muslim* archive

Cancel any time

£3.30 per month

www.criticalmuslim.io

CM35

SUMMER 2020

CONTENTS

MUSLIM ATLANTIC

'American Griot' in performance

MUSLIM ATLANTIC

INTRODUCTION:
WHAT IS THE MUSLIM ATLANTIC?

Daniel Nilsson DeHanas and Peter Mandaville

As we tell stories about Muslims today, what kinds of worlds do these Muslims inhabit? When we speak or write about contemporary Islam, which geographies serve as the backdrop? The Atlantic Ocean region rarely comes to mind as a space of contemporary Muslim life. Other parts of the world have far more obvious claims to Muslim ideas and culture. Islam first emerged in Arabia and spread quickly to the Levant and the Maghreb. With Arabic being the language of the Qur'an, ethnically Arab societies have been deeply intertwined with Islam for its entire lifespan. This is to say nothing of the Islamicate richness of Persian, Turkic, or West African civilisations. And, of course, a broad world region closely associated with Islam is South and Southeast Asia, where Indonesia, Malaysia, Pakistan, Bangladesh, and India have some of the largest Muslim populations in the world. This final set of countries might give us reason to turn our focus to the Indian Ocean, rather than the Atlantic.

Yet the Atlantic holds within it a vast range of stories of Muslim interchange. Since the era of British colonialism, including the forced migration of the transatlantic slave trade, Muslim people, ideas, and cultures have moved and intermingled across an Atlantic space that includes Britain, America, the Caribbean, and West Africa. They continue to do so today. As Zahrah Nesbitt-Ahmed articulates in the story of her quest to learn more about the lived experiences of her Nigerian paternal grandfather and West Indian maternal grandfather, many of their narratives remain largely untold, or even unknown.

In a deliberate nod and with great indebtedness to the work of the British social theorist Paul Gilroy, we call this world region of interchange the 'Muslim Atlantic'. Gilroy's book *The Black Atlantic: Modernity and Double Consciousness* was first published in 1993. It argued that there is a kind of black culture that is not merely the culture of any single nation like the United States, Britain, or Jamaica, but one that instead exists at the confluence of all of these. Gilroy understood this 'Black Atlantic' culture as being forged through a shared history of collective suffering in the middle passage, when enslaved blacks were transported as cargo from West Africa to Britain and then to the Caribbean or the Americas. It was on the backs of these enslaved people that transatlantic capitalism was built and that modernity itself took shape. Black creative expression through the arts including music (such as blues, jazz, and eventually hip hop) and writing became what Gilroy has called a 'counterculture of modernity'.

The 'Muslim Atlantic', as we understand it, is a space that overlaps with and is parallel to the Black Atlantic. Perhaps a third of the Black Africans trafficked across the Atlantic were Muslims, taken from places that include today's Senegal, Mali, the Gambia, and Ghana. Their West Africa was a place of great intellectual and economic achievements: The seat of Islamic learning at Timbuktu was among the world's first universities; the fourteenth-century Muslim emperor Mansa Musa was the single richest person who has ever lived. These forcibly transported Muslims brought with them a fusion of African and Islamic cultures that combined with new influences upon reaching the western shores of the Atlantic.

A good example of such intermingling of cultures was the eighteenth-century griot, or storyteller musician, who would sing tales in an Arabic maqam-style melody and on African stringed instruments that became the guitar and banjo. This history is bought alive in the excerpt from Reginald Edmund and Ronnie Malley's play *American Griot*. Told through the lens of the griot Mamadou, we are taken on a musical journey to the crossroads of Africa and America revealing the shared Atlantic history of Islam and the blues. Seen in this historic perspective, the Muslim Atlantic story is not separate from the Black Atlantic story but instead opens our eyes to its largely ignored Islamic and Muslim dimensions.

Yet there are other sides to the Muslim Atlantic story, involving new kinds of collective suffering that have also in turn generated creative responses. As Tahir Abbas explains, upon entering the twenty-first century, Muslims in the Atlantic region were being subjected to increasingly invasive security measures. The terrorist attacks on 11 September 2001 led to airport security measures affecting anyone with a 'Muslim' name, 'Islamic' clothing, or perceived Arab features, making 'flying while Muslim' a perpetually anxious experience. The American and British-led 'War on Terror' involved military incursions abroad while disciplining Muslims at home, including through Countering Violent Extremism (CVE) in the US and the closely associated Prevent in the UK. The impact of securitisation on the psyche of Muslims on both sides of the water, Shirin Khan recounts, has been profound. Perhaps the most vivid symbol of the securitised era was the orange jumpsuit, worn by hundreds of detainees in Guantánamo Bay, Cuba, many of them imprisoned indefinitely without trial or subjected to torture under extraordinary rendition.

The Muslim Atlantic story unfolds across the Atlantic map of the twenty-first century. It includes the ways that Muslims have been subject to disproportionate surveillance and security measures, setting them apart as cultural pariahs and fostering widespread anti-Muslim sentiment. Indeed, in our current times the Anglosphere Atlantic powers of Britain and the United States seem to be in the grip of an especially anti-Muslim phase. From Donald Trump's 2016 call for a 'total and complete shutdown on Muslims entering the United States' to British Prime Minister Boris Johnson's comments about burqa-wearing women resembling 'letterboxes' and 'bank robbers' — both reflections of surging grassroots movements of white nationalism and nativist populism in their respective societies — these are politically fraught times for millions of Muslims across the Atlantic space. It is unclear whether the Covid-19 pandemic will blunt the momentum of anti-Muslim politics as other issues take priority, or if political leaders will simply renew their targeting of Muslims with an even more sophisticated arsenal of control measures and surveillance technologies.

Those within what we have termed the Muslim Atlantic have responded creatively to new challenges and circumstances. The increasing globalisation of markets, migration, and media has enabled a transnational flowering of Islamic thought and cultural production. These developments have only accelerated with the interweaving of relationships and ideas on social media. Today there are various Muslim scholars, politicians, actors, writers, stand-up comedians, fashion influencers, and musicians who have built wide transatlantic followings. Aina Khan's reportage illustrates that the contemporary Muslim Atlantic is as much about heavy-hitting hip hop artists like Miss Undastood or Poetic Pilgrimage, as it is about formidable intellectuals like Amina Wadud or Ebrahim Moosa.

The Muslim Atlantic is also about Muslims in the ordinary moments of their daily lives. Some have moved across the Atlantic for education or work, or to gain greater freedom. Others have transatlantic personal connections or family histories. And there are many others with less direct experience across borders who nonetheless participate in the Muslim Atlantic on a regular basis. A young British Muslim woman may read online about the achievements of Somali-American congresswoman Ilhan Omar or about London-born Hollywood star Riz Ahmed and his 'Riz test' of Islamophobia. Discussing these on social media with like-minded Muslims, she will soon discover that she has been building networks that span the Atlantic.

While we have been describing the English-speaking Muslim Atlantic, Muslim networks and culture have also crisscrossed the Atlantic in other languages over time. These include French, Spanish, and Portuguese, each with their own (post)colonial histories and different ways of inflecting the Muslim Atlantic world. Hisham Aidi's book *Rebel Music*, for example, explores how the flows and disjunctures of post-9/11 global 'War on Terror' policies have revitalised Muslim consciousness in Afro-Brazilian communities, and have conjured in the work of French rappers new historical resonances between Maghrebi and African-American experience. The scholar Jason Idriss Sparkes provides perhaps the most geographically ambitious historical account of the Muslim Atlantic, locating the contours of an organised and energetic project of decolonial counter-modernity in the traditionalist Sufi milieu of the 'Western Islamicate' of Morocco and West Africa. His recently completed PhD dissertation 'Tradition as Flow: Decolonial Currents in the Muslim Atlantic' argues that the relevance of 1492 as a watershed date in the birth of modernity is not limited to Iberian voyages of exploration to a supposed 'New World' but also necessarily includes the experiences and responses of Muslims expelled from Spain.

Yet even if we simply consider the Anglophone Muslim Atlantic, we will be able to gain a new geographical lens for viewing the world. As we peer through this lens, we will begin to see things differently in at least three ways.

First, the Muslim Atlantic lens breaks us out of our default impulse to think of Muslims in terms of one nation or another. News stories and academic studies alike tend to be framed within national borders, describing how Canadian or American Muslims did this, or French or Algerian Muslims did that. The reality of life is much different. For a great many Muslims, life is transnational in some way or another, whether this means watching Bengali satellite TV, chatting with aunties in Lagos by WhatsApp, or planning travel to Mecca and Medina for *hajj*. The idea of the Muslim Atlantic draws attention to an often neglected set of transnational conversations and underlying histories between Muslims in the US, the UK, Africa, the Caribbean, and the wider Atlantic. This transnational dimension can be as mundane as comparing American and British Muslim fashion bloggers on Instagram, or as weighty as tracing one's Muslim family roots back to enslavement from West Africa.

Paul Gilroy's work emphasises how the Atlantic is neither American, nor British, nor Caribbean, nor African but something built from and existing in the midst of all of these. In the same way, looking through a Muslim Atlantic lens places our focus on the spaces in between. As we see how Muslims draw from — and also question and critique — various conversations and cultural influences from across the Atlantic, we become more aware of the dynamic, hybrid, and constantly re-contextualised nature of contemporary Islam.

Second, looking through a Muslim Atlantic lens reveals black Muslim experience as normative. In the US and the UK, black Muslims have frequently found themselves subject to disrespect by other Muslims. There are different reasons for this in each place: African American Muslims are often seen as associated with the 'heretical' Nation of Islam, while Black British Muslims are more often simply forgotten or ignored. In both countries, for example, it is rare for the visual 'face' of Muslims in a news story or a campaign to be a black Muslim — or at least a black Muslim with political agency. Such problems are deep-seated and can be painful, because they involve the erasure of the historical and contemporary contributions of black Muslims. The Muslim Atlantic narrative provides means for bringing black Muslims back into the foreground of the stories we tell.

If for the moment we focus on African American Muslims, we can begin to see the richness of taking on a Muslim Atlantic perspective. Rasul Miller's essay is an insight into how Black American Islam was reshaped in the crucible of an awakening Pan-African worldview — what Patrick Bowen terms in his 2017 book of the same title an 'African-American Islamic Renaissance' — whose defining impulse involved a conscious (re) entanglement of the black American experience of racial injustice with similar struggles in Africa. The emerging formations of a distinctly black Atlantic Muslimness were central to this movement, and some of its intellectual icons, such as Edward Wilmot Blyden, saw Islam as integral to the making of Pan-African consciousness. Early expressions of organised black American Islam such as the Moorish Science Temple of America founded by Noble Drew Ali in 1913 drew inspiration from the transatlantic black nationalist ideals of Marcus Garvey, and these same currents of thought later went on to inform the creation of the Nation of Islam. The fact that much of twentieth century scholarship on Islam in America — and, until recently, the attitudes of many immigrant Muslims in the United States — viewed black American Muslim culture as an inauthentic aberration reflects both the hegemony of the Middle East and Asia as sources of purported religious orthodoxy and the persistence of pervasive racism within American Muslim communities well into the twenty-first century. Similarly, many discussions of the US Countering Violent Extremism program still fail to appreciate how closely it resembles the security state apparatus of COINTELPRO (including techniques of surveillance and counterinsurgency) that were used to police the Nation of Islam and Black Panthers in the 1960s. Thus, an exploration of the Muslim Atlantic serves to re-centre African-American Muslims and to show that if there is such a thing as an indigenous tradition of Islam in the United States, then it lies in the black American experience.

The killing of George Floyd by Minneapolis police in May 2020 has called us to urgently recognise the importance of black Muslim experiences along with those of other black people. Floyd's murder and the global Black Lives Matter protests that it catalysed have powerfully exposed decades of police brutality against black bodies which had been plastered over and whitewashed. In Bristol, UK, Black Lives Matter protesters gained international attention when they toppled the statue of slaveholder Edward Colston, hurling it into the river. As black Muslim performance artist Tanya Muneera Williams explains in her narrative about growing up in Bristol, the city's street names, buildings, and adornments are brimming with associations to its past as a major slave trade port. Removing the statue of a slaveholder is a poignant symbolic act which echoes across the Muslim Atlantic.

There is perhaps no figure who embodies the black Muslim Atlantic more than El-Hajj Malik El-Shabazz, popularly known as Malcolm X. This is not only because of his historical role in building bridges between struggles against racist violence in the United States and global emancipatory activism, but also because his legacy continues to inspire and animate alternative political imaginaries today. Malcolm is also singularly important in that he helps us to understand how and where the Muslim Atlantic intersects with what Sohail Daulatzai evocatively terms the 'Muslim International'. Insofar as it is composed of flows of peoples, histories, and ideas whose journeys trace back to Africa, the Middle East, and South Asia, what we are calling the Muslim Atlantic implicates a global geography that reaches far beyond the shores of Europe and America. What Malcolm X enables is a route into a Muslim International that is at once centered in the specificity of the black Atlantic fight for emancipation and equality while simultaneously engaging with liberation struggles around the globe. It stands in stark contrast to more conventional modalities of political Islam, if these are understood as the authoritative (often verging on authoritarian) imposition of religious norms in the political domain. The Muslim Atlantic ethos of Malcolm X, therefore, is a form of Muslim politics that finds in Islam first and foremost a radical injunction to prioritise global and universal understandings of social justice. His agenda was clearly relevant to his contemporaries in British Muslim communities, with Malcolm visiting the Birmingham Mosque in England just weeks before he was killed in 1965.

There is yet another way that the Muslim Atlantic lens changes our view: it makes us aware of the centrality of Muslim contributions to what it means to be modern. The Muslim Atlantic story is a narrative of common suffering faced by Muslims across the Atlantic, from those in centuries past who were kidnapped and forced into chattel slavery, to those in recent decades who have been securitised, surveilled, or subject to anti-Muslim hatred. As historian AbdoolKarim Vakil once explained in a keynote address to the annual general meeting of the Muslim Council of Britain, nearly all of the legal and political rights that we have come to expect on the shores of the Atlantic had to be hard won through the courageous resistance of minorities, including blacks and Muslims alongside women's movements, working class movements, and others. The contemporary Muslim Atlantic has become a zone of struggle against securitisation, Islamophobia, xenophobia, populism, and white supremacism. It is through such struggles that new generations of activists rise up and that new legal and political achievements are made.

In our late modern times, we find that Muslims are at the sharp edge of the most fear-laden and hostile of political pressures. Muslims therefore have a central part to play in recovering from these troubled times, forging new values, and eventually re-humanising our societies. When that day comes, today's forsaken griots of the Muslim Atlantic – the non-violent protesters donning orange jumpsuits, the intellectuals risking censure, and the hip hop Muslimahs speaking their minds – will have led the way by producing a new counterculture of modernity.

REALISING A MUSLIM ATLANTIC

Aisha Khan

In his seminal book, *The Black Atlantic*, Paul Gilroy argued that models of cultural nationalism that are typically associated with ideas about individualised nation-states and national belonging present notions of difference that are immutable and cohesive, and which thus segregate people into mutually exclusive groups. Accompanying ideas about exclusivity, immutability, ethnocultural purity, and 'cultural insiderism', the rhetorical strategy that defines identities as distinguished by absolute rather than relative differences, mask or negate the forms of interaction in the Atlantic world that produce *inter*cultural and *trans*national formations and synergies. The misdirection of nationalist paradigms that promote exclusivity, immutability, and purity, and which become received, if misguided wisdom discourage alternative ways of understanding identity formation—notably the social construction of race and ethnicity—as produced through what Gilroy describes as 'inescapable hybridity and intermixture of ideas'. To eschew cultural insiderism and its associated boundaries opens spaces for what Gilroy calls an 'outernationalist' revisionist approach. The contribution of this approach is no less than the revelation of what Gilroy defines as, 'hemispheric if not global' forms of consciousness, such as pan-Africanism and Black Power. This approach constitutes a crucial challenge to assertions of uniformity and absolute, unqualified alterity, perspectives that divide nations and a nation's peoples.

Such an approach also drives Gilroy's critique of the concept of modernity as it is deployed in nationalist historiographies and representations of nationality. He offers a counterhegemonic configuration of Caribbean (Black Atlantic) modernity that probes political dialogues about power, agency, and autonomy. For Gilroy, the idea of modernity is a particular kind of conceptual space, one that contains the drawback of serving as a refuge for black political culture when it is 'locked in a defensive posture' against the injustices of white supremacy. When dedicated to origins, genealogical myths, and 'ornate conceptions of African antiquity', black consciousness is ever on the defensive, Gilroy argues, a posture that reiterates that 'tradition' and 'modernity' are polar opposites, the former inhabited by blacks and the latter by whites. Tradition and modernity are thus separate barometers of value, measuring degrees of development, progress, and aspiration. In this context, an emphasis on tradition erases the Caribbean's history of slave plantations; when tradition serves as an alternative to modernity, representing, for example, a refuge against the assaults of modernity's racism, the debilitating aspects of the colonial past is sidestepped. In this usage the concept of tradition is ahistorical, Gilroy argues, denying slavery's complexity and significance except as 'the site of black victimage', something to be escaped. Such a position denies the central role that plantation-based slavery played in modernity, as well as the hybridity and flux that produce intercultural and transnational formations and synergies. Instead, and quite mistakenly, regressive binary oppositions like 'tradition' vs 'modernity', 'purity' vs 'impurity', and 'us' vs 'them' are sustained.

   Like Gilroy's vision of the Black Atlantic, the Muslim Atlantic is necessarily and by definition a phenomenon of diaspora. Both 'Atlantics' share empirical realities of passage and intermixture that are emblematic of this region's historical experience and cultural production. As a conceptual framework, the Black Atlantic tells, or retells, a particular story, one born out of ideologies about inherent otherness defined by the boundaries of nation. The Muslim Atlantic has no single author, nor is it presently a cohesive conceptual framework. Yet there are, as it were, the raw materials of history and some themes in this history, themes that intersect with those of the Black Atlantic and which may help to realise the Muslim Atlantic as a model of reality that we use implicitly to make sense of the existing external world, and a model for reality that is explicitly designed to imagine and organise that world (here I borrow from Clifford Geertz 1973). I am employing 'realise' in these two senses: to comprehend something and to achieve something. The remainder of my discussion will explore how the Muslim Atlantic might be realised, thinking in terms of such Black Atlantic foundational themes as nation, modernity, hybridity, race, sea passages, and sugar plantation heritage.

As historian Greg Grandin puts it, slavery was the 'back door' through which Islam came to the Americas. Although there is no consensus among scholars about the exact numbers of Muslims who crossed the Atlantic between 1501 and the end of the nineteenth century, estimations by Greg Grandin, Susan Buck-Morss, and John Tofiq Karam. range from 4% to 20% of the approximately 12,500,000 Africans who were enslaved throughout the hemisphere. An important consideration in all of these estimates is the regions from which many of the enslaved were captured: Senegambia, Upper Guinea, Lower Guinea, and the areas around the Senegal and Gambia Rivers. Among the inhabitants who were Wolof, Fulani, and Mandinka, many, according to Karam and Grandin, were Muslim. But given the geographic range throughout West and Central Africa that these populations inhabited, as well as the ethno-linguistic group variations they represented, some scholars think in terms of Islam in the plural: a spectrum of Islamic beliefs and practices that went from coexistence with neighbouring animists and the amalgamation of pre-Islamic and Islamic practices, to jihadist orthodoxies exercised especially throughout the seventeenth to nineteenth centuries. Grandin describes this as a period rife with reformist jihads directed towards the culling and modification of various sorts of local religious syncretism. Another consideration is that early generations of Muslims in the Atlantic world brought with them genealogies of fourteen centuries of engagement with the West, the last five of which included the Americas, which also involved other, New World peoples and cultures. This Muslim version of the Atlantic hybridity that is key to Gilroy's formulation has been the subject of scholarly discussion about how and by whom 'Muslims' are defined, and how important heterodoxy and orthodoxy are in making these determinations. Even the term 'Islam' is itself a sizeable generalisation, encompassing, among other referents, Arab, Ottoman, North African, Spanish, Indian, and Far Eastern. And this, Jerry Toner writes, is just in the Old World.

These questions about the ways that hybridity can destabilise master narratives that definitively categorise religious traditions and those who adhere to them are complicated by the perspective of some scholars that in the Atlantic world, as historian Sylviane Diouf puts it, 'Islam brought by the enslaved West Africans has not survived. It has left traces, it has contributed to the culture and history of the continents; but its conscious practice is no more'. The significance of this disappearance from 'collective consciousness,' argues Diouf, is that enslaved African Muslims have been overlooked in the scholarship on Africa in the Americas. Like all enslaved Africans in the Americas, Allan Austin observes, enslaved African Muslims remain in the vast majority anonymous, or, at best, named property on owners' lists. The public record of their persons and their lives is lost to history. Literary scholar and historian Allan D. Austin points out that African Muslims became slightly more visible in the United States about the time of the Civil War (1861-1865) but 'a kind of suppression of information' about them ensued, lasting for over a hundred years. Notable examples of this erasure are evident earlier in the 1856 American novel, *Benito Cereno*, by Herman Melville, who did not identify his main African characters as Muslims, although they were; in another 1856 American novel, *Dred, A Tale of the Great Dismal Swamp*, by Harriet Beecher Stowe, who also did not identify the protagonist, 'Dred,' as a Muslim, despite that his parents were Mandingo; and, finally, as Austin analyzes it, Toni Morrison was 'curiously coy' in her use of Muslim names for her characters in *Song of Solomon*, and did not acknowledge 'their religious provenance that brought a Muslim spin' to that novel. One important consequence of these kinds of sidelining or erasure, for Austin, was 'an early disidentification between Antebellum African Americans and Muslims' that began to be lessened only with the rise of the Nation of Islam in the second quarter of the twentieth century, or, as Sylviane Diouf has it, in 1913 with the rise of the Moorish Holy Temple of Science founded by Noble Drew Ali. A member of this temple was Wallace Fard Muhammed, who would later go on to found the Nation of Islam.

This issue about visibility and the relationship between Africans' racial identifications and religious identifications in the Americas is yet another dimension of what we might call the survival problematic of Islam in diaspora. This survival problematic can feed the hybrid formations and intermixtures to which Gilroy calls attention, or cast them into doubt. For example, political scientist Ali Mazrui theorises that the Atlantic world's African diaspora had 'two routes toward re-Africanization': one route was through Pan-Islam and the other route was through the Rastafari Movement. Islam took hold in North America and Rastafarianism took hold in the Caribbean. The reason that African diaspora communities in the

Caribbean did not gravitate toward Islam are twofold, Mazrui contends. North American racial thinking collapses 'black' and 'brown' into a single category of identity, thus Muslims of various non-'white' heritages all could identify with Islam. By contrast, historically in the Caribbean, 'race consciousness does not as readily equate Black and Brown' as it has in the US. Counted as 'white,' Arabs in the Caribbean have been more privileged socially in terms of the structural inequality that characterises the region. Thus the Arab origins of Islam, Mazrui argues, were viewed as 'being in conflict with Islam's African credentials'; this did not encourage diaspora Africans to identify with Islam. Diouf takes a comparable position about racial thinking and Islam but from a different angle. She argues that accepting enslaved Muslims as Africans would have threatened the North American racial order. 'It was more acceptable to deny any Africanness to the distinguished Muslims than to recognise that a "true" African could be intelligent and cultured but enslaved nonetheless.' This is not a case of diasporic Africans turning away from Islam, but such dichotomising could have contributed to subsequent conventional wisdom about the connection, or lack thereof, between Africans and Islam.

A second reason for the lesser presence of Islam in the Caribbean is that along with the Levantine diaspora in the Americas, the mid-nineteenth century brought another population of immigrants to the Caribbean: indentured labour from the Indian subcontinent. In the majority Hindu, they also included Muslims. Indians' presence, which began in 1838 in then-British colony, British Guiana, gave rise to what would become a conventional association between Islam and Indians rather than Islam and Africans or Arabs. Mazrui sees the result of this subcontinental overshadowing being 'a much slower pace of Islamic conversions among Caribbean Africans than among African-Americans.' This dominant, dichotomised representation of Caribbean Muslims as Indian and not as African did not produce a picture of uniformity in Caribbean Islam, however. Indian Muslims brought with them a range of schools of thought, including Sunni, Shi'a, and Ahmadiyya traditions, which were, in turn, influenced by centuries of practice among Hindu neighbours and family, both in India and in the Caribbean—in a sense, a kind of built-in 'outernationalism', Gilroy might say. This might indeed be considered an example of the diasporic hybridities and interculturation to which Gilroy points, but as Gilroy's Black Atlantic also contains, there must be in any model of a Muslim Atlantic tension stimulated by debates that call for (certain expressions of) uniformity that seek to promote (certain expressions of) 'insiderism'. Thus, imagined mutual exclusivities between Afro-Caribbean Muslims and Indo-Caribbean Muslims persist, as do debates among Caribbean Muslims in general about which school of thought and its beliefs and practices is authentic and legitimate.

The long-entrenched epistemological distinction between Afro-Caribbean Muslims and Indo-Caribbean Muslims refracts in contested and negotiated ways that reflect two important and interlinked dimensions: their relation to their respective social and cultural pasts, and their contemporary relations with each other in relation to the Caribbean states in which they reside. I have written about this in detail elsewhere, so for my purposes here I will simply reiterate that the ethno-national boundaries that designate 'India' and 'Africa' loom large in regional understandings of how Islam is defined according to its practitioners' genealogical tracing back to their respective homelands. India symbolises one kind of Islamic authenticity, based on Indo-Caribbean hagiography about the abiding efforts of early generations of Muslim Indian indentured immigrant labourers on sugar plantations to keep their religious knowledge and traditions alive under the duress of want and discrimination.

Africa symbolises another kind of Islamic authenticity, based on Afro-Caribbean valorisation of forms of consciousness and personhood – identity – striven to be asserted through the abiding efforts of enslaved Africans on sugar plantations to keep their forms of knowledge and traditions alive under their own duress of want and discrimination. Arabia symbolises yet a third kind of Islamic authenticity, based on the interpretation by some Afro- and Indo-Caribbean Muslims as being shorn of the *bidaa*, or, in popular understanding, illegitimate innovations that the cultures of origin lands can foster and which may permeate Islamic beliefs and practices. In this sense, for some, Arabia is transcendent, projecting a purified, and thus proper Islam. Each of these geographical locations – India, Africa, Arabia – plays a role in the imaginaries of Muslims about how to best (most correctly) practice their religion in terms of particular school of thought, customary traditions, and worldview. These cultural-geographic divisions especially reinforce Afro- and Indo-Caribbean ideas about ethno-racial exclusivity and immutability in their service to the post-independence political cultures of nation-states, which in this region historically have capitalised on competing constituencies (voting blocs) of Afro and Indo, represented by putatively inevitable differences of cultural constitutions, sensibilities, values, and points of view—importantly, including religion—and rewarded with resources and opportunities geared to meeting those allegedly distinct needs. All of these challenges remind us why categorical distinctions take special effort, and why, even in diaspora, where presumably everything is breaking up into flexible, hybrid rearrangements, some orthodoxies, scholarly as well as religious, remain.

Compounding these ideologies of race and nation ('black'/'brown'/'white'; Africa/India) is another key factor in striving toward realising a Muslim Atlantic. It is that of Islam's elusiveness in its earliest New World diaspora: the debates about the nature of its survival over time among African Muslims and thus its identification as being recognisably 'Islam'. As I noted above, most scholars agree that throughout the Americas, Islamic beliefs and practices became absorbed into other, more populous religious traditions, gradually fading from 'collective consciousness'.

As Diouf sees it, historians Brinsely Samaroo and Carl Campbell have argued that by the mid-nineteenth century a lively and effective African Muslim presence in the Caribbean had ebbed. As Diouf sees it, in 'Haiti, Brazil, Jamaica, and Trinidad, the Muslims and Islam were integrated into the religious life of the black population, just as any other African religions were. They were not accorded a special status but were not forgotten either; they just became another component of the religious and social world'. Islam's 'traces' were manifest in, for example, the representation of the ancestral and spirit worlds, and also materialised into paraphernalia that had ritual and other sacred significance. Historian Joaõ José Reis writes that after Brazil's abolition of slavery in 1888, 'formerly enslaved Muslims could still be found as isolated practitioners of their faith' and that some of these Muslims 'became well known makers of amulets' (ritual objects that offer protection for the owner through otherworldly means), although this craft reflected 'a very unorthodox Muslim way of life'. Reis's perspective may have been reinforced by his awareness of the influence that amulets have today on the occult in Brazil. The main point here is that according to the accepted scholarship, the possibilities for Islam's Atlantic world presence range from eventually non-existent to eventually simply hints of itself.

Vast geographical expanses, extensive passage of time, great cultural heterogeneity, and religious viability characterise the flow of Muslims and Islam to the Americas. Islam's 'whole', its substance and its symbolism, is greater than the sum of its parts; its history, heterogeneity, geographical range, and the apprehensive imagery long associated with it from the Western gaze transcend Muslim individuals and communities of practitioners. This gestalt, or whole that exceeds the sum of its parts, helps put into perspective what realising a 'Muslim Atlantic' would entail, and mean. To remain within Gilroy's vision, this gestalt must never project uniformity or impermeability yet it must remain empirically evident; it must honor the *trans*ness of diaspora yet not lose sight of regional specificity; it must be decisive about what recognition of Islam's various 'parts' signifies (schools of thought, debates about practice, genealogies) while also giving those parts equal weight, at least as far as the particular historical and socio-cultural contexts will allow. Heterogeneous populations of African Muslims in the Americas have made for diverse ways of being Muslim even while all may subscribe to certain common denominators, typically taken from the Qur'an and the Hadith, by which they define and interpret Islam. Thus, the difficulty of drawing precise lines around our categories renders these issues vexed at the start.

Gilroy's revisionist objective was to envision a geographic and conceptual space that could negate nation-state based cultural nationalism and its bigotries and instead emphasise exchange and inclusivity. Nationalist paradigms are less emphatic for Muslims in Caribbean diasporas because there is no dominant narrative of entrenched Islamic history in this region. The region's first century's free Muslim seamen and other labourers, including enslaved Muslims, greatly diffused over its five-century history in the Americas, and the Islam of present-day Caribbean societies is associated either with Indo-Caribbean Muslims or Afro-Caribbean Muslim converts, or 'returnees'. That said, all brought their Islam with them on transport ships headed across the Atlantic Ocean. Equally applicable to both groups is historian Peter Linebaugh's comment that ships were 'perhaps the most important conduit of Pan-African communication before the appearance of the long-playing record'. Dilution over diasporic time and space; cultural tropes that emphasise passage through uncertain borders across water rather than the often more visible borders across land; the governmentality of Euro-colonialism in the Caribbean, whose societies were defined by a dominant mode of production dedicated to a single commodity and a shared heritage of that commodity – plantation-based sugar and its byproducts. All of these compete with the idea of 'nation' and exclusive, entrenched national identities linked to it. This is not at all to say that nationalism does not exist in the Atlantic world. Far from it. But it is to suggest a generative tension among ideas about fluid and putatively firm identities that are empirically evident, as Gilroy pointed out more than a quarter century ago, and fluid and putatively firm identities that are ambiguous and not easy to pin down. These tensions are also a sound foundation for theory building from more hypothetical processes: in Gilroy's conceptualisation, the 'reflexive cultures and consciousness' of indigenous Amerindians, Europeans, Africans, and Asians were never 'sealed off hermetically' from one another; rather, he explains, they were, and remain, lived daily in direct contact.

But, again, it is the nature of that contact that is up for debate, not least among scholars trying to capture, or recapture, what the Atlantic constitutes as an object of study. So let me consider, first, what we might think of as the *di*vergence perspective on the relationship between New World Africans and Islam, which is a more contentious relationship, given what I have said above about the losses and uncertainties of historical Islam in the Atlantic world, than the one perceived between Indians and Islam. Then I will consider what we might think of as a *con*vergence perspective on the relationship between Islam and the 'intermixture of ideas' Gilroy describes as both historical and contemporary, African and Indian, that both flow through and create – realise – a Muslim Atlantic space. Gilroy's focus is on Atlantic popular culture – notably music, luminaries of literature and philosophy, and the forms of cultural production that music and great thinkers generate. With different foci, the Muslim Atlantic also might be able to transcend or cross the ideological divides of exclusivity, immutability, purity, and 'cultural insiderism'.

Although it is not a key word in Gilroy's analysis, the concept of 'creolisation' is at the heart of his discussions of hybridity and intermixture. As employed by Atlantic world scholars, creolisation refers to the encounter between two or more cultures or cultural traditions (religious belief and practice, kinship organisation, aesthetic style, cuisine styles, and so on) and the mutual transformation each undergoes in relation to the other. Creolisation does not represent even exchanges but, instead, typically contentious engagements that occur within the context of unequal relations of power, in which certain cultures or cultural traditions will predominate and be socially valorised accordingly. In arguing for the impact that Islam made among diasporic Africans in the New World, if not its tenacity, Diouf contends that African Muslims 'did not participate in the creolisation process that commingled components of diverse African cultures and faiths with that of the slaveholders. By their dress, diet, names, rituals, schools, and imported religious items and books', Diouf argues, 'they clearly indicated that they intended to remain who they had been in Africa – be it *emir*, teacher, *marabout*, *alfa*, *charno*, *imam*, or simply believer … they shaped their response to enslavement, defining how the Muslims lived it and reacted to it. The people they had been in Africa determined the people they were in the Americas.' She quite rightly recognises that the Euro-colonial Caribbean plantocracy's view that African Muslims were superior to African non-Muslims was a racist view; still, African Muslims 'seem to have distinguished themselves', being 'promoted and trusted in a particular way' by that same plantocracy. Standing out in this particular way may be another indication that African Muslims withstood creolisation, which Diouf perhaps sees in metaphoric terms as a kind of cultural homogenising.

It is true that the archival record shows that many African Muslims in the Atlantic world, free and enslaved, made conscious efforts to maintain their religious worldviews, and also that the plantocracies were aware that some Africans in their midst were Muslim, based on the regions from which they were captured and other such indicators as Diouf notes. But this divergence perspective raises a few questions. For one, most scholars would agree that all Africans in the diaspora arguably tried to maintain their religious traditions, and that all of these religious traditions have had more or less residual effects over the generations.

The question is why would Islam be more impervious to the forces of creolisation than other religious traditions, especially given that scholars, some quoted above, have written about the fusion of Islamic and non-Islamic beliefs and practices, fusions that absorbed Islam into a religio-cultural matrix in which it was frequently overshadowed. Another issue is that as scholars understand it, creolisation is not necessarily a conscious process or purposeful endeavour. Cultural transformation within unequal relations of power happen whether or not people want it to, and whether or not people are aware of it while it is happening. There were indeed many instances and expressions of refusal of imposed and dominant epistemologies, slave revolts being a prime example, but these, as such, would typically not be categorised as exemplifying or contradicting 'creolisation'. And because creolisation is basically a way of theorising the workings of culture, no one who lives within that culture can opt out; intentions to remain outside of, distant from, or impervious to can be successful, but they are not the norms of lived experience; they must have catalysts that motivate within particular moments. Certainly, how people define their personhood in their original homeland, including in the parts of Africa that would end up in New World diasporas, informed, but did not determine, the people they would continue to become in the Americas. That said, like Gilroy, Diouf is making an important argument about power and agency, and the creativity that emerges from acts of self-assertion and self-realisation. Again, the challenge for a 'Muslim Atlantic' is to interpret agentive acts and forms of consciousness in ways that acknowledge all forms of agency – including claims to mutual exclusivity, purity, and immutability (to which no religion is a stranger) – while drawing together common denominators that can tell a new story.

Just who gets to tell that story is also a contentious issue. One important example of drawing explanatory templates from Islam and the question of who espouses them is the dialogue between historian Sultana Afroz and anthropologist Kenneth Bilby. Afroz bases her argument on a reasonable premise: that researching Caribbean history should not rely solely on the records of European slave traders and ruling authorities; that the work of African scholars based on African sources must also be part of historiographical narratives. This raises an important point about sources as situated forms of knowledge, and why and when certain ways of knowing may be more subject to elision than others. But Afroz holds steady a model of clearly distinguishable Caribbean (Afro-)Muslim communities, whose dedication to Islamic values and practices, she contends, informed and inspired the resistance to oppression among all enslaved Africans as well as among Maroons: communities of escaped enslaved Africans who were a vibrant and politically important presence in many slave plantation societies in the Atlantic world, notably including, for example, Jamaica, Brazil, and Surinam. But even if we dispense with the idea of obvious and cohesive communities, Afroz's claims merit at least further investigation. Perhaps not as many as 'numerous', but certainly some leaders among enslaved Africans could have been 'crypto-Muslims' – marabouts or imams. Moreover, it is a useful question to ask what the implications might be of calling an uprising a 'slave rebellion' versus a 'jihad' for the way we understand both, and thus the ways that historiographical narratives about the Americas are produced. At the same time, Afroz draws a clear line around Islam in the Atlantic world with her look askance at the attribution to obeah of the heroic efforts and miraculous achievements of elslaved freedom fighters, and her interpretation of African traditions of making offerings to the ancestors as in fact being Islam's voluntary giving of alms. Yet as I have written elsewhere, the story of the inaugural moment of the Haitian Revolution is its catalysis by Haitian national hero (and perhaps apocryphal figure) 'Boukman', who was both an *houngan* (Vodou priest) and imam. This memorialisation captures the ambiguity of a Muslim identity; there is no necessary either/or choice that can be made, unless as an ideological imposition. The messiness of lived experience and of commemoration typically belies categorical summaries.

In his critique of Afroz, Bilby describes her work on the Islamic heritage of maroons in Jamaica as 'feats of imagination'. His central charge is that Afroz lacks evidence to support her claims that Maroon cultural heritage derives from Islam. Bilby objects to attempts, including by academics, 'to appropriate the glory of the Maroon epic'. He is also disturbed by work that gives primacy to interpretations of Maroon history that conflict with Maroons' own understandings, which he sees as resulting in 'severing the Maroons of today from their own past'. But in addition to the Islam of West and Central Africa, Maroons' past may have involved Christianity, as well, despite Bilby's skepticism that Christianity, or Islam, had much influence on Maroon religious tradition. This may forever be unknowable as a certainty, but creolisation processes among enslaved Africans began even before passage across the Atlantic. Bilby is right that all historiographies must be considered when one is attempting to know a community or a people. Taking seriously the point of view of one's interlocutors is an ethical decision a researcher makes about their relationship with those interlocutors. But it establishes neither fact nor truth. Afroz takes the perspective of the whole: Islam, undifferentiated, yet 'invincible', as her essay's title 'Invisible Yet Invincible' contends. Bilby all but discounts Islam's influences in Maroon life, which he seems to suggest jeopardise Maroon understanding of their history and sense of personhood. Both positions assume the primary importance of facts: Afroz's facts are based on a particular take on religion and Bilby's are based on a particular take on history. But these authors' positions also promote their respective dedication to what could also be read as a kind of intellectual purification, where the lived experiences of ambiguity overlap, and changing imaginaries (creolisation?) take second place to ideal(ised) representations.

In a similar vein as Afroz's doubt about the connections between Islam and obeah, Diouf draws a distinction between Islam and African religious traditions vis-à-vis religious syncretism. She argues that 'unorthodoxy and tolerance of foreign elements...are characteristic of the successful African religions that are still alive today. They became creolised borrowing features from a diversity of religions and synthetising them'. By contrast, although 'in Africa, Islam and traditional religions are not exclusive', Diouf notes, 'there are limits to what Islam can absorb'. Syncretism is not acceptable. For Diouf, creolisation comes through religious conversion, which, she says, was not the case with Islam's survival in the Americas; instead, Islam's survival was 'due to the continuous arrival of Africans - including the recaptives and the indentured labourers after the abolition of slavery in the British and French islands'. Such survival of 'Islamic traits' was either recognisable by the adherents of African religious traditions, who, for example, 'make direct references to Allah, the Muslims, or Arabic', according to Diouf, or although Islamic origins may have been forgotten 'they are present and almost as visible'. This visibility, however, demonstrates that 'there was no fusion [creolisation] but rather co-existence, juxtaposition, or symbiosis'.

Ultimately, the tension lies between Africans' diversity and African Muslims' cohesion, given that 'whatever their origin, [Muslims] all shared a number of characteristics that made them stand out,' writes Diouf. For example, they were 'frugal, ascetic people'; they led a 'discreet and devout lifestyle'; they all shared 'a language, a writing system, a set of values, and habits' that transcended ethnic group, caste, and region; they shared a similar education. Enslaved African Muslims purportedly also disproportionately occupied high status plantation jobs, despite their lack of familiarity with 'the rules and regulations of the plantation world' and the language spoken in it. Thus, Diouf surmises, they must have had 'particular qualities that enabled them to climb quickly up the social ladder of the plantations'. This is while Hisham Aidi and Manning Marable argue that in the US, for example, enslaved African Muslims not only were differentiated from non-Muslim Africans by colonisers, they also 'distanced themselves from their non-Muslim counterparts ... often eagerly claim[ing] Moorish, Arab, or Berber origins', revealing an 'air of superiority' on their part.

Diouf seems to be arguing that in Africa, Islam and non-Islamic religious traditions were receptive to one another, but in the Atlantic world Islam exercised influence without itself being influenced. Observable traits and special dispositions notwithstanding, however, the key to African Muslims' fortitude was that 'their minds were free'. They may have had mortal masters but they were, existentially, servants of Allah. In other words, in the Atlantic world, and the Americas more generally, Muslims' consciousness was impermeable: they did not succumb to what others, such as Bob Marley in 'Redemption Song', call 'mental slavery'. This sense of free minds, of consciousness, is a different, although not contradictory, kind of awareness than is the 'hemispheric if not global' forms of consciousness that Gilroy envisions. This is perhaps because Gilroy starts with populations already vastly diverse, as he well recognises, who may be grouped under the rubric 'black' in their formation, through cultural production, of a 'Black Atlantic', which is impossible, in Gilroy's formulation, to capture within such boundaries as 'nation' and 'race.' Diouf and scholars who make similar arguments start with a delimited entity, Islam/Muslim, which, as I noted earlier, can act as a 'nation' even though it is not one in the conventional sense of the word. The key question is: what are the ideological stakes involved in arguing for or against the fluidity of boundaries, group cohesiveness, and 'cultural insiderism'?

For Gilroy and his colleagues, the revisionist agenda is, in part, a struggle against (racial) delimitation and containment. For Diouf and her colleagues, the revisionist agenda is, in part, a struggle against (religious) denial and elision. Yet, arguably, both demand a kind of recognition, a correction of political-sociological blind spots and their consequences. Given this shared goal, can a 'Muslim Atlantic' call upon what we might term a convergence perspective that emphasises the ways that Muslims' experiences and representation in the Americas differ from those we are more often accustomed to hearing from Europe and North America? In other words, can a 'Muslim Atlantic' deliver theoretical paths to the kinds of openness, fairness, inclusivity, and valorisation of the *inter* rather than *intra*; that is, unity without uniformity? Can there be such a thing as a nation without borders, and is a 'Muslim Atlantic' such an entity—an *ummah* that is not simply 'global' but reimagines 'nations' as another kind of entity, as extraneous to geo-political states?

Given the tenacity of boundaries and distinctions that evoke group separateness and racial-cultural exclusivity, envisioning a convergence perspective that can produce models of group cohesiveness and racial-cultural inclusivity also takes effort. The challenge is to create a category of lived experience that maintains the openness, anticipation, and fluidity that lived experience is made of. This may take further research into the syncretism and creolisation that historically, culturally, and socially have tied Islam to Atlantic religious traditions for half a millennium. But perhaps even more crucially, it will take a shift in perspective about what we already know. Reading Diouf, we know that in Africa, India, and the Atlantic world there were, and remain, contact zones in which Islamic, non-Islamic, and pre-Islamic beliefs and practices intermesh, such as shared or converged deities, rites, lexicons, and ritual objects, or as fusions within individuals themselves, as the narratives about the Haitian Revolution's most famous figures of resistance, Makandal and Boukman, aver.

We can think of these processes and people as beyond the bounds of creolisation or as consummate examples of it. And if we think in terms of creolisation, we can envision such transformations as producing new forms of exclusive ownership of culture and identity, or always-in-motion, communally shared cultures and identities. We can work to imagine what kinds of shared differences emerge from interactive dialogue and mutual awareness, or, by contrast, see those differences as inimical. There is not much in the world that is self-evident. From various subject positions and perceived stakes, we work to make things seem that way.

Muslims come in many forms — recognisable, contested, and unrecognised. Thus it stands to reason that we approach Islam as multilayered, receptive, flexible, as always in process even while practitioners and observers may view Islam as more stable. This is one example of the unceasing tension between phenomenological and ideological optics.

In the spirit of Gilroy's emphasis on popular culture, notably music, as illustrative examples of the reality and utility of a 'Black Atlantic' reading of the Atlantic world, and corrective to the misdirection present in the ideas of 'nation' and 'nationalism', perhaps we can end on a note taking inspiration from a classic, top-selling song by American Funk music band Funkadelic, with whom Gilroy is surely acquainted, whose members included the important musician and record producer George Clinton. The song, 'One Nation Under A Groove' (1978; Junie Morrison, George Clinton, and Garry Shider), contains a political message that suggests a 'nation' whose groove makes it open and all-inclusive, a meta-nation, one might say.

As a model for the Muslim Atlantic, one *ummah* under a groove seems a logical, and laudable counterpart to strive for.

This piece quotes and refers to many authors. An accompanying version with full footnote citations has been published in parallel on The Maydan at themaydan. com/2020/07/realising-a-muslim-atlantic/

RETURN TO ALMADIES

Amandla Thomas-Johnson

Long before the French came here, the Cap-Vert peninsula – on which Dakar, the capital of Senegal sits – belonged to the Lebu people. The Lebu are a primarily fishing community, whose life has revolved around the Atlantic. While the city has grown in most parts of the peninsula, to this day many Lebu still live in coastal settlements dating back hundreds of years, such as Camberene and Yoff. At the western extremity of the peninsula is Almadies, a neighbourhood of Dakar which is home to a holy cave frequented by those belonging to a predominantly Lebu Islamic sect. It has been named in homage to Seydina Limamou Laye, who in the nineteenth century claimed to be the Mahdi, the redeemer of Islam expected towards the end of time. After drawing a large following, he made a second claim: that his son was the second coming of Jesus – a 'Black Jesus' as some here call him.

In more recent times, however, Almadies has become one of Africa's most exclusive addresses: Swollen white mansions, a strip of upmarket beachside restaurants, a cumbersome American embassy, and a golf course. But it is also the continent's last address. For beyond the ruins of an abandoned hotel, next to a row of palm trees whose withered leaves are permanently pinned back by the wind, is a narrow strip of sand which marks the westernmost point, not just of Senegal, but the whole of Africa, and of the entire Old World altogether.

Its significance goes unnoticed by those who live here. Accessing the Almadies point usually involves an attempt at bribing a security guard, or sneaking in early before he gets to work. Since I moved to Senegal from London two years ago, coming to this point has become a rare pilgrimage of sorts. By standing here at the westernmost point of the Old World, that ancient place where Egyptians built pyramids, Genghis Khan swept down from the Mongol Steppe, and from where Christopher Columbus set sail, that old landmass which my ancestors used to call home, before they were captured, put in chains and forced into the hellish hold of a slave ship, I was standing – symbolically at least – at the closest point to the New World. 5,839km to Port au Prince, Haiti, a wooden arrow sign near the land's edge indicates: Kingston, Jamaica – 6,312km.

My parents came to London via various islands in the Caribbean, including St Vincent, Tobago, Trinidad and Aruba. My mother, a community leader and teacher, arrived as part of the Windrush generation. My late father was a writer and publisher. Both were Pan-Africanists, and by this I mean that they were active in movements advocating for the political unity of Africans and people of African descent, wherever they happened to be.

Pan-Africanism is nowhere near the national agenda today as it was in the 1950s and 1960s, when it was perceived as a necessary bulwark against colonialism, racism and capitalist exploitation. It's probably about time they thought about it again because those evils still exist. I've seen them in the Andes, in the calloused hands of Hector Pinedo, a peasant farmer who is the king of the Afro-Bolivianos community in Bolivia; in the ramshackle wooden tents of Black Mauritanian refugees, victims of ethnic cleansing; and in the coarse banknotes of the colonial currency I use to buy mangoes at market here in Senegal.

I have had little choice but to revisit Pan-Africanism. In particular, I have been tracking the life of, and writing about, Kwame Ture, formerly Stokely Carmichael. Born in Trinidad before moving to the US, Ture lived in Guinea, Senegal's southern neighbour for many years. His life serves as a reminder that so many of the major Pan-Africanist figures of the twentieth century were actually from the African diaspora. Thinkers like Henry Sylvester Williams, WEB DuBois, Frantz Fanon, Aime Cesaire and Marcus Garvey were major contributors to the dream of African freedom.

While the diaspora has looked to Africa, the extent to which Africa looks back at us is another question. In 2016, the African Union refused to upgrade Haiti's membership from observer to associate member because: 'Only African States can join the African Union'. Not all African states share the same attitude. Ghana has invited people of African descent to return home as part of its Year of Return in 2019. This is in keeping with the spirit of Kwame Nkrumah, its first president, a major Pan-Africanist leader, who was a bridge between the continent and the diaspora. As for Senegal, does it have a political Pan-African consciousness that also embraces the diaspora? A majority Muslim country, Senegal could also be said to be the true site of the Islamic *maghrib* – the westernmost point of the Muslim world, and a potential bridge to the other side of the Atlantic. Is the country a model for the Black Muslim Atlantic?

Based on my appearance, Senegalese people commonly mistake me for being Senegalese. They will address me in Wolof, the main local language, and even when I make it clear that I do not speak it, they are so adamant that they often continue to speak it anyway. Once they are convinced that I am not from here, things start to get tricky. When I explain that my family are from the Caribbean, I am met with blank stares. They don't know where it is or how I ended up there. I attempt to explain further, mentioning the trans-Atlantic slave trade. They know that once upon a time slaves were captured and taken to a land far, far away. But for them that's where the story ends.

Slaves were brought in large numbers to Goree island, which sits just off the coast of Dakar, before being shipped off to the New World. A UNESCO World Heritage Site, it is the central part of any trip to Dakar, especially for those from the diaspora. Indeed, there appears to be something restorative and defiant in the idea of returning and retracing what might have been your ancestors' last footsteps towards the land's end. Given the suffocating conditions of the middle passage and the barbarity with which they were treated on the plantation, our slave forbears weren't supposed to survive, let alone have descendants. But here we are.

To get to Goree, however, slave descendants are virtually required to renounce all claims to be African. While holders of African passports have a special discount for the short boat trip to the island, slave descendants, whose ancestors were brought to Goree involuntarily, screaming and kicking, pay the same as Chinese or White European holidaymakers. My attempt to explain this absurdity to the port's employees floundered hopelessly. They looked straight through me as though I was not there. Their faces were blank. Between us was a gulf of language and understanding. Rather than recognise the connection between the slaves, their descendants and the continent, as it ought to have done, this policy only perpetuated the rupture.

Having passed between Portuguese, Dutch, British and French hands, Goree has distinctly colonial architecture that is both charming and haunting. Women sweep the cobblestone streets, which were laid by slaves, brick by brick. Washing is hung out on the balconies of elegant stone houses, formerly occupied by slave traders. Families sit down to eat and sleep in rooms that were once grim slave quarters. One of those former slave holding centres has now been turned into a museum called the House of Slaves. It retains the cramped, airless cells the slaves were kept in and a restored double staircase that leads up to the apartment where, just above their heads, the owner of the house, an Afro-French madame, resided in pomp.

Tour guides are very careful not to offend the sensibilities of the, mainly European, tourists and so avoid informing them that their empires were built on the backs of the Black bodies once held within its walls. Slavery was something of the past with no further consequences. In fact, the last time I was there, a guide offered a revisionist history. He claimed it was Africans and not Europeans who bore the brunt of responsibility for slavery. That European powers established a global system based on fomenting war in Africa, trafficking millions of human beings across the Atlantic Ocean, subjecting what survivors there were to forced labour on plantations, and deriving huge profits, appeared to have been lost on him.

At the far end of the House is the infamous 'Door of no return', through which slaves passed before boarding the awaiting ships. While indicating, literally, that no return was or is currently possible, the door's name also suggests that the door itself marks the end. As the slaves disappear beyond this narrow doorway, they are shut out of history. What then becomes of them is hardly explained. Out of sight out of mind.

Goree's blindness towards its own past is further exemplified at another museum, which is housed in an old fort on the other side of the island. On the way in, we are greeted by portraits of a number of 'celebrities' who once visited the island. It reads like a who's who of imperial plunder. There is Pedro Alvares Cabral who claimed a large chunk of South America for Portugal, which is now known as Brazil, inaugurating hundreds of years of indigenous slaughter and importation of millions of African slaves. Also starring is Afonso de Albuquerque who conquered Goa in India and the Malacca in Malaysia, and was the first – and certainly not the last – European to raid the Persian Gulf. Outside the museum is the physical centrepiece of the rewriting of Goree's history: La Place de l'Europe, a plaza restored by the European Union at a cost of £130,000. When it was inaugurated in 2018, the Senegalese appeared to have had enough. Social media users asked whether it would be fitting to have a Hitler street in Israel or a Serbian Square in Srebrenica. Meanwhile a prominent activist was arrested for attempting to sabotage the opening ceremony. The mayor of Goree and former president's nephew, Augustin Senghor, reassured onlookers that because of its history, Goree was not just a Senegalese island but also in fact 'a European island'.

But this placing of Goree and Senegal within the mainstream of European history comes at the expense of the diaspora. This isn't just about me and other slave descendants, this is also about Africans. To neglect the history of slavery is to be oblivious to its consequences, of which the underdevelopment of Africa and the colonisation of the continent are the most important. It is also to ignore the plantation, where the seeds of racism and capitalism were sown, and where African slaves rose up in order to defeat those forces.

A stumped history diminishes the possibility of future action; Senegal continues to linger in the dark shadow of Europe.

A look at the political life of Leopold Senghor, Senegal's first president, suggests this was not by accident. It was under Senghor that Goree was transformed into a monument to slavery. One of the most significant French poets of the twentieth century, he once described the Cap Vert peninsula, home to Dakar, as 'an outstretched hand to all Negroes who were scattered throughout the Americas'. Indeed, Senghor knew the diaspora well. While a student in 1920s Paris, he was introduced to the writers of the Harlem Renaissance and soon after co-founded the Negritude movement, along with Martinican poet Aime Cesaire and French Guianan poet Leon Damas. Emerging as a reaction to colonial racism, it promoted a brand of cultural Pan-Africanism, which affirmed the values of Black civilisation. But he was anything but Pan-African when it came to politics. After leading Senegal to Independence in 1960, he became a standard bearer of *Françafrique*, advocating for France's continued influence in its former colonies. In the early 60s, as Pan-African unity appeared on the horizon, Senghor headed up a bloc of countries committed to retaining the colonial borders of the newly independent African nations. Called the Monrovia group, it included most former French colonies and Nigeria. On the opposite side were the Casablanca bloc countries, led by Egypt's Gamal Abdel Nasser, Guinea's Sekou Toure and Ghana's Kwame Nkrumah, which shared a grand vision for a united, federated continent, as a way of fostering peace and overcoming colonial domination.

Senghor's vision won out with the creation of the Organisation of African Unity in 1963, which affirmed independent statehood. While Senegal would go on to achieve relative political stability, colonial borders would wreak havoc up and down the continent. Back in Senegal, meanwhile, Senghor set out to crush his political opponents, many of them Pan-Africanists. Some were tortured, imprisoned and forced to go underground. Omar Blondin Diop, the young radical who had returned to Senegal after participating in the 1968 protests in Paris and had cultivated links with the Black Panther Party, died in suspicious circumstances while imprisoned on Goree island. One of Senghor's most formidable opponents was Pan-Africanist thinker Cheikh Anta Diop, whose ideas seemed to strike at the very heart of his project. He wanted local languages, not just French taught in schools; to overturn the Eurocentric education system; and for Senegal to do away with France and become a haven for Pan-Africanism. When he emerged as a serious political contender to Senghor, he was imprisoned. When later his ideas gained popularity, he was banned from teaching at the University of Dakar.

In keeping with Negritude, Senghor invested extravagantly in culture and staged high-profile Pan-African festivals, attracting diaspora luminaries such as jazz great Duke Ellington and Barbadian novelist George Lamming. But this appreciation only really applied to the realm of 'high culture', Keyti, one of Senegal's foremost rappers, recently told me over lunch. Senghor would have had little time for hip hop, now one of the dominant cultural forms of the African diaspora. 'He was out to create the civilised Negro,' said Keyti, who is nevertheless a fan of his poetry. Frantz Fanon, who had watched with dismay as Senghor sided with France in the Algerian civil war, tore into his policies. '"Negro-African" culture grows deeper through the people's struggle, and not through songs, poems, or folklore,' he wrote in 1961. In the early 1980s, after twenty years in power, the old poet left Senegal for France where he was to live out the rest of his days, while serving as an 'immortal', one of the elected members of the Academie Française, the sacred guardians of the French language. He died in Normandy in 2001. That outstretched hand to the diaspora that Senghor likened Dakar to was, in fact, nothing more than a closed palm.

Yet as influential as this official narrative might be, it is not the only vein that runs through Senegal's varied society. Cheikh Anta Diop still has an ardent set of followers. Artists are painting a new path. Those associated with pre-colonial kingdoms have their way. And there has been something of a Wolof revival in recent years. Then there are the country's powerful

Muslim Sufi brotherhoods. They operate largely independently of the government, run a parallel Arabic education system, have a legacy of anti-colonial resistance and as a result a competing historical narrative. Do they have a vision of a Black Muslim Atlantic?

Although I may never know whether my own ancestors passed through Goree, I do know that, sometime in the early nineteenth century, a couple of hundred kilometres down the coast, my maternal great-great-great grandmother was forced onto a slave ship bound for the Americas. The ship left from what is today known as The Gambia, a tiny country that sits inside Senegal save for a narrow Atlantic coast, and which shares the same languages and peoples. Sat there shackled in the dark with disease and death and vomit all around her, she would have been terrified, as the ship buckled and tipped on the waves of the Atlantic. But after a couple of months the worst seemed over. The ship had passed Barbados and entered the placid waters of the Caribbean. Then it began to sink. As it went down the slaves were released. Preserving their lives was to preserve a very valuable commodity. Those from the hills were unable to swim and quickly sank, their arms flailing hopelessly. Mothers lost their babies. They were just off Bequia, a tiny island in the Grenadines. Perhaps she thought she would be easily captured and enslaved there because she swam the other way – to St Vincent, some 9 km away. There was no time to rest after she made it to shore. There was slavery there too. She had to run. Of all the places she could have fled to, she settled on the edge of Kingstown, the island's capital, at the foot of some hills on which was built the island's main British fortification. I don't know whether she knew this or not, but I like to think that she did, and had the audacity to live there knowing that she was safely sheltered in the shadow of the bristling cannon that pointed out to sea above her head.

The story has come down to me, thankfully, because of the longevity of the women in my family, formidable individuals who in their own way each seem to embody what little I know about my foremother. Her fortitude was in her daughter Eva, who used to walk tens of miles each day to market and who died at 102 in the 1960s; her defiance in Edna Howard, Eva's daughter, who by refusing to give up her seat at the front of the Cathedral one Sunday morning, led to its desegregation; her freedom in Norma, Edna's daughter and my grandmother who died 2019 Christmas Eve aged 95; and her resilience in Yvette, my own mother.

Most were unable to evade the plantation as she did, however. They were the ones who dropped down dead on the sugar cane fields, who were raped and whose kids were carried away in the middle of the night. They were my ancestors, too. Far from being a few fields in the colonial backwaters of the West Indies, the plantation generated the profits that allowed Britannia to rule the waves and expand her empire. It kick-started the capitalist system that has now led us to ecological catastrophe and birthed the structures of racism that today keep so many Black people in US prisons, stuck in Brazilian favelas, or sinking in boats in the Mediterranean. But out of the brutality of the plantation sprung resistance. Some like the slaves of Haiti rose up and burnt the place down. Others, like Harriet Tubman, escaped and then helped others to freedom. The damned of the earth outfoxed and, at times, thrashed the most powerful empires the world had ever seen.

Had I truly understood the significance of slave defiance, including that of my foremother's, it perhaps would have been much easier as a young Black male growing up in 1990s London. Having a greater grasp on that history might have made it easier to cope with the rite of passage that is dealing with society's racist expectations. Then the fad was relentlessly depicting Black men and boys as dangerous, their grainy mugshots plastered on tabloid newspapers, on BBC Crimewatch. Maybe I thought that it had nothing to do with me, that I was a respectable negro. A few stop and searches, one for allegedly hijacking a London bus, and the experience of people crossing the road when they saw you coming, quickly put an end to that.

Then there were the fetishists. Apparently, I was supposed to talk a certain way, dip my shoulder a certain way when I walked, because that's what being Black was for the kids at my majority-white school. The confusion was compounded by the reality that I could see around me, that we as Black people lived in the most deprived neighbourhoods, attended the worst schools, and occupied the most underrated jobs, when we were not unemployed.

Perhaps it was supposed to be this way. If not petty criminals and part-time drug dealers, Black males — especially West Indian boys like me — were destined to be confused, scared and misunderstood. Perhaps this was the curse of the plantation, I began to think. Had those beatings and whippings and hot iron brandings imprinted violence onto your very being?

And what about that void in our family history, where we lost our name, our language and the memory of where we came from — did that portend an empty future? Was the destruction of our past a precursor to our own destruction? Or to put it another way, as Theologian William R. Jones once asked, was God a white racist?

Not for Malcolm X. For nearly every deracinated youth like I was, his autobiography had some bold answers. Malcolm's politics were firmly rooted in the plantation. In fact, slavery was a subject he came back to again and again as he tried to rouse his audiences. 'I wish it was possible for me to show you the sea bottom in those days – the Black bodies, the blood, the bones broken by boots and clubs', he would say. After he had applied this jolt to the system, he would explain that the plantation wasn't something in the past, it was the current reality for Black people. More than just a site of suffering and pain it was a place of resistance and resilience. He made this allusion by describing himself as a modern-day Field Negro, that unruly slave who had nothing to lose and who would give his master hell.

As those Haitian slaves set out to defeat Napoleon in the most lucrative slave colony the world had ever seen, Malcolm X was out to tear down a global system of racism, capitalism and imperialism and to restore Black dignity, to make us beautiful, powerful and noble. His politics were 'anti-plantation' as Tanzeen R. Doha and others have put it.

Malcom X would take this a step further. Writer Ta Nehisi Coates puts the significance of slavery like this. 'Remember that you and I are brothers,' he writes to his son in *Between the World and Me*, 'are the children of trans-Atlantic rape. Remember the broader consciousness that comes with that. Remember that this consciousness can never ultimately be racial; it must be cosmic'. That consciousness led Malcolm X to Islam. And in time it would lead me there too. I was moved by how he redeemed the plantation past and connected it to the lived realities of Black people today and then onto The Transcendent, the ultimate source of hope and justice.

His vision also attempted to fill that historical void that lies between us and the continent of Africa. To become Muslim was to repair that broken chain, he argued, because so many African slaves had been Muslim. The exact figures are hard to come by, but Sylviane Diouf, author of *Servants of Allah* proposes that 15–20% of the 15 million slaves brought across the Atlantic were Muslim. Many of us would have had Muslim ancestors.

My maternal great-great-great grandmother could not have imagined that 200 years after she left these shores, that one of her descendants would return to them, let alone as a Muslim. When that boat sailed away and she saw the waves pounding this coast for the last time, there was no guarantee that she would even make it to the other side. And that wasn't enough, she then had to swim and then run. 'You are the result of their Duas [supplications]', a friend whose ancestors were also taken from these shores once told me.

The universality of Malcolm's message was just as important as the personal redemption it seemed to provide. As far as I was concerned, any faith worth its salt had to transcend human differences and geographical boundaries. Some of Malcolm's last footsteps, as he embarked on an ambitious schedule of global travel in the months leading up to his death, took him across two interlocking geographical zones. High profile visits to Africa, including to Ghana to meet President Nkrumah and to Egypt to meet Gamal Abdel Nasser, were an expression of his Pan-Africanism. His Hajj to Mecca, his meeting with Saudi Arabia's King Faisal and striking up a relationship with Egypt's Al-Azhar University offered signs of a Pan-Islamic politics.

This was a bold attempt, if there ever was one, to bridge Black solidarity and Islamic brotherhood, and expand the possibilities of third world solidarity. They were shared struggles. The forces of white supremacy that Black people were resisting against at home in the US threatened those in the Muslim world, too. He was also trying to say that the spiritual message of Islam necessitated a struggle against universal injustices outside of the Muslim world, the most important of which were those that stemmed from the trans-Atlantic slave trade.

'Malcolm did not see religious belief and antiracism as mutually exclusive', writes Souhail Daulatzai in *Black Star, Crescent Moon: The Muslim International and Black Freedom Beyond America.* 'Instead, he saw them as deeply enmeshed, for he saw the struggle of Black peoples in the United States as a responsibility not just for the continent of Africa but claimed that it "must also be the concern and the moral responsibility of the entire Muslim world – if you hope to make the principles of the Qu'ran a living reality"'. Malcom's worldview, which fused the Old World and the New and ran from Indonesia to Illinois, and from Pretoria to Palestine, was empowering. He saw an invigorating potential when the consciousness that resulted from the Black experience – of slavery, racism, colonisation and resisting white supremacy – was catalysed by the spiritual message of Islam. He was shifting the centre of Islam's moral vision across both sides of the Atlantic. This was the Black Muslim Atlantic.

As much as this grand vision caught my imagination at the time I embraced Islam, I was being shaped more by real-world events. A few months after I became Muslim, two hijacked planes crashed into New York's World Trade Centre. I saw overnight how the tabloid front pages changed from Black boys in hoodies to bearded brown Muslim bogeymen. There was no escape.

The West's obsession with Muslims had begun and so had its War on Terror. It was, and still is, an immensely challenging period: the self-censoring, the scrutiny, the holding your breath every time there's an 'incident', hoping that it wouldn't be one of us – again – because you know what will follow. I wasn't directly affected by the War on Terror as much as others, partly, ironically, because of my appearance. I have yet to experience a Schedule 7 airport stop and search or had the Muslim equivalent of MI5 tap me on the shoulder. But I have felt part of a community under attack. The misreporting of Muslims was an important factor in my decision to become a journalist in the first place.

But out of the military interventions, extraordinary rendition, torture and drone strikes came a global consciousness. People in Pakistan, Palestine and Somalia now mattered to me in a way that they hadn't before. I was now supposedly one of them, a Muslim like them. I soon realised, however, that the idea of a global Muslim community – an *ummah* – in reality only went so far. The prayers and compassion of Muslims rarely extended as far as Black Africa or to Black Muslims. There was no racism in Islam, we were told, because Prophet Muhammad had a Black companion. Genocide in Darfur hardly prompted an outcry. Gradually, I began to orientate away from an Arab and South Asian-centric geography to one that was more focused on the Black world. Moving to Senegal and revisiting Pan-Africanism cemented this further. But does the Black Muslim Atlantic exist in my new home?

Given their mass appeal, Senegal's Sufi Muslim brotherhoods are the best place to start.

The largest in Senegal and The Gambia is the Mouride brotherhood, which was founded by Sheikh Ahmadou Bamba, a scholar and saint who led a nonviolent resistance against the French. His exiles to Gabon and Mauritania in the late nineteenth and early twentieth century inspired stories of miraculous escapes and adventures. One such tale involved him jumping off a boat to perform his prayers on a carpet floating on the sea.

His image is ubiquitous across Dakar, painted on walls and on car stickers. His followers, dressed in bell-sleeved robes, can be seen sitting on dusty street corners performing zikr and singing his hymns long into the night. Mouridism is very much the popular faith here. When al-Ghazali said: 'Ah, to have the faith of the old women of Nishapur!', that simple, non-intellectual faith that still yields humility and humanity, he could easily have been talking about the Mouride masses, women and men, old and young. The movement runs many of the small *daara*, the local Qur'anic schools, part of an alternative to the French-language education system. Sometimes consisting of little more than a thatched roof held up with tree branches, little children can be seen hunched over long wooden tablets carefully writing out passages of the Qu'ran. Presidential candidates court the Mouride Caliph, who sits atop a vast hierarchy, wielding powers both spiritual and temporal. Spiritual guides called marabouts can direct their faithful who to vote for and heal them. The Mourides are also rich. Peanut production has been in the palm of their hands for the best part of a century. It is Senegal's third biggest export today. Their flock work the lucrative fields for they believe it to be an act of worship. Hard work and service are core values.

The biggest symbol of Mouridism is the holy city of Touba. A small village just 60 years ago, it is now the second largest city in Senegal and operates as an independent city state with no governor, no police force and where no one pays tax. At the heart of this modern-day Medina, is one of Africa's largest mosques, which contains the mausoleum of Bamba. Millions throng there each year to take part in the Grand Magal, a major pilgrimage, the Mouride multitudes circumambulating the grand mosque in a way similar to the *hajj* in Mecca. The movement has an extensive international network. The Senegalese street vendors you might come across under the Eiffel Tower, outside the Colosseum or on the corner of Las Ramblas in Barcelona are most probably Mourides, as are the ones found on the streets of Harlem in New York.

Mouridism has done much to indigenise and appropriate Islam, opening it up for the Wolof-speaking Senegambian masses. But its vision hardly extends beyond Senegal and the Gambia, let alone the diaspora, making it difficult for outsiders to penetrate. It is undoubtedly an African Islam – but not an Islam for all Africans.

The Tijaniiyyah of Medina Baye, another Sufi brotherhood, are somewhat more worldly. While originating in Algeria, the order spread thanks in part to Elhaj Oumar Tall, a ferocious ethnic Fulani leader who resisted the French and carved out a vast if not short-lived empire in West Africa in the nineteenth century. Tall performed the *hajj* in Mecca, met Ibrahim Pasha of Egypt in Damascus, and married a granddaughter of Uthman Dan Fodio. But it was under the religious leader Ibrahim Baye Niass that the order flourished. Wandering tirelessly along the dirt tracks and through the remote villages of West Africa he is said to have bought many to Islam during the course of the twentieth century. He would broker links with African leaders, and was an informal advisor to Kwame Nkrumah, Ghana's first president. Today the Tariqah claims to have in excess of a hundred million members across the world, mostly throughout West Africa.

Medina Baye, the seat of the movement, and where Niass is buried, offers a snapshot into an African Islam. Tall Hausa men gracefully stride with gowns that billow about them in the hot wind; brightly-dressed women raise their hands and mutter prayers inside the mausoleum of Niass. Turbaned Mauritanian men gather their sky-blue robes as they solemnly stand in prayer; and local *talibes* in tatty T-shirts break into worshipful song as they sweep dirt from mosque carpets. In a small room inside the vast compound of Sheikh Mahy Cisse, one of Niass's grandsons, accents from North London mingle with those from Brooklyn, and a former senior member of the Nation of Islam cracks jokes. Medina Baye attracts an international cast who come in search of spiritual enlightenment and to study under its teachers, some of whom are sent from Al-Azhar in Egypt.

The Tariqah has a strong presence in the US, and, unusually among Sufi orders, teaches that any adherent can experience direct communion with God, not just spiritual elites. You can get by in English there, but it's better to speak Hausa or Arabic. Fulani and Wolof are also helpful. French doesn't get you very far, because, I was told, it is perceived to be 'too European'.

Muhammad Ali, who has been studying Islamic sciences since he arrived from Brooklyn six years ago, said American racism had alienated him. Coming to Africa and studying under a Sufi master, he said, had given him a sense of self-worth. Zakiyyah, his mother, whom I met earlier this year at their Brooklyn apartment, said she had come to Islam through Jamil Al-Amin (H. Rap Brown), who rose to prominence alongside Kwame Ture

(Stokely Carmichael) as part of the Black Power movement and the Student Non-Violent Co-ordinating Committee (SNCC).

I am not a Tijani but I appreciate their spiritual depth and reach. Despite its anti-colonial origins, the movement eschews politics, and so doesn't embody Malcolm X's vision of the Black Muslim Atlantic. Nevertheless it has a Pan-African geographical presence, including in the diaspora and appears to be empowering to slave descendants who are a part of its community. It is also possibly one of the largest Black organisations in the world.

My foremother left Africa with a simple, straightforward faith and way of looking at the world. I've returned as someone quite different, towing grand ideas. Perhaps they are too bold. But maybe they can only be that way.

As I stand at the Almadies point 200 years after she left, in some ways I haven't returned at all, because we are still dreaming of freedom.

Dakar's Atlantic shoreline extends to the Almadies Point, the westernmost tip of Africa

CLOSED MINDS

Ahmed Younis

The minds of Western Muslims, American and British, are being closed. It is the result of many factors. Chief among them is the Arabisation of Muslim identity and its attendant approaches to teaching and learning. When I was young, Arabs came from the Arab world to proselytise. Today, white men travel to the Arab world and return as Arabs, albeit with accents, proselytising. Cultural associations with banking theories of religious education led to the paralysis of the Muslim mind, and the rise of Muslim cultural supremacy as a counter to Western or white supremacy. Muslims in America are broken. World events have overtaken the natural trajectory of maturation of communal life. What was possible in America for Muslims has been trampled by incoherence and confusion. Blinding traditionalism and ethno-cultural ghettoisation are the norm. As American and British Muslims, we carry the burden of our immense failure together.

Through the development of a regressive, culturally specific, *identitarian* milieu of Islam, the UK offers us a strong example of the closing of the Western Muslim mind. A land with no constitution and little restraints on the ability of government to spy on citizens, subject them to disinformation, and a history of brutal colonialism – British Muslim life is uniquely complex. Adjacent to an increasingly racist mainland Europe, life for young British Muslims grows ever more difficult. Media reports of children whitening their skin in the UK to avoid bullying serve as an example of how the cultural dynamics of oppression differ across the Atlantic.

Yet, American and British Muslims are broken in many of the same ways, but I will focus on one. Deeply mired in the confusion of oppression, the vast majority of both conservative and liberal Muslims have abdicated their agency as citizens of their nations and communities in lieu of cultural comfort. More importantly, we have abdicated our agency in faith. Islam, as socially constructed in today's America, is a cacophony of ethnic, quasi-magical, heart-warming beliefs completely divorced from reality. Pietistic affectations of identity rule the day. Beards, canes, cultural clothing, and randomly placed *inshallahs* define public perceptions of piety. Women fight with all their might against a male religious establishment that demonises feminism and declares a woman's mind a private part to be hidden and guarded.

Halal meat has replaced halal ideas. No grocery store could sell the rotten pietism that has come to predominate our mosques, organisations, and communities masquerading as ideas. In all camps - Islamist, neo-traditionalist, fans of military dictatorship, those who claim to be progressive - women are in the back or absent altogether, LGBTQ community members are not welcome, and cheap quasi-religious slogans are peddled for donations among the politically aggrieved. Why is that so? Why is it that, aside from a few spaces, regardless of political stripe or school of thought, western Muslims exhibit such backwardness in the development of their Muslim identities? How did we lose all capacity for critical thinking? Would a Muslim scientist in America agree to denial of access to a men-only lab? Why does she accept it in the Mosque?

It is important to pause at the phrase 'critical thinking' for a brief moment at the outset. When we speak of critical thinking, critical pedagogy, or critical theory, we are not speaking of the process of criticising but rather that of critique. Criticising is sourced in egotism, and a perception of being better than the one being criticised. Critique is sourced in love and willingness to participate in the co-creation of a more vibrant, beautiful and just reality. To critique, is to deconstruct language, meaning, context, philosophy, ethics, and power relations in an attempt at understanding the thing for what it really is. It is a substantive endeavour that brings the positionality of the individual to the table of paradigm shaping and decision-making. It is filled with emotion yet not emotive. The purpose of critique is not to vent, it is to articulate one's belief in the viability of an alternative. As critical theorists, when we try to investigate – what a thing is – bound up in that meaning is – what the thing can become. Critical theory requires critical thinking. As critical theorists our primary commitment is to the unrealised, untested feasibility of a thing as the primary impetus for engagement.

The power of critical thinking, being in control, and starting at a position of self-confidence, are what make a person psychologically self-sufficient and ready to walk the walk in difficult and easy times, in company or loneliness, guided by principles and faith, seeking empowerment, fulfilment and reward from God, Only when the inner core is filled with this type of strong personal attitude can an individual be ready to join, cooperate and associate with others without losing themselves.

This duality of internal development and social action is often missed at the grassroots level. Masquerading in its place is rote memorisation and amateurish spirituality that bank good feelings. Many Muslims find their situations involving a modicum of injustice. If not in their personal lives, such as bullying, war, and immigration bans, they identify with the meta-narrative of injustice toward Muslims globally. This injustice, whether economic, political, or civilisational, breeds a deep sense of frustration and paralysis at the inability of a person to change their situation. When one finds no solutions to their reality they often take upon themselves the identity of the oppressed as an end to itself. Oppression becomes identity, which is always advantageous to the oppressor. Alterity is elevated to an end in itself breeding a discourse of impossibility. For Muslims, this impossibility applies to the reform of faith as well as society. Impossibility is social and personal paradigmatic paralysis. It rests upon the theology of non-movement which believes what we have is better than what can come. Never venturing to challenge the balance of the status quo for justice.

The discourse of the impossibility of changing the world is the discourse of those who, for different reasons, have accepted settling for the status quo. It is easier to cosy up to the tepidness of impossibility, rather than to embrace the permanent and almost always uneven struggle for justice and ethics.

For neo-traditionalists, this ideology of permanence appears as theology. An excellent example is that of Ibn Rajab's *Refutation of Those Who Do Not Follow the Four Schools* translated by Musa Furber, a white convert living in the Arab gulf. In it, Ibn Rajab, the famous Hanbali jurist, resorts to the frequent use of the charming phrase 'insolent imbeciles' for those who disagree with his position. Ibn Rajab argues that in order to properly practice Islam, one is obligated to choose a school of jurisprudential thought and strictly follow the writings and analysis of the chief jurist (and subsequent jurists) of that school of thought.

Do not think even for a moment of talking yourself into believing that you perceive something that this Imam was unaware of, or understood something that he did not reach. Put all your efforts into understanding the words of this Imam concerning all the issues of knowledge, not (just) the issues of Islam. Do not think. That is the charge of neo-traditionalists of all stripes in three words. Be they white, Arab, Black, it makes no difference. Their charge is to not think lest one sway from God's intention. Claiming the need to keep static Arab cultural traditions and interpretations of Islam for the preservation of the faith regardless of the political is the mechanism by which we make non-movement faithful. We are the caretakers of sameness. Among Muslims, white men touting the unfettered objectivity of traditionalism reign supreme in the West among immigrants and their progeny. The great paralysing forces of religion, identity, and nationalism intoxicate the masses of Muslim followers allowing their domestication by those who preach non-movement as authenticity. Through a discourse of permanence we justify our physical and intellectual abuse by our own religious leaders. Theologies of permanence discourage a commitment to intervention upon the world in order to change it. The belief that we will never change our reality is a symptom of hopelessness. It is difficult to parse a conceptual distinction between losing hope and losing faith. If we define Islam by its non-movement how can it be a force for social movement toward justice or personal development? To be paralysed in this way is opposed to human design. And thus, a deformed understanding of being-Muslim in the modern comes to fruition.

Most Muslims agree that Islam can influence the development of the world in a positive way. Surprisingly, most Muslims also believe that Islam does not change and cannot reform to meet the needs of the day because its authenticity lies in a far away history. Those two ideas can't coexist. Our intoxication with a golden age paradise of Islamic moral excellence renders us driving from the rear view mirror. This is how rocket scientists, brain surgeons, and tech gurus are convinced that they cannot reason through their faith and faithfulness to meet the needs of the day. They abdicate to the nearest convincing authority. Then, in a feat of parasitic excellence, become a follower, then the best follower, then teacher of the new followers. Everyone is following toward a mirage that never existed and cannot come to fruition in the modern while maintaining Islamic ethics.

All brands of organised Islam have come to believe that a lack of critical consciousness among their followers is more Islamic than a critical posture upon the world and the word. Islamists and neo-traditionalists spar on social media. At the core of their ideologies and banking pedagogies of education, they prefer sameness of ideas and conformity. Despite one team shaving their moustache, they are the same. They engage in conceptually bankrupt positions that value allegiance over ethics. They fetishise their political leaders who dress soldiers in ancient Ottoman war garb. They turn to religious leaders who dress like saints with flowing robes of majesty and piety. Looking for a connection to something, anything to regain honour to their identities is their primary mode of identity acquisition. Power is their aim, if it needs to be Ottoman rather than Saudi, so be it.

In his work *This is Not Propaganda*, Peter Pomerantsev presents Svetlana Boym's idea of restorative nostalgia. Restorative nostalgia 'strives to build the lost homeland with paranoiac determination, poses as truth and tradition, obsessed over grand symbols and relinquishes critical thinking for emotional bonding. Unreflective nostalgia can breed monsters'. As Muslims, we have been tricked into believing that our primary goal is to re-build lost greatness. Abu Bakr Al Baghdadi and Hassan Nasrallah, supposed sectarian opposites, are arguing for the exact same thing: Muslim supremacy through the resurgence of a faith-based state. They both manage, before Baghdadi was killed, territory and run governments in the hope that one day they will conquer all others for Islam. Why? Who commissioned us with that? Regressive traditionalism of paranoiac determination is not the domain of Muslim social/religious conservatives alone. The tricks of domestication among all Muslims are the same. The process of domestication and blinding to reality in the name of lost greatness is universal.

In today's America, the most famous Muslim leaders are bifurcated between two constantly competing tribes. The first, and perhaps the most avant-garde, is the camp of neo-traditionalists. Among them are those who have taken it upon themselves to preach against democracy and individual agency. They stand against the wisdom of the masses by convincing them to align themselves with those who oppress them in the name of stability. The stability of government and the stability of faith. From the corpus of faith they argue that citizens don't have a right to respond to their injustice because their leaders know better what is in their interests. They cite ancient text to convince people that their intellectual and civic contribution is not needed. Rather, they argue that acquiescence to oppression is faithfulness. Closely aligned with dictatorships that arm private militias sparking the destruction of countries in the Global South, they claim to be the arbiters of Islamic ethics in our time. Despite their good intentions, they work to make us dumber, quieter, and more acquiescent. Through their lectures, retreats, *halaqas*, universities, sermons and students they argue that the original scholars of their respective schools of thought yielded to no personal subjectivity. Their original scholars were super-human in their capacity to maintain eternal objectivity for all times and places. The objective power of their reasoning should bind our discourse a thousand years later and bind our lives, politics and social relations. Only the individual at the top of the hierarchy of a specific school of thought can engage in critical reasoning to meet the needs of the times. One man, always a man, per school of thought or their representative in your local community is allowed to agitate, to think, to construct a more just reality.

Neo-traditionalists chime in on the appointment of accused rapist Brett Kavanaugh to the Supreme Court arguing that there were not four witnesses to his alleged rape of Christine Blasé-Ford. They aim to team up with other evangelical neo-traditionalist Americans of varying faiths to limit the freedom of citizens and design societies that reflect their sense of morality. If they could make all of reality gender segregated, they would. It makes them more comfortable. They don't shake hands with women, unless they are white women who are not Muslim. Like Vice President, Mike Pence, they are not confident in their ability to be honourable, so they prefer not to be in a room alone with a woman that isn't their wife. Lest they be tempted by the devil to be indecent, they prefer that all females cover to keep them from yearning to transgress.

The second tribe, which holds much more active power across the grassroots of American Muslim life, is the disorganised coalition of varying stripes of Islamist inspired acronym organisations. This camp is much more versatile than neo-traditionalists in their ability to politically engage the modern and build progressive coalitions. Their woke brand allows them to neatly move into the space of liberal political action while maintaining mosques, organisations and realities that are dominated by Arab men, cultural traditionalism and banking theories of education. Islamists like to promote women who appear to be models for how they prefer other women to act. They also claim to be the advocates of democracy. They do so, however, through ethical contortions of unmatched proportion rendering their wall of magic of beliefs impenetrable to reason. When Fethullah Gulen was Recep Erdogan's friend American Islamist academics and their supporters wrote books praising him. When Erdogan turned on Gulen, they joined Michael Flynn, Paul Manafort, and Rudy Giuliani arguing for extradition to Turkey. When a military dictatorship in a Muslim majority society rips up a constitution they light the mosques of the West with fiery speeches that weave scripture, political philosophy, and folklore. When an Islamist government does it, America's Muslim Brotherhood activists go on vacation to Istanbul. They dare not critique the policies of Saudi Arabia lest they be denied entry for the annual money making *hajj* expeditions that float their families financially for most of the year.

Despite the clear split among leaders, followers in the United States flow between the two camps assembling an identity that bobs and weaves according to the passions of the scholar of the day. One will often find among Islamists and neo-traditionalists the frequency of citing Hadith, the sayings of scholars, or the analysis of jurists (lawyers) more than Qur'an. This, in turn, leads to the invocation of time-specific traditions, norms, habits, instances, or even coincidences as a component of the corpus of canonised knowledge. The banking theory of education is the primary mode of engagement between both groups rendering those who emulate and reinforce what once was as the most capable of leadership. Each student races for the most immediate opportunities to acquire certified deposits of knowledge leaving no room for their personal reflection and analysis. This is why often we find the students of Islamists and neo-traditionalists being more conservative and regressive than their teachers. They are excelling in what they've been taught. Their organisations are not democratic, their ideas are not progressive but don the garb of liberalism.

Let us explore some common denominating pillars of Western Muslim regression. Then, provide a competing paradigm that can perhaps liberate us from our intellectual and thus spiritual slumber. At the outset, none of this is personal. I have great respect for the people critiqued below.

Critical thinking is taboo in Western Muslim life. It is not permitted. Those who challenge the ideology of their respective community are quickly blocked from leadership positions and relegated to the liminal state of the un-mosqued. Muslim spaces in the West are factories of cultural reproduction masquerading as religious knowledge. Unique among Western religious groups is reverence for white converts among congregations of immigrant-cultured affluent young professionals. Whether Islamists or neo-traditionalists, whiteness holds great value in Western Muslim life. No one from any camp dare argue for Islamic reform, lest they be deemed too liberal, which is communal code for not good for your children. They surely don't dare do so in opposition to a white convert with moderate Arabic skills, because mediocre white Muslim men are committed to making Islam great again.

The most famous British neo-traditionalist is Abdul Hakim Murad, original name Timothy Winter, of the Cambridge Muslim College. In a series of videos, he argues that 1,400 years of scholars investigating the issues we deal with today should displace our individual thinking. Sound familiar? It's an Ibn Rajab remix. Winter, like other neo-traditionalists argues that ideas of reform elevate fallible human critical capacity beyond its appropriate scope limiting the wisdom of Islam. He goes so far as to say that positions, such as mine, which encourage incorporating the wisdom of scholars as input to our subjective experience and final determination is a form of shirk (belief in a God other than God alone). To think and make our own decisions is shirk? Not much movement possible there. Winter argues that challenging the scholars and the import of their subjectivities upon our reality is a form of believing in a God alongside God. He goes on to explain that challenging or diverging from the opinion of these scholars is tantamount to back-biting, in reference to the Qur'anic image of eating the dead burned flesh of the scholars of Islamic history. Why do we terrorise ourselves away from thinking? People come to believe that thinking will land them in hell, literally. Message delivery by a white man with a British accent, who converts to Islam, carries great weight. So thousands decide not to think, lest they weaken their faithfulness.

The encouragement to not individually engage the ethics of Islam and apply them to our lives is often tied to an understated, but widely whisper-disseminated conspiracy among neo-traditionalists. Religious leaders convince Muslims that liberalism is coming for their faith, cultural norms, and gender identity. Like Trump, they whistle to the base that the world wants to change them. Religious identity under threat from dilution becomes yet another catalyst for non-movement. In our current reality, Western Muslims achieve authenticity by rejecting change.

Leaders often find themselves stuck between actions that were once upon a time sanctioned under Islamic law and their unethical application in the modern. They convince their neo-traditionalist and Islamist congregations that there is divergence between the normative principles of Islam and the legal regimes of the societies in which we live. For instance, in Southern California, there are circles of Muslims who use Muslim lawyers to create cohabitation agreements circumventing bigamy laws allowing for multiple wives. The same folks oppose the use of cohabitation agreements to circumvent the once upon a time ban on gay marriage but find no ethical challenge in using them for polygamy. When challenged on the illegality of their actions and the possibility they are engaged in human and sex trafficking, they revert to claims of Islamic authenticity. They move in on the uninformed Islam-illiterate masses for business. Convincing a wealthy community that wants to contract out of their rights in America pursuant to pre-purposed pietism is a great business model. As long as someone says it is more authentically Islamic, they are willing to cut the deal. Convincing American Muslims that they should give their daughters an inheritance that is less than they deserve pursuant to state law, they appear as the arbiters of an objective past looking for reincarnation in the modern. A magical world akin to Willy Wonka's where girls get less chocolate, because they are girls.

Our scholars waffle. They don't loudly condemn Imams who groom underage girls and they step aside when others defend female genital mutilation. When accused of excluding women from communal leadership they claim that sister so and so spoke on issues that relate to women. They preach equity and not equality for women. All in the name of protecting, conserving, and preserving. The most liberal neo-traditionalist will say that Western Muslims should not openly support gay marriage because it will dilute the concept of marriage and will send a message to Muslims that we accept homosexuality. Thus, they argue, Muslims should not allow ethics to determine how they stand on issues of justice. So we stand for injustice in the name of conserving with paranoiac determination what was once (1,000 years ago) the ethical tenor of society. Injustice for justice is peak hyper-reality.

Surely this approach to understanding Islam doesn't come from the US or the UK. It originates in the Arab world where all attempts at finding authenticity in the face of coloniality led to deformations of religion and culture. Like Napoleon insisting upon the Egyptian religious establishment to criminalise all sin to prove their civility, Western Muslim leaders import social regression to prove their God-given superiority to surrounding culture. One would assume there are issues upon which there would be sharp divergence between Western and Arab-world Muslim scholars given the very different realities they live. Allow me to walk you through the neo-traditionalist condemnation of sex slavery to highlight the chaotic incoherence Muslims are faced with in the US and the UK.

In his book *Refuting ISIS*, Shaikh Muhammad al-Yacoubi, a major Syrian religious and intellectual figure, articulates his argument against the terrorist organisation from his perspective of Islamic law. I once met Yacoubi at the White House, a kind and sincere man. Shaikh Yacoubi is opposed to ISIS and is rightfully applauded as a moderate. Yacoubi tackles ISIS and their use of sex slavery. He explains that there is no harm in heads of state of Muslim majority societies from signing international treaties that obligate them against slavery. If other nations were to break their contracts and begin enslaving Muslims or non-Muslim citizens in Muslim nations, then it would be permissible for the Muslims to retaliate accordingly against the violating nations.

Wait, what just happened? You mean we revert to juristic opinions (rulings) of people in times when the rules of prisoners of war in Islam were significantly more progressive than the existent legal regimes. And we will use them to justify the use of sex slavery today? Really? Yacoubi is saying that there are modern conditions or circumstances that permit the use of sex slavery as a sanctioned Islamic activity in 2019.

That an agreement with a non-Muslim leader or nation is a departure from the normative Islamic position, that there are circumstances in which slavery is permitted, is nothing less than an injustice toward Islam. They will insist it is tradition. They will insist it is fiqh. How could this possibly be? The idea of retaliation is so out of place in the spirit of the Qur'an and the Prophetic tradition as applied to our time that it should be challenged as a poisonous philosophy of conflict resolution. What is the purpose of this confusion and inability to articulate an ethical stand with moral clarity? What does it do other than satiate the insecurities of the masses? How can self-decimation in the modern be Islamic?

We have socially constructed our Muslim identities in a way that ostracises us from normalcy, beauty, and reasonableness. Notice the inability to articulate reasonable dialectics between genres of ethics and law with use of phrases like - these agreements do not nullify. This is how we construct an argument against ISIS? It falls so far short of what is needed for our time. How can anyone exercise agency as a Muslim if this is the guidance we receive from the most learned among us? The ones who challenge the terrorists from the bowels of faith.

I am reminded of Paulo Freire's admonition that 'to affirm that men and women are persons, and as persons, should be free, and yet to do nothing tangible to make this affirmation a reality, is a farce.' We can't even get our leaders to affirm that as persons we should be free to condemn sex slavery without any confusion. We cannot stand for this freedom in the twenty-first century because we are afraid of the degradation of Islam. We are afraid that if we go against any component of what has come to be in history we will ruin our religion. We fear diluting or breaking Islam in some way. Our fragility is turning us into backers of ugliness in the name of beauty. What we are offering the world is fundamentally not reasonable, and not ethical! I am not talking about some liberal conception of Western ethics – I am speaking to the core of the construction of the Islamic in the modern. It should be clear and without question that any form of slavery in our time is un-Islamic and unacceptable under any rationale or analysis. This is doable – there is no requirement of the scholar to fault what has come before us to say that as of now, there is an absolute moratorium on all forms of slavery in all times from this day forward. Period. Full stop (for the Brits). Nothing else is needed. What is offered here, instead, is the deformation of Islam in the name of tradition. A glimpse of Umberto Echo's hyper-reality where we are constructing things to appear more real than what is real. As if Walt Disney was the head of their school of thought. We are dreaming of paradise and creating a living hell in the name of Islam, in the name of God.

Yacoubi then goes on to vociferously condemn the sexual enslavement of Yazidi women by ISIS, which is welcome! The confusion, however, ensues in an endless series of hedges and dance-steps to accommodate camps of ideology and their emotional states of defeatism. One of his reasons for opposing the slavery of Yazidis and the sexual abuse of Yazidi women is that even 'if ISIS was to implement the principle of retributive justice, the Yazidis have not enslaved any Muslims to warrant such retaliatory measures'. What? How is this reasonable? Could this not be seen as a display of complete and utter confusion and inability to clearly state an unequivocal moral position to represent Islam in the modern? What is a young person in Southern California supposed to learn from this line of reasoning? That we do inhumane things if the other side does? We meet sex slavery with sex slavery? Yacoubi is bringing the culture of desert Arabs 1,400 years ago directly into the realities we are living today. How can anyone take us seriously with this kind of thinking? This can't be our best effort in the West in an era of international law and human rights norms. We will be war criminals if the other side commits war crimes? That's Islam in 2020?

So, a young Muslim in America goes online to understand what is happening and she is met with this analysis as the authoritative take on the issue. Allow me to note here that social media is a very important medium for communication in Western Muslim life for two reasons. First, until the advent of social media, American Muslim leaders were regional figures. Getting to scale financially and communally was a difficult task in the 80s and 90s of American Muslim activism. Second, there is very little reading at the popular level of Muslim community life because most Muslims believe that truth lies in the secret Arabic code of ancient texts. In that sense, the works of modern scholars write are not read by the community, thus there is a mismatch between the scholar class and the masses. Generally, scholars of all stripes live good lives. They are reasonable and open to private disagreement and discussion. Their influence, however, is rarely correlated to their intellectual output. Some of the most famous American Muslim scholars have translated a couple ancient pamphlets at best. Their scholarship is sourced in banking ideas and quotations not in research and the development of knowledge that benefits the masses. Their role is to ornament the past, resulting in a bejewelled and bedazzled Islam that appeals to our need for respect in the face of oppression and emotional displacement. Instead of glasses to envision a more beautiful future, we place blinders on ourselves like donkeys averting distraction in Cairo traffic.

With the advent of websites, blogs, YouTube, and social media, American Muslim leaders developed direct access to congregations across the country and around the world. People like disgraced (sexual abuse) Imam Nouman Ali Khan or the disgraced Tariq Ramadan (accused of multiple rapes) could not succeed in getting to scale on both sides of the Atlantic without technology and social media. This opened potential audiences and donors. All of this is to say, never underestimate what looks to young people as a fatwa on Facebook. They carry great weight at the popular level. There are almost no other sources of Islamic knowledge at the popular level of American Muslim life. We don't read books. We have Imams that read for us and then spoon-feed us like children to make us feel that everything will be ok. And we like, then share their incoherence to ensure we've done our part.

Let us point to an American example of the same insistence on incoherence as identity. Imam Zaid Shakir is one of the most prominent American Muslim leaders alive and with Shaykh Hamza Yusuf is a founder of Zaytuna College. A voice of sanity, reason, love, encouragement, hope, and faithfulness, he is loved by the masses and I love him. With an ability to speak to young people and a life of service to community and nation (Air Force) – he is a critical component of the current Muslim American experience. He is also a neo-traditionalist. In a Facebook post, dated 13 August 2015, entitled 'ISIS, Sex Slaves and Islam', Imam Zaid Shakir attempts to allay the fears and horror of American Muslims in what they see ISIS doing. His first post on the subject was ten paragraphs long and appeared to be a reasoned and intentional intervention. The purpose, I assumed, was to help the community deal with a *New York Times* article highlighting the use of sexual slavery by ISIS. Imam Zaid opens with a call for concern among Muslims arguing that ISIS 'presents its practices as normative Islam and accuses the masses of Muslims who reject their draconian interpretation of the religion as ignoramuses or cowards who are afraid to identify with real Islam'. Yes, this is welcome. But notice the centre of gravity in the framing of the analysis is that which has become normative in the construction of the Islamic is real Islam. Real Islam? Normative to whom, where, when, and in what situations? Who are the holders of this real Islam? I shouldn't ask that, I already know the answers. The Imams.

The first thing we should understand about slavery is that it is not an integral part of Islam such as praying, fasting, the prohibition of interest, etc. As such, it is amenable to being rejected without any sin falling on the one rejecting it. For this reason, every Muslim nation has legally outlawed slavery. The fact that slavery is not an integral part of Islam also means that fatwas associated with it are amenable to change with changing circumstances.

Is that really the first thing we should understand? In the twenty-first century, the first thing we need to understand about slavery is that it is not integral to Islam? Why is the first sentence not – the first thing we should understand is that there is no place for slavery in Islam. At no point does he clearly and directly reject it under all circumstances. All fatwas are amenable to change, every single one! They are the product of humans practicing law in a time and place pursuant to their limited subjectivity. The baseline opinion of neo-traditionalists is that fatwas are not amenable to change? Every Muslim nation is now our guiding light for legality and ethics in the modern? These bastions of injustice and oppression are where we get our guidance on how to be Muslim in the modern? If every Muslim nation legalised sex-slavery does it suddenly become Islamic? Is Islam like customary international law where action that is not opposed becomes normative or is it based on some ethical parameters (maqasid) from which we begin our analysis? If by integral part of Islam you mean creed, then creed comes from the Qur'an not from fatwas. There is nothing in a human being's opinion that rises to the level of something that is integral to Islam. That means all fatwas without any exception can and should be challenged and are binding upon nobody but the mufti of that specific fatwa. The way Imam Zaid writes it, one would think that the core components of Islam's creed come from fatwas, they don't. They come from God. This amplifying of the role of Imams as intermediaries of the Lord and the consequent Catholicisation of Imam culture is one of the primary reasons Muslims are afraid of thinking. Especially when they see pictures of their leaders dressed in flowing white robes presented to the world as equals to the Pope. Then, like Shaikh Yacoubi's intervention, Imam Zaid goes off the rails of reasonableness and ventures into the realms of hyper-reality:

> For those who argue that Islam has retained sexual slavery as a deterrent to other nations from going to war against Muslims; in the current context, the

actions of ISIS are being used to fan the flames of war against Muslims. In that the ruling to re-institute slavery has lost its deterrent power, the ruling itself collapses.

Wait, what? It is as if when we talk about Islam we forget everything we know about humanity. We shut off our minds to please God. The rationale for why Islam should not retain sex slavery is that it is not de facto functioning as a deterrent to attacks against Muslims? As opposed to saying: the idea of sexual slavery as a deterrent for the actions of others is an unethical concept sourced in the morality of a different time that does not have any bearing on the way we live today as Muslims. We as Muslims do not engage in immoral action because others choose to do so against us. Our religion is a religion of ethics, we are not interested in reducing the level of freedoms a person enjoys on this earth for political gain.

Imam Zaid argues that the reasoning for the ruling allowing sex slavery is no longer valid because its pre-requisite conditions have not been met. This is why the intelligent faithful must turn their minds off to maintain their faithfulness. This makes no sense. There were so many reasonable avenues to take in his analysis. He can argue that the ethical standards of society at the time of the ruling are no longer relevant. Or that the ugliness and taking of human dignity has no place in a way of life that submits to the majesty of God. He could argue that this ruling was only viable in light of Qur'anic ethics because the custom of the time was more oppressive than the reality the rulings constructed. Or, that these issues are for governments to manage. He could then underscore that we as Muslims in the West are clearly bound by the normative ethos of US and international law. No, none of that.

This kind of unreasonable thinking is what has Muslims leaving Islam in droves, and encourages those who don't choose Islam as a way of life to look at us as though we are transplants of an ugly history. Exactly what Imam Zaid is trying to combat is what he is facilitating. Allowing our differences with ISIS to appear as mere legalism, we mainstream malignance. Al Qaeda's condemnation of ISIS was stronger than this! It facilitates for extremists to convince young people to join their ranks, the opposite of its intended purpose. Muslims in the West are losing the essence of our faith because of our inability to engage the modern with authenticity and intelligence. Zero reflexivity. We don't look inward. Instead, white converts argue that slavery in Islam was better than trans-Atlantic slavery. Imam Zaid continues his analysis.

Another relevant legal principle is consideration of the future harm resulting from implementing a ruling. This principle is subordinate to the principle of removing the means that lead to an unlawful end, even if those means, in some cases, are themselves lawful. In the case of ISIS and slavery, one of the frightening implications of their actions is that it is turning people away from Islam in unprecedented numbers.

Notice how all authority and all determinations of what this religion is and is not revolves around the law and the principles of analysis in application of the law. We are still mired in the law to the extent that it no longer makes any sense. Then he says that removing a means that leads to an unlawful end is necessary in Islam. This is correct as a principle oscillating in a vacuum. What is the means he is referring to? Sexual slavery. Wait. Are these means permissible if they lead to a lawful end? What is the unlawful end he is speaking of? Turning people away from Islam. Not enslaving humans in sexually abusive situations? One of the most prominent Black Muslim leaders in American history offers a fatwa on sex slavery and the reasoning for why it should not be used by ISIS is that it leads to people leaving Islam? How can this be?

> Our religion is not this hideous Frankenstein-like creation being cobbled together by ISIS and their ilk and endorsed by some Islamic studies professors at Princeton University. It is a beautiful gift of a sophisticated civilisation, however, that gift will not be understood or understandable when the principles that allow us to make sense of various rulings are cast aside.

How is a religion that is open to sex slavery in 2020, if the necessary pre-requisite measures are met, not a Frankenstein-like monster? There is nothing sophisticated about the civilisation he presents to us. Nothing. Notice the side slap to Western academia. Without providing explanation he lumps universities in concert with ISIS and their ilk. The understated dog whistle is clear. Feminism is coming for your deen. Don't let the liberal West change your faith. Don't let them get you to hate yourself. In Southern California Imams who were born in Southern California refer to

America in the third person. Why would we resist change? Are we for sex slavery? Is that what we stand for?

When Imam Zaid's opinion was published many in the community were not comfortable. In response to the critique of his analysis, white Islamist convert Jonathan Brown, of the al-Waleed Center for Muslim-Christian Understanding at Georgetown University, volunteered himself as a defender of Imam Zaid. Brown argued that no self-respecting scholar could do more than what Imam Zaid offered because it would require a nullification of scholarly analysis and consensus over time in the development of Islamic law. He argued that any expectation of Imam Zaid calling for the complete abolition of slavery is not reasonable. That's a Georgetown professor, another white convert, insisting that you cannot be a respectable scholar of Islam if you call for a complete prohibition of sex slavery. What is a kid in a mosque in a random town supposed to think? Well, we took care of that. They aren't allowed to think.

Allow me now to conclude with a final example of how to deal with this issue. This example serves as a stark contrast to the approaches offered above in that it is sourced in pedagogy of critique and critical analysis. In his seminal text, *In Pursuit of Justice: The Jurisprudence of Human Rights in Islam*, Maher Hathout tackles the issue of slavery in Islam with its own chapter. The chapter opens with a claim to the authority of international law in citing both the UN Declaration of Human Rights and the Universal Islamic Declaration of Human Rights. Immediately, there is a clear and unambiguous statement of affirmation that what is normative international law should be seen as a core component of the rights and freedoms guaranteed to all people. Including for Muslims and by Muslims. We are not excepted as chosen by God to deviate from the ethical norms of our time.

The second paragraph, trying to relay the immediacy felt by the author, of the chapter is an admonition of Muslim majority societies for taking too long to institute corollary national laws that reflect the international standard. 'Furthermore, the illegal practice of slavery continues to the present day in different forms. Also, the exploitation of domestic workers and illegal trafficking of women all over the world continues to be a modern-day manifestation of slavery.' There is absolutely no hesitation whatsoever. Notice the ascription to international normative principles over opaque and archaic legal rulings 1,000 years old to set the tenor for the conversation. He also allows slavery to be defined according to its modern manifestations. There is no confusion on where this chapter is going or what ethical ground it stands on.

> This chapter seeks to address this issue from an Islamic perspective, highlight-ing the contrast between the Qur'anic text and the actual, historical practice of slavery by Muslims. From a doctrinal, Islamic perspective, we firmly con-demn slavery as an affront to the natural state of freedom in which God cre-ated human beings and to the very first pillar of Islam (the declaration of faith), which indicates that no person or power has the right to enslave people.

This is the discourse of an ethical Muslim in our time. This is a discourse that attracts beautiful, intelligent people who want to bring about justice and beauty in the world as Muslims. This is a discourse that accedes to our equality with all other people and honours human dignity. At the outset Hathout strikes a clear demarcation between God's authority and the actions of Muslims in history with no hesitation. Muslims are not holy. Only God is holy. This passage defines Hathout's approach to everything that requires analysis – always starting with the Qur'anic ethics. He then condemns slavery in all forms for all times from now until the last day of humanity. Insisting on his obligation to God to only pursue justice and to stand against oneself if justice necessitates, Hathout doesn't mince words. There should be absolutely no slavery. Why? Because it is against the *Design* of the ultimate *Designer* – it goes counter to the natural order of humanity. He believed that freedom is a necessary pre-requisite to true faithfulness. It is the declaration of faith, the first statement of being a Muslim that nullifies any argument for slavery. Not the ins and outs of underground tunnel work of incoherence in order to see the light.

The Qur'an never legislated slavery, but legislated abolition. The issue here is not so much why slavery should be, quite rightly, prohibited today, but the fact that we need to go beyond the historical Qur'anic context as we interpret Islam with regard to contemporary issues and problems. Universal normative principles such as justice and equality and freedom, which have a clear basis in the Qur'an, are the primary, underlying sources of an Islamic human rights framework. We need not rely exclusively on traditional Islamic Jurisprudence, especially with regard to the slavery issue.

Hathout returns to Qur'anic ethics and offers an analysis of what the overall trajectory of the Qur'an is regarding slavery. Surprisingly, neither Yacoubi nor Shakir ever state simply that the Qur'an advocates the abolition of slavery. Hathout offers an extensive verse-by-verse analysis of slavery in the Qur'an and what the objectives of the verses analysed together encourage. Abolition. If there is a clear basis in the Qur'an to argue for a more humane engagement with reality and argue for more freedoms and dignity for humanity then it is incumbent upon us to do so! The statement that Shaikh Yacoubi and Imam Zaid couldn't make is the one Hathout makes because he does not subscribe to Winter and Ibn Rajab's admonition to not dare and think. Thinking critically is faithfulness. Hathout encourages us to not rely exclusively on Islamic jurisprudence as it exists, rather we should be engaged in the work of meeting the aims and objectives of that law in our time. We should actively participate with our God-given agency in defining what it means to be Muslim today.

> Freedom is a natural right of all human beings. Freedom is inherent in the creation of man by God, and is a component of human dignity ... From an Islamic perspective slavery is a socially constructed institution and not a hereditary one. All children are born free.

All children are born free is neither astrophysics nor neuroscience. Yet neuroscientists and astrophysicists need their Imam to find the words to condemn sex slavery in our time. Zaid and Yacoubi insist that the principles that make Islam beautiful are the ones associated with the promulgation of law and placed upon jurists as a methodology of exegesis and jurisprudential commentary. Hathout derives the principles he uses for analysis directly from the Qur'an. Hathout's pedagogy is a critical pedagogy of Islamic liberation theology. Where faith exists to free us from ugliness not mire us in webs of confusion. It seeks to empower the believer to engage God in real-time. By giving agency to the believer it is possible to construct Islam in the modern in a way that allows the light of the Qur'an to shine upon the world through the actions of Muslims. There can be liberation from the socio-cultural realities of 1,400 years ago! Hathout makes clear that what is socially constructed can be deconstructed, including the opinion of jurists. Yes, I understand this is anathema to neo-traditionalists.

Justice derives from the equality of all human beings, with their moral freedom and human dignity, as created by God, but it is manifested in their equality before the (temporal) law, with equal legal rights and duties. The state must treat all of its citizens with equity and cannot restrict the freedom of any human being by enslaving them. To do so is to limit the human condition. Justice according to the Divine plan is based on our equality as human beings, without which, the whole narrative of human experience is meaningless from an Islamic standpoint. The state does not have the right to take away from freedom and dignity granted by God, even if it claims to be a state that represents the will of God. The Imam is under the same limitation. A Muslim cannot deny her God-granted freedom to be a believer of ethics that are coherent with the times.

If the discourse of American and British Muslims and the discourse of Muslims in Muslim majority societies is exactly the same then we have failed. If freedom of thought, movement, association, worship, participation in politics, and diversity – if with all of these blessings and tools from God – we re-create what has been created then we have failed. Not just failed on the level of sociology. We fail on the level of faith, on the level of our ontological purpose in being created. Failing in our worship of God. When what we create resembles what can only be created under the most extreme conditions of oppressive backwardness and regression, then we are not meeting our obligation as Muslims. Our obligation for the global community of Muslims in the future is to push as far as possible in our journey for renewal, growth, and renaissance to a more impressive understanding of both the word and the world. Not with the intention of displacing the journeys of other communities and societies. Rather, pursuant to the recognition of our obligation to do the best we can with what we have. And we have been given a great deal! The process of seeing our faith as embodying a theology that liberates humans will culminate in our collective critical consciousness.

As of now, Muslim tech executives, physicians, and engineers gather around their Teslas in the parking lots of mosques in Orange County, California. Their tradition is to hand scoop biryani onto jumbo slices of halal beef pepperoni pizza in gender-segregated gatherings on Ramadan nights. This, to them, is Islam in America.

THE MUSLIM INTERNATIONAL

Sohail Daulatzai in conversation with
Peter Mandaville

Peter Mandaville: We're engaging with you in the context of a project we've been working on over the last couple of years called 'The Muslim Atlantic' in which we explore the intersection of questions of race, gender and securitisation within Muslim communities in North America and Europe. But, of course, you can't talk about something like the Muslim Atlantic without recognising that the Atlantic in question is not only northern, but also southern. It includes the Caribbean, West Africa, and South America. The breadth of the geography in Lupe Fiasco's song, 'The Show Goes On', really captures it for me.

And so I wanted to start by asking you what this concept of the Muslim Atlantic means to you? What does it invoke for you? How should we think about it in the context of a broader set of contemporary discussions of coloniality and decoloniality?

Sohail Daulatzai: It's an excellent question and a really compelling frame to think through the kind of ideas, currents and forms of resistance that have trafficked across the world. I think it's a really provocative frame that is clearly indebted to Paul Gilroy's monumental and influential Black Atlantic. And it's one of the things that I tried to address in my work because Gilroy's *Black Atlantic* is clearly thinking about space and geography, pushing back against the concept of the nation-state as a kind of limiting space for thinking about redemptive Black possibility. Which I think is an incredibly edifying and astute point. But as I wrote about it in *Black Star, Crescent Moon*, Gilroy is in some ways reproducing the very problem that he sought to address by replacing one geography – the nation-state – with another one, the Black Atlantic.

That said, I do think it's still a very generative and productive way to think about the histories and enduring legacies of the so called New World and the violences that it has inaugurated, which are undeniable and, seemingly intractable. So for me, the Atlantic and the Black Atlantic in particular is a very redemptive kind of reclaiming. It provides a particular and productive space for thinking about that violence and the forms of resistance that were sought and mobilised against it.

But in thinking about Gilroy's work and the kind of horrors that modernity inaugurated, I was wondering about how do we also think about Muslim or in particular Black Muslim longing or aspirations embodied in someone like Malcolm X, or so many others? And so I thought that it was important to provide a more robust account of what was happening within, across and beyond the Atlantic. And I felt like another way of thinking about these kinds of histories, circulations, and networks was to think about — and I think we'll talk about it later - this notion of the Muslim International.

So I do find the Muslim Atlantic very powerful, because I do think that when we think about the histories of the Africans who were enslaved, and the presence of Islam amongst the Africans who were enslaved, it's very hard to ignore that centrality. And then also, when we think about the histories of migration, forced migration, exile, refugees, coming from parts of the Global South, from Muslim majority countries as a result of a whole set of forces, such as war, colonialism, and empire, you start to see a very rich and vibrant space potentially emerging. So I find it very compelling and enriching. But I would just want us to be attuned to the spaces that are imagined and conjured beyond the Atlantic that make these redemptive visions so resonant.

PM: It's been remarkable to me to observe the persistence and, maybe of late, even a resurgence of interest in the figure of Malcolm X. But it's also hard not to notice that there seem to be so many Malcolms in the sense of different constituencies and 'users' — if we can put it that way — of him and his legacy: many people finding in his life and his work varying trajectories and different forms of utility for their own positionality and their own activism and politics. I want to ask you to reflect on your understanding of how he is understood differently in the United States today, compared with

Europe or North Africa. What is at stake in thinking about and then recognising these differential uses of Malcolm—up to and including, as Hisham Aidi points out in his work, the fact that there are Western governments that have built counterterrorism/countering violent extremism programmes around a certain appropriation of the figure of Malcolm as someone who at some level embodies a 'usable' form of moderate Islam.

SD: I think it is a great question. And I think, if I'm going to be optimistic about thinking about these multiple uses of Malcolm or the multiple entry points that people have to try to think through Malcolm, what this reveals to me is that Malcolm was a complex figure who was addressing and trying to connect some very important and serious dots.

When we think about Malcolm there are so many ways that he is remembered: as a Pan-Africanist, a Muslim, a colour-blind universalist, a Black nationalist, a Civil Rights icon, some would even go so far and say a Marxist. So there are these differing and even contradictory ideas about Malcolm that circulate, so that for example, and I'm speaking in somewhat broad brushstrokes here, but Leftists tend to ignore that he was a devout Muslim. Or Muslims - and here I am speaking primarily about immigrant Muslims from what we call the Middle East or West Asia and South Asia - they tend to centre on Malcolm's *hajj* and tend to see him as a colour-blind universalist and ignore how vigorously Malcolm continued to struggle against white supremacy even after *hajj*. Then there are Nationalists who tend to erase his Third World internationalism, or the way in which Malcolm is thought of as a Civil Rights hero even though he was vehemently opposed to Civil Rights as a framework for thinking about Black redress.

So Malcolm falls through the cracks in some ways, and I think it's always important to re-centre him and to again, think about the kinds of dots he was trying to connect. Because I believe that the hermeneutical war that is ongoing around Malcolm is a genuine one, and that the aspiration to 'claim' Malcolm as it were, is because the violent forces that he was speaking out about are still very much alive today. And in some ways, much of the Black Radical Tradition that he was not only a part of but that he also helped inaugurate, has been decimated. So I think this struggle over his meaning is a result of the urgent necessity of his thinking.

What's hopeful or at least promising is that Malcolm left us with a robust, vibrant body of work – meaning his speeches, his writings, and his diaries right? These are undeniable – so that any attempts to try and reframe him could be addressed if we engage Malcolm through deep study. And that's something I tried to do in *Black Star, Crescent Moon*, which is essentially a book about Malcolm X and his enduring influence across politics, social movements, and the arts.

For me Malcolm is important because he laid bare the global nature of white supremacy, and he tied the domestic struggles around race and white supremacy to the anti-colonial struggles taking place around the Third World, imagining Black people in the US not as a national minority but as part of a global majority. And in doing that he strongly opposed the Civil Rights logic that tied Black peoples' fate to the American project of empire, and the idea that America's enemies were therefore Black people's enemies. Instead Malcolm understood that a more robust reckoning with white supremacy had to be undertaken, a struggle that was global. As Malcolm would often quip, and I'm paraphrasing here, if you wanted to understand what was happening in Jim Crow Mississippi you would have to look at the Congo or Cairo or Palestine. Or in Malcolm's words 'what the police do locally the military does globally'. These are profoundly insightful claims and even theorisations about the nature of domination and the white supremacist glue that binds them. That is why for Malcolm the problem of Black suffering had to be internationalised and not nationalised or domesticated, because as he saw it, Black people getting a 'piece of the pie' here in the States was not only an illusion or an elusive quest, but even the attempt at it was going to perpetuate a racist global system and imperil if not eradicate anticolonial struggles for liberation through a tacit if not explicit support of US foreign policy and interventionism.

And so I think Malcolm and his thinking has deep implications for today, especially in the ways that various Black and other non-white communities – Muslims included – either so readily identify with American-ness, or worse buy into its assumptions about the rest of the world and America's role in that world. Malcolm striped the veneer off of the narrative of American exceptionalism that saw the US as distinct from Europe and not part of that legacy of empire. Instead, for Malcolm, US global hegemony was and is violently complicit with the histories of European colonialism, and that is why I place him in the pantheon of other radical internationalists such as DuBois, Robeson, Claudia Jones, Fanon, Lamumba and others. And I think Malcolm, like these others, sounded the alarm and provided dire warnings that unfortunately too many of us have not heeded to this day.

And that he did this as a believer? As a practicing Muslim? That is deeply inspiring and profound in its implications – because to me his life was a shining example of how the Qur'an could be made a living reality and Islam the religion of justice that it is.

PM: This was very much reflected to me in a long conversation I had with Imam Talib 'Abdur-Rashid, from The Mosque of Islamic Brotherhood in Harlem. I had asked him about the various groups that come through there all the time on something like 'Malcolm pilgrimages': people wanting to be in places he was and to walk the streets that he walked. And Imam Talib related to me a version of exactly what you just laid out. Some who come looking for Malcolm don't want him to be black, others don't want him to be Muslim, while still others need Malcolm to be very American and less international in his orientation. And Imam Talib just shook his head as he said to me, 'I don't really know what to tell them, because whatever it is they're looking for, Malcolm either wasn't that or he was so much more than that'.

SD: Absolutely. And I think part of those blind spots have to do with how we think about what a kind of radical politics could look like. And so then it's very difficult for people to think about a particular kind of radical politics coming from a Muslim. Right? But there are then folks who want to strip that away from him, and make him a kind of a humanist, a universalist figure.

Malcolm wasn't a universalist. I mean, this is the kind of claim that many Muslims seek to make: that Malcolm had a universalist vision, right? I'm arguing that Malcolm was an internationalist, which, to me is something fundamentally different. But I think what calling Malcolm a universalist hinges on is this inability to see a radical political framework emanating from somebody who identifies as Muslim, which then deracialises not only Malcolm and the Black Radical Tradition he is central to, but it also ignores how white supremacy deeply structures an unequal global order. I think to me in some ways, there's something there that I'm always interested in exploring: what are the kinds of blind spots that different constituencies have – Muslims included – to thinking about radical politics, coming from somebody who closely identifies with Islam or being Muslim?

PM: We think and talk these days a lot about the emergence of something like a post-Western world order. How in that context should we think about the significance and future of what you so evocatively term the Muslim International? What does that mean going forward? What sorts of possibilities are present in it?

SD: I think it is important to mention that on the question of a post-Western world order, I remember as we entered the twenty-first century many people were talking about the BRICS countries - Brazil, Russia, India, China, and South Africa – as a kind of counterweight to US power. And if we think about those countries today look at where Brazil is now with Bolsonaro, Russia with Putin, India with Modi, and China with its own forms of authoritarianism. But at least four of those five BRICS countries that were supposed to be this counterweight to US power or Western power, have become either completely complicit with it or deepening and replicating forms of violence. And so, when I think about what a post-Western order is or is not, I wonder if it will still be structured by a kind of Westphalian system and forms of governance that has at its foundations the idea of racial capitalism? And is the nation-state still the predominant form for thinking about collectivity and redress?

And I ask these questions because if a post-Western world is to exist, then I wonder what it would look like, because if it is one that is still structured by racial capitalism will a non-Western entity or force or set of forces continue to carry on the traditions of an international order structured by dominance and unequal relations between regions and countries? And if so, who is dominating? And who will continue to be dominated?

PM: All of the evidence we have to date suggests the answer to those questions are: Yes. That is precisely because the countries that were supposedly the emerging alternative poles are themselves some of the greatest and enthusiastic underwriters of precisely those racialised politics.

Take for instance contemporary China as an example of mass internment or annihilation of Muslims at the hands of a state.

SD: Right. As I tell my students, the West is not a geographic or spatial designation. There is nothing that Europe, the United States, Canada, Australia, or Israel have in common spatially – they are not in the 'West' in any way. And so the West is instead an ideological and dare I say, a racial designation – a frame for thinking about the centrality of white supremacy to liberalism, modernity, democracy and rights. So, if a post-Western world is only going to replicate or even deepen those violent forces but with a 'non-Western' face, a kind of ventriloquism for whiteness, then I am not sure we're in a fundamentally different place. In fact, an argument could be made that it's worse, as we are only masking who or what our real enemy is.

And so that is why for me the Muslim International became something productive to gesture toward and to imagine as an alternative to a Western world order. As I talked about in *Black Star, Crescent Moon*, I was thinking about how through the kind of convergence of Black radical thought in the US, struggles for decolonisation and the Muslim Third World, that particular worlds, and even worldviews, were being shaped by this convergence, so that the Muslim International for me was and is a space for worldmaking where the possibilities of other imaginings and redemptive visions could be conjured.

And so in looking to think through and against the legacies of European colonialism and empire, as well as the emergent Leviathan of US empire with its own settler logics and legacies of slavery, what I was trying to do with the Muslim International was to one, name something that already existed, and two, to name something that was yet to come. So that it was both a horizon of possibility and also an imagining of a kind of futurity.

For me, the Muslim International was about forging alternative epistemologies and orientations that were markedly different from the Western liberal humanist order. And this just didn't mean only in the traditional realm of politics, but also in the realm of the political – so that it encompasses both state and non-state actors, artists, filmmakers, writers, intellectuals, exiles, refugees, and movement builders who could then deploy these alternative epistemes within the political and aesthetic realms to create new forms of sociality and a radically different world order.

Interestingly, I remember doing a talk at Columbia University and a scholar whose work I deeply admire asked what to me was a profound yet simple question: what is the purpose of naming this? And it struck me more for what it revealed. Because to me the urgent necessity of naming the Muslim International came from the inability of the world to think or even fathom the possibility that Muslims could resist, challenge and create in profound and powerful ways that were not always already dismissed because these insurgent practices didn't conform to or adhere to what is already proscribed and circumscribed by what it is thought that Muslims do. In other words, there are a whole host of ways that forms of resistance, creativity and militancy by Muslims are rendered illegible and even erased because it is assumed that Muslims can only protest in this way or that way. Now of course this is a deeply problematic and anti-Muslim way of thinking. And I'm not necessarily ascribing it to this scholar who asked the question, but this thinking is fairly commonplace on both the Right and the Left, and so I felt the need to give these ideas and imaginings some coherence without formalising them in a narrow way that would reproduce the very problem I set out to address. Because for me the Muslim International is not a monolithic space, and is instead a space of radical difference, multiplicity and even contestation over the question of liberation and emancipation. And it is important for it to remain a dissident and insurgent space that encourages transgression and that foments forms of sabotage – aesthetically, politically and otherwise.

PM: So is it your sense that the generative possibilities of the Muslim International have been foreclosed by the present configuration of global power, neoliberal economics and the racialised settler practices that are so intrinsically wrapped up with them? I should add that I ask this from the perspective of someone who views global neoliberal power as something that is not simply Western in the sense of being confined to (or originating exclusively in) something called Europe and North America or Australia but something – à la Hardt & Negri – that is increasingly planetary in scope. So is the possibility of something different as expressed by the Muslim International foreclosed now? Or do you still have some sense that perhaps through formations yet to come the Muslim International might continue to have that emancipatory potential within it?

SD: Yes, I absolutely do believe that. I clearly think that not just Muslims, there is a whole host of people who, across the world, particularly in what we can call the Global South, and various communities in the United States and in Europe who are under rabid assault. But if we are going to talk about the Muslim International, I do think that it is under attack: the artists, the movements, the organisers, the writers, the intellectuals, even the very idea of it is being violently assaulted. And so there is and has been a definite assault upon where we are positioned. And we are not the only ones. But despite being under duress, I still believe that there are spaces. And I know that folks are still actively thinking about and trying to imagine other possible futures beyond the current reality. So I'm very hopeful about it. Because that is what the Muslim International rests upon is a kind of utopic possibility.

When I wrote *Black Star, Crescent Moon*, my editor at the University of Minnesota Press said 'wow, your book really ends on a depressing note.' Because you know, I end with a chapter on the incarceration of Imam Jamil Al-Amin (formerly H. Rap Brown). And I talked about how, especially in the last two chapters with Muhammad Ali and him, the way in which the Muslim International was in the crosshairs of the US security state. But to the extent that the Muslim International resonates with you, Peter, if I could ask you that question … How do you feel about what possibilities exist?

PM: Well, one of the few hopeful things happening around me in the United States as a result of what our country is living through right now is to see elements of engagement and partnership and solidarity start to emerge between groups who under previous political configurations and framings, were not able to find common cause, but should have been natural allies for a long time. And so, when you start to see certain kinds of conversations happening between, for example, supporters of the Black Lives Matter movement, and, say, immigrant Muslim Americans – in other words groups not previously engaged with each other and to some extent even pitted against each other – then that is where I start to have a little bit of hope.

And so let's think about that on a on a global scale, let's think about that kind of subaltern solidarity as a form of internationalism. And it makes sense to talk about it in terms of the Muslim International if we want to explore one particular expression of a way of thinking about how particular experiences of racism and violence get transformed into an emancipatory project. In other words there's going to be a certain specificity to what that has looked like for Muslims, and Muslims of diverse backgrounds, different geographies, and varying cultures. But this is why I think your framing of the Muslim International for us in the book is so powerful: you ground it in the particularity of Muslim experience, but it's not exclusivist in its orientation. It is something capable of seeing itself in the specificity of other kinds of injustices and wants to engage with and work alongside those. And so the more I see Muslim activists and thinkers getting out of their communalist, sectarian, or *madhabi* bubbles and saying, 'my struggle is your struggle,' that is where I continue to have some hope.

SD: Absolutely. I mean, that is key to how I described the Muslim International, a space of overlapping diasporas and intertwined histories where solidarity is not a given but is something that is built. And so to go back to your previous question about where we can see the Muslim International now, I think there are various examples of it. For me it's embodied in the Black, Arab and Desi Muslims involved in the Black Lives Matter Movements, and also the Ferguson-Gaza solidarities around the killing of Michael Brown, which were part of a longer history of Black-Palestinian Solidarity that dates back to Malcolm X, SNCC (Student Nonviolent Coordinating Committee) and the Black Panther Party. I also see it in the Muslims who were part of the Standing Rock Sioux protests against settler-colonialism here in the United States. And also in the work of numerous activists against the institutionalisation of CVE (Countering-Violent Extremism) programmes and the military-police nexus within Muslim communities, as they fought against racist programmes that has not only furthered the surveillance of Muslim communities, but has also deepened police powers against non-Muslim Black and Brown communities here in Los Angeles and throughout the country.

In terms of artists, I saw it in the powerful video of Yasiin Bey who underwent the force feeding procedures at Guantanamo Bay that was timed with the first day of Ramadan and the hunger strikes of prisoners here in the States at Pelican Bay and other prisons. And I remember talking to him about it and the timing of it which brought together these multiple and intertwined histories and communities around the world. I also see it in the brilliant work of the artist Bouchra Khalili, the UK-based rapper Lowkey, and also in the comedy of Aamer Rahman.

I think there are so many examples that we can point to such as these that are not about a transactional solidarity, but rather a transformative solidarity that deepens our understanding of the brutal forces that we face and the connections between them. Because in thinking about the Muslim International as a set of emancipatory practices of worldmaking, it's important to recognise that these more contemporary examples that I'm pointing out have deep historic roots in both the political and artistic battles that were waged by artists and activists for decades, if not centuries. And it's not that these contemporary artists and activists are simply influenced by those in the past, it's that the forms of violence and the conditions of suffering that they are now trying to address also have deep historic roots in slavery and empire that have been perpetuated, reproduced and normalised.

So I think pointing out these examples is vital because they compel us to think historically and to act on a world that refuses to see them as such. Not that they are doing it for recognition. Not at all. In fact they are engaged in this work as acts of refusal. But it does point to the urgent need to do a kind of work of historical recovery, which is something I continue to be deeply invested in. In fact, I'm currently exploring what I'm calling the 'ghost archive' of the Muslim International through other mediums such as film, video, and other experimental forms. And I'm really interested in how, for example, do instances of potentially radical formations and utopic possibilities continue to haunt the current moment. And how do they become useful for animating the kinds of struggles that we need to have today? How do they become at least windows into thinking about alternative possibilities and utopian futures?

I think these are important questions because I think the question around emancipatory politics and Muslim agency – and the forms that such agency can or cannot take – continues to loom large because there is an assumption that 'the Left' is something that is antagonistic to Muslims, or vice versa. Or even more troubling, that Muslims cannot be involved in a truly liberatory politics. Both of these assumptions are deeply disturbing in their own right. And so then it's just easier to set up the 'straw man' of a reactionary Islam and the bogey-man Muslim against which to define supposedly genuine Left or radical politics. For me the Muslim International is not only part of and also parallel to the various attempts of the Third World project and the Black Radical Tradition (in particular in the post-World War II era), but it also helped to give shape to these, whether it was at Bandung, the Non-Aligned Movement, the Tricontinental or any of its other formations.

And so I think this historical presence has to be reckoned with, for it has profound implications for what we think of radical politics and justice today. Because if we are going to continue to excise – or exorcise - Muslims from those histories and see Muslims as antithetical or even antagonistic to emancipatory politics, then we will replicate those very same problematic notions in our current political projects and movements, while also playing into the very logic of anti-Muslim racism and the 'Long War on Terror' that sees Muslims as a problem for politics, as a threat to justice (however that is defined), and therefore as an enemy that must be vanquished.

TERRORISM

Tahir Abbas

I have been working on the study of extremism, radicalisation and terrorism for over a decade and a half, largely focusing on the topic through a sociological lens. Naturally, this affords me the opportunity to explore a range of social problems at the heart of the malaise. Much of what I have to say, however, tends to go against the grain of dominant thinking, which is not surprising, as much of the leading themes focus on ideology as the cause – as if it was as simple as that. Ideology is, evidently, important, but for the vast majority of those who go down a path towards violent extremism, it may or may not figure. For the average young Jihadi or far-right extremist, theirs is a reality shaped by their lived experience in their places of birth. It is the very few who are the ideologues with clear aims to entice vulnerable others to the call. Indeed, most of the issues relating to the problems are a function of various aspects of social breakdown, as well as the ontological and epistemological foundations for much of what passes as knowledge and expertise in this field. In this essay, I reflect on the realities of terrorism by exploring recent events in relation to both Islamist and far-right terrorism, the associations between them, and the divergent ways in which they are discussed in the media but also in politics. Themes explored will be questions relating to masculinity, identity, urbanicity, nationalism and the ongoing implications of the global war on terror. At the heart of many of the concerns is the overriding concept of racism and aspects of racialism and racialisation that emerge alongside it.

1.

In March 2019, fifty-one people were shot dead during Jummah prayers at two mosques in Christchurch, New Zealand's second most populous city. These Muslims from all over the world were gunned down by a self-confessed, manifesto-publishing, white supremacist with transnational far-right motivations, associations and aspirations. In any sociological analysis of the causes of extremism and radicalisation, it is a matter of fact that the background of the individual is scrutinised. In exploring patterns of socialisation, identity formation as well as issues relating to alienation and exclusion, it is possible to get a handle on the development of an ideological perspective that leads an individual to pursue acts of horrendous violence in the name of some greater cause. In this case, the primary suspect is a self-identified white supremacist, who viewed the world in Manichean terms, regarding Islam and Muslims as a combined category of a movement and its people who are not merely a blot on the landscape but deserve to be depopulated. This is because they somehow present a risk to the survival of the white nation itself. There is no perspective on the nature of this whiteness; that is, its own internal diversity or the historical legacies of class formation, colonialism, orientalism, eugenics or white nationalism that have defined the space occupied by whiteness. But this perspective is also an odd combination: palpable fear is presented in relation to the 'other', whose motivations are to seemingly take over through population expansion. At the same time, there is a decrying of these 'others' for their primitive, backward and hateful natures, thus seemingly legitimising ethnic nationalism and white supremacism.

Some would regard this as a reality of Islamophobia. They would be accurate in this instance. Islamophobia is not merely a response to a sense of cultural dilution at the hands of some regressive other. It extends into notions of ethnic cleansing of groups. There is much to expand on the nature of the motivations of the main suspect behind these attacks, which align with the activities of other individual actors apparently acting on their own. All have carried out an act of ultra-violence in the name of defending against the loss of privileges associated with whiteness at one level but also the fear of being overtaken by hordes of primitives. These kinds of ideas have motivated far-right extremists in the last few years in the number of places in the Global North, including in Norway, Canada, England and now in New Zealand. The reasons for these are structural, cultural and political.

Over the last two decades, men have faced considerable challenges to their positions in society, especially in the labour market and in educational terms. This is the result of the improving positions of women in these settings but also because globalisation means that the average young white man has to compete far harder than ever before and where his privileged urban post-industrial patriarchy can no longer be sustained in the light of an increasingly interdependent world. The rage against the loss of supremacy results in the venting of a certain fury against these now significant others. There was a time, well before the events of 9/11, where multiculturalism and diversity were seen as assets that contributed to the wellbeing of nations, where differences among people result in an enriched lived reality that benefits all in the pursuit of human values. But multiculturalism became distorted when the political and media classes began to shift attention away from these notions because they associated the concept with a risk of polarisation, radicalisation and ultimately terrorism. It is not beyond the realm of many who have a public school education to think that too much diversity can lead to the fragmentation of the nation itself. Alas, the experiment with diversity was over before it began, which has led to further polarisation and entrenchment in various physical concentrations within urban spaces. What social scientists will explore as the nature of downward social mobility, housing policies and gateways that limit access to certain forms of accommodation as explanatory factors in what leads to patterns of residential clustering, certain opinion-makers and political voices would argue that this outcome is solely an example of self-styled segregation. This is a blatant falsehood and a deliberate misdirection. It ignores history, past public policy and ongoing patterns of socio-economic inequalities that affect all. And in the final domain, the question of politics has become far more pervasive than ever. Populism, nativism and ethnic nationalism go hand-in-hand as a ruse to mask the failures of domestic policy and the ongoing shenanigans of interventions in faraway lands in pursuit of some greater foreign policy objective that routinely leads to catastrophe and destabilisation in those spaces as the norm.

In the pursuit of attention-grabbing headlines, sensationalist messaging presented as newsworthy items, and the bold ideological motivations of certain press barons (it is no surprise that Australian news and media output is almost entirely under the sole purview of Rupert Murdoch), Islam and Muslims are demonised on such an extensive basis that to be Islamophobic is to be normal. It takes a critical mind to distance oneself from what politicians and media outlets are actually saying, but for the less critical such words are gospel. The attacks in Christchurch were not the result of a random mental health victim on a rampage. They were calculated, cold and clinical. The assailant had a clear agenda — as he identified himself in his own writings. He aimed to sow fear and discord by broadcasting his actions all over the world. He alluded to Eurocentric heroism, which borders on ethnic cleansing — a 'kebab-removalist'. The air, thick with Islamophobia, gave him the licence he felt he could legitimately mobilise into political violence and terrorism. The sympathetic voices embolden some while radicalising others. And, thus, the circle is complete.

It is not always the case that far-right extremists take a pilgrimage of sorts before they are somehow radicalised, turning their newfound ideological perspectives into weaponised political violence and terrorism. The case in relation to the New Zealand shooter appears to be unusual in this regard. There is a real chance that he was radicalised during his travels, possibly in the Balkans, although this is conjectural rather than factual at this stage. In the course of time, it will be possible to determine where and how he was first radicalised, but it is clear that his radicalisation was significantly enhanced online. Undoubtedly, his references to the siege of Vienna by the Ottomans or the idea of 'kebab-removalist' in particular appeal to a certain anti-Muslim sentiment, the later with contemporary connotations, namely the war in Bosnia. What extremists find in this region is the memory of the Ottomans who held power over a period of six hundred and fifty years, during which they were able to annex territories that are now in the Balkans, South-East Europe, the Caucasus, North Africa and across the Middle East. But in many of the areas of Middle Europe today, these Ottomans are seen by some as invaders who only pillaged villages and raped women.

In the wider context of growing Islamophobia across the world today, these anti-Islam and anti-Muslim voices grow louder at a time when politicians in Hungary, Slovakia, Slovenia and Poland evoke populist sentiment. This is especially the case as many of these countries were directly affected by the Syrian refugee crisis that began in 2015, and which saw over half a million people walking through the Balkans on their way to countries like Germany. In general, the far-right in Europe does focus on the historical dynamics of Ottoman history and Christian Europe. For example, Anders Breivik made clear links, seeing himself as a Knight Templar, saving

Christianity from the invasive Muslim 'other'. These notions appeal to young men who are at the fringes of their societies, burying themselves in the discourses of the far and radical right online, with its focus on hate towards differences, women and groups with diverse sexual preferences or leanings. All of it supports the projected inherited importance of the average white male who has to club together with greater cause in order to a) save the 'white nation' from 'invasion' through immigration and mixing and to b) eliminate these 'other' undesirables as they are breeding at excessive rates and unless checked they will fully absorb the 'white nation'. There is a tragic absence of historical, political or social depth to these perspectives, which are effectively ideologically instrumentalised to create a 'race war'. The likes of Breivik and the New Zealand white supremacist want a reaction to their terrorism that starts this 'race war'.

2.

Speaking at a press conference where he announced the death of the Islamic State group (IS) leader Abu Bakr al-Baghdadi on 27 October 2019, US President Donald Trump threatened to 'drop' captured IS fighters on the UK border if the government did not start repatriating them from Syrian camps. 'They came from France, they came from Germany, they came from the UK. They came from many countries', he added. 'And I actually said to them, if you don't take them, I'm going to drop them right on your border and you can have fun capturing them again'. Earlier that month, US forces removed Alexanda Kotey and El Shafee Elsheikh, part of a group of IS members known as the 'Beatles', from a camp in northern Syria. The aim was to prevent them from escaping captivity, but also to potentially take them to Guantanamo Bay. Both Londoners, Kotey and Elsheikh were radicalised in their twenties. Their alleged IS crimes are some of the most heinous imaginable. But little is understood about how they came to be transformed into deranged executioners.

Much has to do with psychological processes that began once they arrived in Syria, although it is widely accepted that young people such as these two join radical Islamist groups due to ideological convictions. Yet, the socioeconomic issues behind their motivations are often overlooked, as is the wider political and cultural fabric of the societies in which they are born and raised, and in which they face systematic patterns of racism, disadvantage and exclusion. During its zenith, Islamic State informed potential recruits that what they endured on a daily basis meant they were not welcome in Britain. Living in Iraq or Syria would solve all of their woes. Through a widespread campaign of information dissemination and ideological communication, young people from poorer locations responded to the call. Accounts of anti-Muslim hate rang particularly true for the vulnerable people that IS was targeting. Approximately nine hundred Britons made it to Iraq and Syria as the UK government celebrated preventing one hundred and fifty or so from making the journey, as a senior Prevent official told me. The Prevent strategy has been in place informally since 2003 and formally since 2006, but despite efforts to put up an engaging front, the policy remains controversial. There is a clear and direct relationship between the social outcomes endured by young Muslims in urban areas across Britain and the degree to which they sympathise with violent Islamism.

The social problems facing British Muslims are aggravated by the utterances of populist figures. Islamophobia grows when political actors seek to gain capital from their insensitive contempt. Sentiments from US President Donald Trump, which inspired the 'send her back' chant in reference to a critical Muslim congresswoman, create huge damage, as does UK Prime Minister Boris Johnson's suggestion that Muslim women donning the niqab look like 'letterboxes or bank robbers'. Such views also embolden elements of the far-right, who come to believe that their perspectives have legitimacy. It is too easy to lampoon, jest or simply snub through poisonous opprobrium. Far-right groups grow due to the same set of structural challenges encountered by British Muslims, but also because of messages they hear in the media and in politics. In a climate of fear, hostility and intolerance reinforced by polarising politics and economics, there is a process of reciprocal radicalisation, boosted by populism. It has the effect of normalising Islamophobic attacks, which are predominantly directed towards visibly Muslim women. The high rates of unemployment, poor health, limited housing and relative educational underachievement faced by many are ignored. The fact that half of British Muslims live in the poorest 20% of areas in the country is disregarded. Structural disadvantages, combined with direct and indirect forms of racism normalised through austerity and Islamophobia, are significant social issues that receive scant attention. The sole emphasis on political ideology leading to radicalisation is therefore misleading.

Islamophobia, however, is not restricted to social and political life. It also infuses policy-making. A vast trust deficit remains between the UK government and British Muslims. This has grown since the 'war on terror', made worse by the fact that the only meaningful terms of engagement the UK government has with British Muslims are through the discourse of extremism and terrorism. Undoubtedly, Muslims in Britain have far greater dilemmas than radicalisation, but nowhere is this fully understood or wholly appreciated in developing policies. The wider drift towards authoritarianism, exclusivism and protectionism afflicting liberal democracies more generally is of concern. In this climate, the UK government has blurred the line between moderate and moderated Muslims. Critics of the dominant policy outlook are sidelined by those who seek to maintain the status quo in relation to counter-extremism in particular. This suggests a certain paranoia and pressure to conform to prevailing diktats, and to kowtow to dominant (mis)understandings of Islam and Muslims, both locally and globally. The solutions to these issues are not half as complicated as would be imagined. Rather than concentrate on the symptoms, the root causes must be fully addressed. There is no point focusing on the fever if the virus is still in place. A focus on social and economic conditions is essential to ensure that all groups are able to share in the fruits of opportunity and mobility. This would diminish the number of people vulnerable to both Islamist and far-right radicalisation.

Ideology also needs to be addressed, but this would be an easier task with the number of vulnerable people made smaller. It is also incumbent upon community and civil society organisations to maintain their efforts to engage with government and with wider communities to break down the walls of misunderstanding, intolerance and bigotry. All of this is entirely logical, but a million miles away from the dominant threads of counter-extremism policy. To deal with the answers to both Islamophobia and radicalisation, there needs to be much better UK government thinking on these urgent issues, but also greater honesty on the part of commissions, think-tanks, scholars and activists. To appreciate what stimulates these young people, it is important to understand the harsh truths facing groups, especially in the poorer parts of the country. More should be done to remain sensitive to the social and economic realities of life for British Muslims.

3.

Sudesh Amman, a first-generation Sri Lankan Muslim, was shot dead on the streets of south London by undercover police officers on 2 February 2019. Released less than two months after serving half his sentence, Amman attacked three people with a knife he had purchased moments earlier. Questions were asked about what caused this event and how it can be prevented in the future.

There are numerous cases of young people now in prisons for various offences related to spreading material associated with terrorist groups, whose aim of radicalising others in the hope of generating further support for acts of violent extremism led to their conviction. These young men, once locked up for their offences, are generally released after serving half of their allocated time. However, these prisons can act as an incubator, where impressionable young men are surrounded by hardened ideologues with an even more chequered history. In the case of Amman, and as reported in relation to others, deeper radicalisation can occur, in the process further damaging the minds of these young men. In imprisoning someone for offences related to terrorism, it takes them away from particular stimuli, but by being in certain institutions of incarceration, there is a real possibility of these prisons acting as a breeding place, where the radicalised can learn from others. Elsewhere, there have been problems of torture and abuse at the hands of captors that have played significant roles in radicalising individuals who became influential leaders within their domains. Abu Musab al-Zarqawi was an insignificant car mechanic before he was radicalised in prison and then became the number one Al Qaeda figure in Iraq from 2005 onwards. Abu Bakr al-Baghdadi was an inconsequential teacher with a background in theology. He too was radicalised in prison, ultimately becoming one of the founding actors within the Islamic State.

In many ways, when a young British Muslim has radicalised, it is already too late. The problem is the belief systems they now carry have warped their sense of themselves and their position in the world. It is true that this ideology is problematic, but it is not new to the study of violent jihadism. It has always been part of the eschatological framework of particular interpretations of script. The problem is why so many young people are seemingly drawn to it. And this is the crux of the matter. If ideology is the pull in this equation, the push is individual and structural factors that are somehow enabled at a particular moment. While the lure of ideology is potentially always there, attempts to fight it are limited because the push of structural and individual factors is too great. Halfway measures that intervene just before 'the bomb goes off' only do so much. The case of Amman, therefore, is not unsurprising in the context of the problems of knowing what to do with radicals in Western Europe and often getting it wrong. Having witnessed, experienced and seen it first hand, too many working within the fields of deradicalisation, counter-extremism and counterterrorism start with the premise that an individual on the verge of carrying out an act of violence can be 'reverse-engineered' if their psychological state of mind can be altered by education or emotional support. This approach has amiable ambitions. However, upon the completion of this intervention, and as individuals are returned back to the communities, they face the same vulnerabilities of being exposed to all of the pressures that lead some to a narrow path of self-realisation through self-annihilation. There are much wider structural issues that relate to investment in rebuilding communities that have faced decline over the last few decades, especially in parts of the country traditionally home to post-war ethnic minority communities, now in their fourth and fifth generations. By being trapped in spaces that reduce opportunities rather than open them up, creating narrow cultural domains rather than present opportunities to learn and share with others from different backgrounds, with internal questions relating to intergenerational disconnect, with communities having been effectively left out of the race for success, which is essentially racialised and gendered, the risks remain.

The government, in its usually reactionary manner, wishes to increase sentences or to ensure that those who have been imprisoned complete their sentences. This works well with presenting strength and receiving the support of parts of the country that equates toughness with results. At the same time, there will be those who decry counterterrorism policies that are quick to incarcerate individuals based on a presumption of intent rather than actual evidence of action or its potential. All of this will also embolden far-right groups and their counter-jihadi rhetoric. But all of this is also to forget that the reality of extremism is that it is a function of social conflict in a more general sense, which is to say that these young men are products of society. They are made in Britain. And it is the fissures and the cleavages of society that permit young men to fall through the gaps. As austerity deepens and as insecurity in relation to the future of Britain and its populations continues to heighten, the vulnerabilities in relation to the potential for young people to be drawn into extremism will only grow. No deradicalisation intervention can succeed without the appreciation of the wider social contexts in which radicals are made. And it is this lack of awareness and misdirection, in some cases fuelling confusion and misalignment with respect to what to do in such situations, that leads to attacks against academics, think-tankers and policymakers who seemingly get it wrong every time. The fact of the matter is that while thinkers spend the time and energy to work through an argument, it is in the hands of policymakers to introduce laws to make the difference. However, too many political actors play politics with people's lives. They would rather engage in populist overtones in the pursuit of power. Combined with a certain media, in particular, at the behest of the billionaire press barons, an intractable situation leads to more harm than good.

Terrorism, while a social construction, is also primarily a function of the lived experience facing groups and individuals with particular gripes and grievances that for various reasons cannot be met through the democratic process. This is why there will always be terrorism and extremism in societies that necessarily include groups with interests that conflict in a hierarchical social structure with those at the bottom of the social ladder, with some that have already fallen through the cracks of criminality, most at risk. They are so because of their vulnerabilities, not because of their inherent tendencies. Amman's shooting in the middle of a London street by undercover police officers was in many ways distressing. The perpetrator was a hugely disturbed young man who had been thoroughly let down by a whole host of actors. In prison for distributing terrorist propaganda, with a history of petty crime, he was thrown into the heady mix of Belmarsh prison, and then released halfway through his sentence with little or no support. In fact, in many ways, due to the permanent mark on his record, and his pariah status as a former inmate, his psychological and emotional well-being would have been in even more of a vulnerable state but with no one to act in support.

Radicalisation and deradicalisation, extremism and counter-extremism, terrorism and counter-terrorism are all subjective and highly contested concepts. While we can argue about what they mean in reality and the implications they raise for a social world in which people find themselves, young men face all the vulnerabilities of life but with little or no focus on their needs, wants and wishes in a fractured, atomised and hugely polarised world. Theirs is a malaise that grows insidiously but blindly for far too many lest we revisit the scene of a young, dead Muslim man on the streets of Britain the next time an event such as this south London attack happens all over again.

4.

The 19 February 2020 horrific attack on two Shisha bars by a far-right extremist in Germany led to several questions relating to concerns around motivation, activation and implication. It was the third attack by far-right extremists in nine months – this one by far the deadliest.

In many respects, eugenics is making a comeback. Increasingly, politicians across Western Europe are feeling comfortable with expressing sentiments that would ordinarily be defined as racist. These views espouse the idea that there is the inherent difference between particular racial categories, with the white category at the top of this tree. Invariably, it places people of a darker skin at the bottom of this hierarchy. The historical attempts behind these efforts were to maintain the status quo concerning slavery and later colonialism, but it subsequently developed into the concept of scientific racism, the zenith of which was the Nazi Holocaust. The policy of elimination targeting Jews, communists, leftists, homosexuals and all others who would reject the values of the Third Reich is attributed solely to Hitler. The reality is that similar sentiments were not uncommon in North America and elsewhere in Europe where eugenics was being seriously considered, and pursed, in august academic and research institutions.

In mid-February 2020, the British government moved quickly to dismiss Andrew Sabisky who had been appointed in response to calls for 'weirdos and misfits' to join the heart of government by the neoliberal, libertarian chef advisor of the prime minister, Dominic Cummings. It emerged that Sabisky posted racist messages online, with some of his writing confirming that he viewed particular minority groups as somehow inferior and undesirable, including where depopulation through sterilisation would be seen as a viable policy. This was no aberration, however. Numerous Conservative party politicians have been accused of Islamophobia, which is akin to racism. The current Prime Minister Boris Johnson has described minorities as 'piccaninnies' bearing 'watermelon smiles'. It is also well-documented that President Donald Trump favours the ideas of eugenics, even applying it to his marital relations, suggesting that in mating with Eastern European stock, he would be producing superior children. All of this suggests the normalisation of racism and a particular logic of white supremacism.

For what is currently known about the incident in Hanau, A 43-year-old German man shot and killed nine people while injuring five others in two shisha bars. Most were Turkish and Kurdish men and women, with a Bosnian, Bulgarian and Romanian in the mix. He later returned to his home, first shooting his mother before committing suicide. This suggests a combination of problems relating to ideas of the self and the other, and the internalisation of a particular kind of racism that pertains to the view the white groups are superior but they are under threat due to growing minority populations in particular urban centres, with their respective high birth rates and in-marrying. The motivations of this particular man were to prevent the dilutions of whiteness, as he saw it. But it is also clear that the assailant had particular mental health issues, something that is also significant amongst Islamist extremist actors. But the emphasis on reporting in the media is on ideology and religion when it comes to Islamist terrorists. The emphasis is less on ideology and more on mental health or other personal matters for far-right aggressors. This is a fundamental failure of reporting, especially in the mainstream press, although the reality is that with more and more examples – Breivik in Norway in 2011 and Tarrant in New Zealand in 2019 – it is now impossible to ignore what is palpably clear and apparent. The Hanau attacker, Tobias Rathjen, published a manifesto citing fear of immigrants and disdain towards women.

In trying to understand how far-right extremists become motivated, there has been much emphasis in the recent past on the idea of lone-wolf extremists. That is individuals who operate at the fringes of society, but effectively on their own. It is now clear that many of these attackers have an online presence, which allows them to develop their ideological perspectives as well as learn of methods and processes concerning attacks. But while this radicalisation occurs online, real-world connectivity is nevertheless important to understand. It is clear that we live in an era where racism towards minorities, Islamophobia and anti-Muslim sentiment targeting a particular category of a minority that is already facing a host of social, cultural and political pressures, has become the new normal. This racism fuels the fire of right ideologies of white supremacism, cultural superiority and notions of exclusivity which is seemingly threatened by the realities of migration and the settlement of minorities. Politicians in the Global North are routinely demonising such groups for political gain, but it is clear that those at the very fringes of society are mobilising these sentiments into far more sinister outcomes. It reflects on the individuals who face the consequences of rapid transformations to the local economy and society, and who are invariably men who no longer receive the trappings of advantage associated with their gender. It also reflects on an ideology that receives broad acceptance elsewhere in social life. There will be many in Europe, who are increasingly becoming worried by these recent developments, where random Muslims are seemingly targeted, whether it is shisha bars or praying in mosques. These people are being pursued because it fulfils an existing agenda driven by hatred, intolerance and racism. While Muslims are naturally going to be fearful about these issues, the vast majority will carry on regardless.

In understanding what is happening concerning far-right attacks against Muslims, three factors remain. First, these far-right attackers are finding fuel for their ideological predilections from the machinations of mainstream society and politics. Second, the counterterrorism and counter-extremism policy frameworks that currently receive considerable attention across the

Global North are ill-equipped to deal with the growing threat of far-right extremism because so much attention was historically placed on the idea that the most sinister forms of extremism are only of the Islamist kind. Third, the reporting on these issues remain skewed, biased or is entirely invisible. It is wholly incumbent upon observers to report on matters fairly and obsequiously. Only then will this topic get the wider recognition it deserves. And that it will encourage those working in this field to understand that extremism and terrorism among different actors share common characteristics. And that, as societies, if we concentrate on those social development concerns for all, then there is a real chance of eliminating the threat of terrorism for all because it is clear that there are patterns of reciprocal extremism in the current climate, and to break this vicious cycle, a focus on local area community development concerns and issues of social inclusion remain paramount.

5.

It is clear from recent events that there remains a concern regarding Islamist extremism, but far-right extremism is becoming a more virulent threat than ever. When the perpetrators are ostensibly Muslim, a focus on ideology and religion fixates pundits and policymakers but when it is a majority white man implicated, attention is placed on mental health, individual questions of psychology and upbringing, while regarding these cases as aberrations. It reflects the multiple roles played by racism in this entire landscape. Young Muslims face the challenges of Islamophobic anti-Muslim sentiment on a persistent basis, and yet it is the very few who respond to the challenges of their real-world existence with violence in the name of some higher purpose. Far-right extremists are motivated by a hateful ideology, while their white privilege is never threatened in reality, even if it is perceived as such. For many, they are unable to cope with a radically changing globalised world and the impact it has on their local lived experiences. Leading politicians speak out against attacks on Muslims in the lamest of ways while making all the political capital they can when the attack is carried out by an Islamist extremist. The media over-report Islamist attacks while under-reporting far-right acts of terrorism. Policymakers are only now beginning to catch up with the menace that far-right extremism has become. Thus, there are numerous biases operating at various levels, including how aspects of counter-terrorism, counter-extremism and de-radicalisation thinking and training are heavily skewed towards the Islamist threat but it is often formulated and delivered by individuals with no real appreciation of the reality of people's lives on the ground. UK ministries are still dominated by an Oxbridge-trained civil service, which has no connection to the world it wishes to preside over, especially that which is affected by extremism, radicalisation and terrorism. Critical and activist left-leaning Muslim or non-Muslim voices are often rendered invisible – for if one criticises the policy and processes of government, in some circles, one is branded as part of the problem itself. Muslims who are quick to cede to the dominant diktat, even promoting it as a career strategy, reap rewards.

Today's world of ongoing Islamist and far-right extremism, while concentrated in urban areas, affecting young men in particular, where ideology is a mask for perceptions of failings in relation to the self, is fraught with numerous challenges. Populism, authoritarianism and protectionism go hand in hand with widening socio-economic inequalities and the democratic deficit that is being felt particularly by men. In this climate, as the challenges far outweigh the opportunities, and where racism continues to reinvent itself unabated, matters will only get worse before they get better.

TRAVELLER

Zahrah Nesbitt-Ahmed

I saw them for the first time the year I turned thirty. Three months apart. There they were, both of them, looking back at me in black and white photos that I held in my hand. One man in a white suit standing next to a car, with another man carrying a little girl. The other – alone in an open space – dressed in a white kaftan and hat. Both unfamiliar to me.

My father speaks very little about his father. What I know I have pieced together from the few passing references, fleeting memories, that he occasionally shares. All I know is that he had three wives. Goggo Larai, my father's mother, who I knew as Goggo or Goggo Jos. Goggo Dije, who I only ever knew as Goggo Kaduna, and Tamalam, whom I never knew. He migrated from a northern state in Nigeria called Jigawa, and made his way to the middle belt of the country, eventually arriving in Plateau. I only recently learned his name – Mallam Ahmadu Adamu – and that he died on Monday 6 June 1966 at the relatively young age of fifty-six.

With my paternal grandfather a mystery to me, it is a similar story on my mother's side of the family. She barely remembers her father. What she does know she pieced together through faded childhood memories and a few nuggets of information her own mother shared over the years. She remembers his curly, wavy hair. She recalls him always being smartly dressed, in pin-stripe suits and two-tone shoes, 'a very, very dapper man indeed. Always smiling. Very playful. Never raising his voice. Never angry. Always jolly, playing, laughing, joking, taking us for rides in the car'.

She wasn't yet ten when he died. She couldn't even recall what his face looked like until her brother gave her a copy of a picture he came across in their mother's house. This would be the same picture I would see, the first chance to see my grandfather, his features, his eyes, the way he carried himself. He came alive to us in that image, which was only a few years ago. That's the first time my mother realised that her brother bore a striking resemblance to their father.

My maternal grandfather, Wilfred St Clair Nisbett, was born 3 or 4 October 1924 on the island of Nevis, a small piece of land in the Caribbean Sea that forms the inner arc of the Leeward Islands chain of the West Indies. His father had died before, or shortly after his birth. After his father's death, his mother decided to return to St Kitts to bring him up. Once back in her home town he was raised by his mother and maternal grandmother. Before he was two years old his mother died, and his grandmother became his primary carer. In St Kitts, like most islanders, my grandfather became a farmer, working a small holding and helping out at harvest time on the island's larger plantations.

In 1953 or 1955 my grandfather left his wife and the small Caribbean island of St Kitts for England. He, like many other men and women from all over the Caribbean, came at the invitation of the British government – the Mother Country – to help rebuild the nation after World War II. He arrived at Southampton in either September or October, and went straight to Birmingham as he had relatives already living there who, when he had alerted them to his impending arrival, had found work for him. Six weeks after he stepped on these shores, his wife, my grandmother, Pearlita Jarvis, docked at Southampton. She stayed in Ipswich with a cousin for a brief period before travelling to Birmingham to join my grandfather. My mother is still not sure what kind of work her father did. However, my uncle believes he was involved in construction – building roads and houses. The hard labour eventually took its toll and he fell ill in early 1968, was taken to hospital and never came back home. He was buried in Birmingham in March 1968. He was forty-three years old.

This was all I knew of my grandfathers. There was still so much I wanted to learn about these two men who lived in different parts of the world – one on the African continent, the other in the African Diaspora – and who were of different religions – one Muslim, the other Christian. Two men who moved through spaces – one migrating internally, the other migrating internationally. I yearned to see their contrasting identities in mine, and feel their histories in my present. It was difficult as I had minimal biographical information to draw on. Their lives were a blank space in the recesses of my imagination and my understanding of my forefathers. I desperately wanted to fill that space, and it wasn't until I looked to black music, that I managed to do so. It was music of that generation that helped me build a connection to my grandfathers.

I envisioned the sounds of their era – flutes and talking drums, calypso, ska. Music is how I tried to represent them and place myself deeply alongside them both. Such sounds are, of course, only part of their story, but it is the part I could most easily understand and use to come to terms in shaping, defining, and constructing what these men may have been like. Sound is also the part I knew I could connect the most with, as music travels everywhere with me.

I started the process of discovery with my paternal grandfather. I knew less about Hausa music. Caribbean music was already a part of me, as I grew up in a home where the sounds of calypso, soca, reggae and lovers rock were on constant repeat. Having been raised in the south-western part of Nigeria, I was more familiar with the sounds of Afrobeat, juju and fuji music, which are traditionally the music of the Yorubaland. Highlife was another genre that was present. So, I dug deep into Hausa music, as a means of re-creating forgotten imagined memories of my grandfather's past.

A predominantly Muslim group in northern Nigeria, the language of the Hausa, which my grandfather spoke, spread widely from northern Nigeria to the Niger Republic and to other parts of West Africa – stretching to Ghana, Cote d'Ivoire, Gambia and Senegal. I would discover that there isn't a single word for musicians in Hausa culture, as the creation of music is more associated with activities – drumming (*kidaa*), singing (*waakaa*) and blowing (*buusaa*). The folk music played by the people of the north is known for its complex percussion instruments, including the one- or two-stringed *goje*, the two-or three-stringed *molo*, the one- or two-stringed *kontigi* or the smaller one-stringed bowed *kukuma* (all lutes), the *kakaki* (trumpets), kuge, and the *gangan*, *tambari* and *kalangu* (drums of various sizes).

Hausa popular music mainly grew from two distinct nineteenth-century traditions: urban classical music, comprised of *rok'on fada* (state ceremonial music) and *yabon sarakai* (court praise singing) and rural folk music or popular music. This reflected the highly stratified structure of the society, in which the emir holds the highest political and social position. *Marookaa* – musicians and praise singers – are the same level as griots, in the broadly lowest rank. Royal musicians, due to the association with royalty, rank near the top of the *marooku* class, while *boori* musicians, due to their associations with card players and drinkers, are ranked at the bottom. Islam also plays a role in this ranking – as royal musicians are 'outwardly devout Muslims'.

Musicians were enlisted for armies and orchestras took up residence in emir's palaces. Ceremonial music is probably the most esteemed form of music in Hausa society, with the emir controlling the occasions for the performance of state ceremonial music. This was often during *sara*, which is the weekly statement of authority on Fridays outside the emir palace, religious festivals, visits from other emirs or important people, and as weddings and births within the emir's family. Instruments, such as the *tambari* and *kakaki* are prestigious royal musical instruments, with royal arrivals announced by the *kakaki*. Hausa music also has a strong praise song vocal tradition drawing heavily on Hausa proverbs in a poetic manner and reflecting free-rhythmic improvisation. In a court praise singers' band, although the instrumental is important, emphasis is usually on vocalisation as the main vehicle of communication.

During the 1930s and 1940s, radio became part of the public urban space in Northern Nigeria, with its sounds flowing onto the city streets through public listening stations for the vast majority of Hausa listeners or homes (for those who could afford it). Although programming consisted largely of BBC programmes made in England, BBC Arabic broadcasts and Indian and English records, Hausa singers, such as Hamisu Maiganga and later, Mamman Shata, were also big in the 1940s and were played heavily on the wireless. Alhaji Mamman Shata was a well-known griot/musician whose vocals were often accompanied by talking drums, such as *kalangu*. Hindi music was also extremely popular in Northern Nigeria – although its popularity soared in the 1960s – after my grandfather had passed away – as more soundtracks from popular Hindi films were introduced via radio and cinema houses.

I imagined my grandfather would have listened to these sounds, these different melodies and rhythms. So, I immersed myself in them – creating playlists of Hausa music that I could access from that era, such as songs by praise singer Dan Maraya Jos including 'Wak'ar Karen Mota' ('Song of the Driver's Mate'), and 'Yan Arewa Ku Bar Barci, Najeriyarmu Akwai

Dad'I' (Northerners Stop Sleeping, Our Nigeria is a Pleasant Place) by
Mamman Shata.

Around the same period, many miles away, the music of St Kitts and
Nevis, which included the big drum ensembles and community brass
bands took off, and frequently accompanied folk singers. Big drum or
string band music accompanied the various groups who performed during
the Christmas period – from Boxing Day to New Year's Eve. Most well
known was the St Kitts Defence Force Band, formed in 1932 (although
some sources claim it was 1938) by Edgar Samuel Bridgewater, which
often served to introduce young men from working class backgrounds to
music. The St Kitts Brass Band founded by William 'Doc' Davis in 1933
was also popular. By the mid-1940s these bands, including the Police
Military Brass Band, would perform regular band concerts at Pall Mall
Square (later called Independence Square) at the Bay Front. In addition to
the big drum, a range of instruments accompanied the lilting, rhythmic
sounds of Caribbean music – guitars including the cuatro, fife, triangle,
and the *shak-shak*, which is also known as the maracas in countries such as
Cuba and Venezuela.

The following decade saw the introduction of the Trinidadian style
steelpans, introduced by Lloyd Matheson, CBE, then an education officer.
The first steelpan band was Roy Martin's Wilberforce Steel Pan. Prior to
that, bands used makeshift percussion instruments. Steelpans quickly
became popular and steelbands became the most coveted sound,
dominating private and public social events and dances. Demand for this
new sound led to the decline of the horn-based orchestra and the big
drum, both of which had previously been in vogue. This surge in
popularity led to an explosion of steelbands, with the most popular bands
featured at major dances and orchestras including the Music Makers,
Rhythm Kings, Brown Queen, and Silver Rhythm Combo.

Then there was calypso. Originating in Trinidad, where enslaved
people employed the narrative style and coded lyrics to mock their
masters and the ruling classes. The music established itself and evolved
into the first modern Caribbean music to make an impact on the wider
world. From Trinidad, calypso spread across the Caribbean, and became
a major part of Kittitian (or Kittian) and Nevisian music with the
introduction of calypso competitions in the 1950s. Until the early 1940s,

'calypso-like' songs in St Kitts were called 'country dance' and *kwelbe*. Veteran calypsonians from this period included the Mighty Saint, Lord Harmony, King Monow, Mighty Kush, Lord Mike, and Elmo Osborne.

While the Hausa's, like my grandfather, mostly migrate internally within Nigeria or to neighbouring west African countries, Caribbean's migrate both within the Caribbean, and to North America and Europe. Principal destinations were New York City and London. And Caribbean's literally brought their music with them when they migrated. Inspired by the fact that migration has been a feature of both Hausa-speaking people in West Africa and English-speaking Caribbean societies, I continued to follow my grandfathers, specifically my maternal grandfather, to Britain, through music.

Indeed, the history of British music – Black British music – cannot be divorced from Caribbean music. The British cultural theorist, Stuart Hall, traced the story and impact of the first wave of Caribbean music to reach Britain, and found that 'since West Indians first began to settle in Britain in large numbers after the Second World War, a succession of black musics have transformed the British music scene'. The Windrush generation – my maternal grandparents' generation – made a significant contribution to British black music – from calypso, ska, bluebeat and reggae, to gospel to lovers rock, from roots and dub, to drum to jungle to rap, dancehall, to techno and house, to UK garage to grime.

Once in the UK, I wondered what my maternal grandfather listened to? Most documentary evidence that is available concerns Trinidad and the evolution of calypso, which, according to Lloyd Bradley, became 'the official sound-track of black Britain' in the 1950s and early 1960s. I thought to myself, did he listen to the music of Lord Kitchener and Lord Beginner – two Kings of Calypso that were on the SS Empire Windrush that docked at Tilbury in 1948.

Calypso to me was part and parcel of the West Indian migrant community and their experiences in the UK. I used it, the same way I used books such as *Lonely Londoners* by Sam Selvon and *Small Island* by Andrea Levy, to offer insights into the early days of the migrant experience, and in my case my grandfather's experience. I kept coming back to Stuart Hall's words, 'this is the music of a minority who have travelled to a strange or strangely familiar place in search of a better life and are determined to survive and prosper'.

I listened to calypso songs such as Lord Invader's 1959 'Teddy Boy Calypso (Bring Back The Cat-O-Nine)' – about racial attacks in parts of the London. As well as, 'Black Power' and 'If You're Brown' about the experiences of being a Caribbean migrant newly arrived in London.

Along with the music also came the house parties and sound systems. Radio stations weren't playing Caribbean music back then. Instead, sound systems were played at house parties – with DJs, rappers and singers and women of the house running the bar in the kitchen. I had heard that my grandmother had thrown these in her home in Birmingham in her younger days – I wondered if they continued while my grandfather was still alive.

Playlists of 1950s and 1960s calypso, as well as ska of the 1960s provided the foundation of what would blossom into my unique relationship with my maternal grandfather. In addition to Lord Kitchner's song it also included 'The Lion's Tick! Tick! (The Story of The Lost Watch)', Marie Bryant's 'Don't Touch Me Nylon' and Millie Small's 1964 recording of 'My Boy Lollipop'. My geography – their geography – made the Caribbean, West Africa, and Western Europe essential parts of my core. This also means my world is one where Black African, African Diasporic, Islamic, Christian, and European civilisations met, clashed, and blended. Shaped by various cultures ethnically divided by slavery and colonialism, I was in a state of uncertainty about my grandfathers. I stared at their photos. The first, my maternal grandfather. The second, my paternal grandfather. A sense of familiarity and excitement now comes over me.

I am still not fully aware of them – the sound of their laughter, the lilt of their voice. But, like my grandparents before me, and even my own parents, I continue to travel – putting down roots in Western Europe, North America, and more recently Southern Europe. With me, I carry our tradition – through the sounds that these two men were probably surrounded with and might even have listened to during their time. Their music, which over the decades evolved into my music of jazz, blues, Afrobeats, reggae, dancehall, grime, hip-hop, pop, and now calypso and soca – genres which travel with me wherever I go, and now so do my grandfathers.

WHITE MUSLIMS,
BLACK MUSLIMS

Juliette Galonnier

In every religious tradition, issues of religious authority and leadership are eminently complex and contentious. The religion of Islam on the two sides of the Atlantic is no exception to this rule, especially since it is increasingly diversified in terms of race, ethnicity, gender, age, migration status and class. Yet, another layer of difficulties comes from the fact that Islam as a religion is racialised in Western societies, which means that it is associated with a number of cultural and moral characteristics deemed inborn and immutable. Muslims are also scrutinised and the politics of Muslim religious leadership involve high stakes: Western states frequently organise the institutionalisation of Islam by selecting or co-opting what they see as acceptable religious spokespersons. This makes the question 'who represents Islam?' a tricky one, since the assertion of religious legitimacy within the Muslim community is complicated by processes of racialisation, stigmatisation and politicisation (state involvement). Taking into account this particular context, we can examine the racialised fault lines that affect the construction of religious authority within the French and American Muslim minorities.

The Muslim minority in France, according to the Pew Research Centre, is currently estimated at 4.7 million, which represents 7.5% of the total French population. According to estimates, over 70% of French Muslims are of North African descent, with large numbers from Algeria. Some 10% hail from Turkey, 9% from Africa and the Indian Ocean, and 2% from Asia, the remaining 9% being constituted of untraceable immigrants and people of various origins, including converts hailing from white or West Indian families. Converts are believed to represent 2 to 3% of the total Muslim population. Because of demographics and past historical trajectories, Islam is often conflated with mastery of the Arabic language and North African culture in French representations. In the process of institutionalising French Islam, Muslim immigrants' countries of origin have also played a key role, as evidenced in the management and funding of mosques, imam training and participation in institutional structures. Such transnational influence has tended to favour the public visibility and institutional legitimacy of Islamic expressions that are strongly backed by powerful States such as Morocco, Algeria, Turkey, at the expense of African Muslims, second-generation Muslims and converts.

The American Muslim minority is smaller than the French one, both in absolute and relative terms. Recent estimates by the Pew Research Centre established that there are 3.3 million Muslims living on American territory, who make up only 0.9% of the total American population. In spite of their small size, Muslims are considered, according to Gallup Coexist Foundation in 2009, 'the most racially diverse religious group in the US'. A 2012 survey of American mosques by Ihsan Bagby found that 33% of American mosque goers are South Asian, 27% Arab, 24% African-American, 9% African, the remaining 7% being a mix of European, Turkish, Southeast Asian, Latino, and Iranian. The American Muslim minority is therefore more heterogeneous than the French one. Within American Islam, the most striking and enduring cleavage is that opposing African-American Muslims on the one hand and immigrant Muslims from the Middle East or South Asia on the other. To be sure, both groups display great internal diversity. In 2005 Sherman Jackson explained in his book *Islam and the Blackamerican*, that 'African-American Islam' and 'Immigrant Islam' do not refer to reified groups, but rather to distinct sets of experiences, memories and practices that have a structural impact on the direction American Islam is taking as a whole. This cleavage also overlaps with class inequalities, contrasted migration histories and urban/suburban disparities.

Relying on my own ethnographic observations and in-depth interviewing with 82 white and black converts to Islam in France and the United States as well as on a collective study on French Muslims of Sub-Saharan and Comorian descent, I conducted with my colleagues Mahamet Timéra, Mahamadou Cissoko, Seydi Diamil Niane, Hassan Oili and Cheikhna Wagué, I propose, to investigate how white and black Muslims relate to religious authority on the two sides of the Atlantic in contexts where Islam is racialised. As minorities within the Muslim minority, white and black

Muslims experience race, religion and the racialisation of religion in peculiar ways. While their accounts and experiences sometimes coincide, they also markedly diverge, as whiteness tends to be valued and blackness devalued in both national contexts.

My interviewees perceived the religion of Islam as a powerful tool to fight racism, and universal Islamic brotherhood was frequently evoked as a means to eradicate or smoothen racial inequalities. Khabir, a twenty-three-year-old African American barber from Detroit, stated for instance that 'being a Muslim is not being a certain race; it is about your soul'. The Muslims I spoke to often articulate their commitment for racial equality in religious terms. At the convert associations I followed, such commitment was clearly stated. Prominent black figures from the classical period of Muslim history were frequently mentioned, such as Hajar and Bilal. In the US specifically, the anti-racist Islamic rhetoric is prominent. Constantly revived through new films and documentaries, the legacy of Malcolm X in particular continues to shape the experience of converts and born Muslims alike. The letter he wrote after his 1964 pilgrimage to Mecca is for instance frequently cited as evidence of the great transformative power of Islam:

> America needs to understand Islam, because this is the one religion that erases from its society the race problem. Throughout my travels in the Muslim world, I have met, talked to and even eaten with people who, in America, would have been considered 'white' but the 'white' attitude was removed from their minds by the religion of Islam. (...) And in the words and in the actions and in the deeds of the 'white' Muslims, I felt the same sincerity that I felt among the black African Muslims of Nigeria, Sudan and Ghana.

Many Muslims in both France and the United States strive to place religious sincerity over racial considerations and consider the Islamic tradition as well-armed to foster racial equality. Yet, several interviewees complained about the discrepancy between Islamic teachings and the reality of Muslim communities. Kathleen, aged thirty and a flight attendant from Detroit, who identifies as black, was sceptical about the prospects of Islamic anti-racism: 'Islam could solve racism in every country of the world. But will the practitioners of the religion be able to do so? That's a different story.' In my samples, white and black Muslims tended to share pessimistic views about the existence of internal racial boundaries among

Muslims. The segregation of mosques along ethno-racial lines, in particular, is a matter of concern for those, particularly converts, who had fantasised the *ummah* as an indivisible whole. Complaining about the monochromatic character of some mosques in Marseille, forty-seven-year-old Gérard, who works as an accountant, explained: 'they don't understand that there is only one Islam. There is not one Islam for the Moroccans, one Islam for the Algerians, one Islam for the Comorians. No!' In Chicago, student Pablo, twenty-two, also noticed: 'we are supposed to be all one, you know. And then we get this separation thing going on: "oh that's the Desi mosque, that's the Nigerian mosque, that's the Palestinian mosque, that's the Syrian mosque." It shouldn't be like that.' For many interviewees, the ethno-racial homogamy of Muslim worship spaces prevented the emergence of an overarching Muslim religious identity that could supersede differences.

With Islam as a religion so heavily racialised as 'Arab' or 'Middle Eastern', white and black Muslims often share the experience of not being identified as Muslims by their fellow coreligionists or by society. Sophie, a twenty-seven-year-old social worker from Marseille, who is blond and blue-eyed and a convert of several years, confessed that many of her coreligionists do not see her as a Muslim. She recounted how the imam at her mosque kept calling her a Christian, even though he sees her pray there on a regular basis. Once he gave a sermon on interfaith dialogue between Muslims and Christians and said he had done it just for her, as a Christian. She was really disconcerted: 'I know he means well but these are the stereotypes that you see over and over and over again. Even in a religious context, he leaps to the conclusion that French = Christian.'

White converts often stand out in mosques. In Marseille, Sophie explains that she is constantly being stared at: 'I don't have the typical face of a Muslim, so, with my blue eyes, I really get noticed!' African-Americans and Muslims of Sub-Saharan and Comorian descent also experience their invisibility as Muslims. French journalist Rokhaya Diallo, who is of Senegalese and Gambian descent, declared: 'being Black cancels my Muslimness in this society. There is a complete invisibility of non-Arab Muslims in France.' Black Muslims do not conform to the stereotyped image of the 'Muslim' in the French imagination and are more closely associated with Christianity. This feeling of being denied Islamic belonging is clearly stated by Banta, a forty-two-year-old Muslim of Malian descent who works as a Muslim chaplain in prison. In an interview conducted by my colleague Cheikhna Wagué, he describes the surprise that his Islamic identity generates among the people he encounters on a daily basis:

> At work, it happens that we meet people who think we are only Blacks. Sometimes, when they ask for the chaplain and I come forth, they don't understand. Some even ask: 'are you a Catholic chaplain?' When I reply that no, I am a Muslim chaplain, they do not understand. They say 'oh really?' Because for them this job is for the *sourakhou* [the Arabs in soninke language].

The racialisation of Islam and well-entrenched stereotypes about who 'looks Muslim' and who does not, affect white and black Muslims' claims for religious legitimacy on a daily basis. These issues are often magnified when it comes to religious leadership and authority. In France, a number of interviewees complained about what they saw as the excessive influence exerted by 'Arabs' over Islam. What is merely the reflection of the demographic composition of French Muslims is experienced by some converts as undue monopoly. Some, like thirty-five-year-old Adam, a convert of Caribbean descent living in Paris, mentioned the arrogant attitude of some of his North African coreligionists: 'most of the time, when I talk about Islam with Arabs, we quarrel... They are like: "how come, you are Caribbean, you are a convert and you want to teach me lessons about my religion?" They are real nuts! They think it is their religion. These guys are convinced that Islam comes from them, that it is them, that it is their stuff.' A convert, Adam denounces what he sees as North Africans hijacking Islamic religious authority, thereby preventing his full participation in religious discussions.

These discourses were also found among first and second-generation Muslims of African descent in France who lament their marginalisation in the Islamic landscape. Aissatou, a twenty-five-year-old student of Mauritanian descent, explained:

> There is this very strong feeling of superiority sometimes, coming from Arabs, over the rest of the Muslim community. It is a pity. Really, I feel it very strongly. North Africans consider that they know religion better than Africans, because Arabic is their main language. Supposedly Islam came to their countries first. But this isn't true! When you look at the history of the

expansion of Islam, you see that this isn't true... As a black African, you always have to endure remarks like 'how come you speak Arabic?', 'you know how to do that?', 'but how do you pray?' I always have to explain how I practise my religion.

On a daily basis, ordinary interactions in mosques or learning institutions shape the boundaries of a legitimate and orthodox Islam, from which African Muslims are implicitly excluded. Their Islam is denigrated as secondary, subaltern and different from 'true Islam'.

In the US, many African-American Muslims also claim that the legacy of African Muslim slaves as well as that of the various black movements that appropriated Islam to turn it into an American religion have been silenced and forgotten. The Moorish Science Temple, Nation of Islam, Five Percenters, among others, are insufficiently recognised by post-1965 immigrant Muslims, who, upon arriving in America, launched their own Islamic institutions while overlooking the fact that Islam had already a well-established history in the US at least since the 1910s. The oblivion of generations of African-American Muslims was particularly disturbing for John, a white convert married to an African-American born Muslim woman: 'I remember a well-educated Pakistani brother said to me a few years back: "my generation (1970-80) was the first to wear *hijab* in America and it was tough to be the people to introduce Islam to America." My wife's eyes open wide in shock and disbelief that this man said this with conviction.' Several converts felt that South Asian and Middle Eastern Muslims hold themselves as the sole repositories of authentic Islamic knowledge and the only ones having the legitimacy to define the boundaries of proper Islamic behaviour. Khabir noted that Islamic legitimacy was often conditioned by obtaining degrees or traveling to the Middle East or South Asia to study: 'it is like if you don't go to the South Asian and the Arab door, you are not a valid Muslim. You are not. That's the impression I get a lot.' He criticises the conflation of Islamic authenticity with Arab/Desi culture and its potential negative impact on black converts' sense of self.

When an African-American Muslim looks in the mirror, they don't want to see an African. Because they think that a Muslim is Arab, Persian, South Asian. You are not Muslim unless you are of these backgrounds. I really get frustrated with that reality. I really do! Before your slave master was a European God figure. Now you think God is an Arab. Now you think God is a South Asian.

White and black Muslims also denounce their tokenistic use as representatives of the diversity of Islam in institutional settings: when applying for mosque funding, when meeting authorities, and so forth. They critique the way they are sometimes harnessed as 'diverse faces' of the Muslim community, while not being given an actual voice in religious matters. In Chicago, strikingly tall and blue-eyed thirty-six-year-old technician Jonathan, who has been part of a mostly-immigrant mosque for decades, noticed this phenomenon: 'If somebody becomes Muslim, and he is Caucasian, they [Muslims] will have him give a lecture about Islam tomorrow.' Imam Suhaib Webb, who is white and converted in 1992, said during a 2013 public talk that he resented the way he was sometimes strategically used. Put on the front stage for advertisement purposes, he regretted not being listened to regarding internal mosque matters: 'they would not consult me over any decision. They never asked me one question. But when it came to a fundraiser, when it came to get a guy on a poster, you know what I mean.'

Such concerns were also voiced by several black Muslims interviewed in France. According to religious speaker Ousmane Timéra, an energetic French man of Senegalese descent, 'they bring Africans but only as stooges. It is just to be able to say "look, we have diversity, there is a Black person with us".' In Marseille, Cheikh Ahmed Ndieguene, a renowned and much appreciated imam of the Bilal Mosque, now systematically refuses to play the role of the token African Muslim.

> Africans don't have their say. They are just being used to say 'see, we represent all Muslims'. The moment I understood this, I said, 'I am done, I won't do it anymore'. For instance, they wanted to go see the prefecture. They brought an Algerian, a Moroccan, a Tunisian, a Senegalese, a Comorian, to say: 'we represent Islam' and all that. It is a way of bringing colour to the picture. I said 'no, I won't do this anymore', because if I agree to come, I contribute to legitimate such discourses.

These feelings of instrumentalisation were strongly expressed during interviews. Yet, while they both denounce racialised hegemony over Islam and tokenism, white and black Muslims' experiences with religious authority differ markedly. While white converts are often presented as valued assets for a community in need of recognition, black Muslims have to endure sustained forms of marginalisation and stigmatisation. Reflecting general trends in the French and American societies, white skin is often valued as a social asset within religious communities. More than other converts, white Muslims are often over-congratulated for their conversion. In addition, a number of white converts have quickly risen to positions of prominence and authority, as board members in mosques, scholars, spokespersons for Muslim organisations, for example. Because a certain amount of prestige is coupled with whiteness, white Muslims are believed to be legitimate faces who can speak in the name of Islam. They can be valued representatives for religious minorities that are stigmatised at the national level and frequently exposed to litmus tests of assimilation.

The valorisation of white converts becomes particularly evident when compared to the marginalisation of non-white converts. This was clearly expressed by forty-five-year-old Souleymane from Detroit. A charismatic African-American convert who teaches Islamic courses in a mosque, he described the intra-Muslim racism he experienced at the beginning of his conversion. During his first years as a Muslim, he was very active in *da'wah* efforts and brought many new converts to the immigrant mosque he attended. Yet, he was under the impression that his coreligionists were only interested in white converts, and dismissive of black converts:

> During that year, many African-American women and men took Islam. And within our community, there were five or six Europeans who came in. There was one, Abu Bakr from Connecticut. When he took *shahada*, all of the Pakistanis, all the Syrians, they stayed, all the Lebanese people were like: '*Mash'Allah* brother, we will get you help and everything.' But he was from the hood, they didn't know! They said: 'Is there anything you want to say?' And he said: 'yeah, there is only one thing I want to say. I have seen other brothers, African-Americans, take *shahada* here and you all didn't care. And me, I will take *shahada* today, all of you all are happy, all of you all are spinning around me. Is it because I am white? Why don't you do that for any of these? This brother here, he took it last week. And that sister, last month.' And he really crushed their whole ego system about the whole thing. His name was Abu Bakr. He became a stronger Muslim after that.

Souleymane was grateful for Abu Bakr to publicly point at the racial and class dynamics within the mosque and unveil the greater appreciation shown to white converts over their black counterparts. Cab driver Umar Lee from St Louis, a forty-year-old working-class white convert, reported the same phenomenon: 'you literally have white converts coming, and I have seen it, within a couple of weeks, or couple of months, they are on the board of directors of the masjid. Now imagine a black Muslim! He has been around for thirty years. He barely gets returned greetings. White guy comes in, and in a month he is on the board.' The undervaluation of African-American Muslims in comparison to white Muslims, especially in scholarship, is a very important issue for Souleymane. His assessment of the popularity of white Islamic scholars such as Dr Umar Faruq-Abdallah or Sheikh Hamza Yusuf is definite: 'even though I have great respect for Sheikh Umar and Hamza Yusuf, it is true that they wouldn't have gained as much exposure if they were African-Americans. Because there are tons of African-Americans who haven't been given exposure.' Ubaydullah, a forty-year-old Islamic teacher from Chicago is an African-American scholar who studied Islam overseas and now teaches in various settings, contrasted the way his scholarship and that of Hamza Yusuf are received:

> Personally, Sheikh Hamza is one of my teachers and I think he is really brilliant. That said, I think his being white did and does confer onto him a certain image of privilege in the Muslim community. When the same thing was from my mouth and from Sheikh Hamza's mouth, maybe it wouldn't resonate in the same way, because people are so attuned to this reality of white privilege. When people are looking for social commentary that they are prepared to take as authoritative or at the very least valid, I do think the fact that he is white has something to do with how they receive his commentary.

The racialised cognitive association of whiteness with knowledge and legitimacy can therefore partly explain white converts' rise to positions of Islamic authority within the Muslim community.

On the contrary, black Muslims have to endure the systematic devaluation of their Islamic traditions and practices. According to scholar Bakary Sambe, black Muslims in France are subjected to paternalism and racism from their coreligionists, society and the French State alike. Their practices are often depreciated as 'folkloric', 'heterodox', if not 'deviant', and they are pushed into the background as 'second-rank' Muslims. The typification of black African Islam (*islam noir*) as a 'peripheral' Islam tainted with local cultures, in contrast to a so-called 'orthodox' and 'authentic' North African Islam, was created and enforced by the French colonial administration. Its persistence in contemporary representations contributes to the invisibility and discredit of Muslims of African descent in French Muslim spaces. As a result, African Muslims in France are perceived as less practicing, less reliable and less authentic Muslims. Maimouna, a French woman of Senegalese descent, who is well-trained in Islamic sciences and has taught Arabic and Qur'an in women study groups in several mosques, mentioned the lack of legitimacy that black people endure when they try to assert their Islamic authority: 'When you teach Qur'an or Arabic, you show up, people look at you and in the back of their minds they think "she is either the cleaning lady or she came to study". They never see you as the professor. They are always astounded that a Black African can speak Arabic and know the Qur'an.'

Some French black imams also described the difficulties they encountered when seeking to establish their religious authority. Cheikh Ahmed Ndieguene, who is now a widely recognised religious figure among Muslims in Marseille, recounted his difficult beginnings as a young imam:

> When I lived on the university campus, I used to be imam there as well. And someone had made a comment. He was an Algerian who liked me dearly so I wasn't shocked. But the comment in itself was interesting. He told me, 'I heard that there is a *hadith* that says that a Black man does not have the right to lead white people in prayer. The prayer won't be valid.' I told him 'well, that *hadith* is not valid' and I explained it to him. I knew that, in his case, it was due to ignorance. But this ignorance took root in a place, in a culture. There are people here who grew up with this way of thinking.

These enduring perceptions, coupled with the lack of religious support from African States to their diaspora and the fact that African Muslims are less socio-economically established than their North African counterparts, contribute to the marginalisation of African Muslims within the institutional field of French Islam. Taken together, these various experiences and testimonies outline the existence of strong logics of stigmatisation and marginalisation of black Muslims, which significantly affect their claims to religious authority and legitimacy.

Building on the various experiences of black and white Muslims, some of the conflicts and contestations that surround the construction of religious authority in the French and American contexts are laid bare. Because of the racialisation of Islam, white and black Muslims encounter difficulties in asserting their Islamic legitimacy in the society and within the Muslim minority itself, where the boundary between orthodoxy and heterodoxy can at times be policed along racialised lines. Both can be used as tokens of diversity in institutional settings while struggling to authenticate their Islamic belonging and authority among their coreligionists. Yet, black and white Muslims encounter contrasted obstacles in authenticating their Islamic legitimacy, the former being often undervalued as Muslims while the latter are often put in the spotlight. It is therefore important to debunk the myth of a homogenous Muslim community and explore the complex dynamics that shape authority and representation among stigmatised minorities. The rich conversations that are taking place on these issues among Muslim communities in both France and the United States and the strong similarities and resonances of these debates across the Atlantic warrant further investigation.

DANGEROUS IDEAS

Abdul-Rehman Malik

We can't conjure, or think, or muse, the idea of a Muslim Atlantic without considering the work of Paul Gilroy and his theorisation of the Black Atlantic: it forms its very DNA. By extension the very idea of a Muslim Atlantic – if it has any genealogy at all – is deeply imbedded in the ways we understand Blackness, the Black experience and emergence of chattel slavery.

There are two 'historical moments' however that don't quite complicate this view but do create a particularly Muslim mood music for the idea of the Muslim Atlantic. One is the sort of myth-making moments some strands of contemporary Islam love to celebrate, the other is largely forgotten, or ignored, a casualty of the 'whitespots' that plague the story of the Muslim past.

The first, as the lands of North Africa are conquered in the name of the emerging Islamic imperial authority in Arabia and the Levant, the famed, and stunningly successful, General Uqba ibn Nafi (622–683) finds himself at the shores of the Atlantic. Generations will be told that he rides his steed into the cold waters shouting *Allahu Akbar*, and looks across to a horizon that reveals no more land and declares, 'O Lord be Thou witness, that I have taken Thy Message up to the end of the land and if this ocean were not in my way I would have proceeded to fight the pagans until none would be worshipped except Thee'. It's one of those moments that no doubt deserves a Gulf-financed biopic with soaring sounds of oud and the banging of dafs. The cynic or the triumphalist might look to this moment and find the genesis of the Muslim Atlantic. I like to think that this story, at the very least, draws us to the idea of Islam as something mobile, adaptable, with the capacity to settle, change and re-form. Uqba may have conquered the lands in the name of God, but the culture – music, art, architecture, literature, theology, philosophy – that those lands produced are dizzying cultural eco-systems, an idea we will return to shortly, that are not merely the product of an imperial Islam.

The second, and by far my favourite, is the account of Mansa Abubakari II, the fourteenth century ruler of – let's be honest – the richest empire in the world encompassing the western coast of Africa, extending into modern-day Mali and beyond. Mansa Abubakari II had an armada of 2,000 ships and, in 1311, desiring to explore the 'other bank' of the wide river we call the Atlantic, handed his throne to his brother and sailed into that landless horizon that Uqba had looked on centuries earlier. He left with ships laden to trade and exchange. The mysterious historian Ibn Fadl al-Umari is said to have chronicled this journey and noted that some made it back from the 'other bank' with stories of vibrant, verdant, rich and populated land. Naysayers discard al-Umari but thanks to recent scholarship the idea of an African passage before the middle passage remains a delicious possibility. Abubakari II's ships are for me a significant symbol of the Muslim Atlantic.

Back to Gilroy for a moment. It's important to keep in mind that Gilroy's idea of the Black Atlantic endures because his conceptualisation is a sophisticated one. The Atlantic is a rich geography not constrained by nations and states. It's not merely a body of water that is crossed for the purposes of exploitation or trade. It is the link between old and new worlds, or between civilisation and savageness. It is a rich *maydan* – field – of exchange, formulation, creation and emergence. The Black Atlantic is also a framework born out of modernity:

> The specificity of the modern political and cultural formation I want to call the Black Atlantic can be defined, on one level, through [a] desire to transcend both the structures of the nation state and the constraints of ethnicity and national particularity. These desires are relevant to understanding political organising and cultural criticism. They have always sat uneasily alongside the strategic choices forced on black movements and individuals embedded in national and political cultures and nation-states in America, the Caribbean, and Europe.

Gilroy uses a number of emblematic symbols to represent the Black Atlantic. Central to his framework is the image of ships:

I have settled on the image of ships in motion across the spaces between Europe, America, Africa, and the Caribbean as a central organising symbol for this enterprise and as my starting point. The image of the ship — a living, microcultural, micro-political system in motion — is especially important for historical and theoretical reasons ... Ships immediately focus attention on the middle passage, on the various projects for redemptive return to an African homeland, on the circulation of ideas and activists as well as the movement of key cultural and political artefacts: tracts, books, gramophone records, and choirs.

I can't help but imagine Abubakari II's 2,000 ships imbedded in Gilroy's evocation. It brings me back to the particular ways the Muslim Atlantic sits in and alongside the Black Atlantic and why that relationship is important when we centre culture in the conversation. In these Atlantic movements, Muslim bodies, identities, peoples are not interlocutors but central to the emergence of the very idea of the Muslim Atlantic. In this fertile field connecting Africa, the Caribbean, the Americas and Europe, engagement with Muslims and Islam as an idea and faith shaped the very emergence of the political, economic and social conditions that create the Black Atlantic. The colonial project, which looked to discover a passage to India and instead chanced upon a 'New World', was accelerated if not borne out of a desire to avoid Muslim power – empires, polities and Islamic governance which needed to be negotiated with, fought with, cajoled and compromised with. The Reconquista and the Inquisition which followed tried to wrest the 'cancer of Islam' from Christendom. The Convivencia – a remarkable cultural moment – collapsed under the weight of religious supremacy, domination and by 1609 eradication. The emergence of the empire-making project of finding a way to India, the institutionalisation of chattel slavery, and the reality of middle passage all emerge out of an engagement-altercation with Islam. As European powers tried to circumvent 'Mohammedan menace' and subdue African bodies as mercantile tools to fuel their economic expansion, they inadvertently carried the very Muslim bodies they wished to eradicate and remove from their midst (think about the 1609 order to expel the Moriscoes, ostensibly converted Christians tainted by Muslim blood), to their colonies. How much did Spain and other powers despise Islam and those who adhered to it. A visit to Seville's Cathedral, built on the ruins of a Mesquita of course, will reveal how the visual imagery of the global Spanish empire encoded and commemorates this ongoing battle. The statue of Columbus over his grave inside the cathedral depicts him spearing a pomegranate – Qarnata – Grenada. The murderous process his voyages started have their roots in the destruction of that pomegranate. Islam's defeat is at the very genesis of the project of conquest.

Much has been written about the emergence of a racialised worldview and in particular the institutions of anti-blackness and its connection to the project of conquest, colonisation and subjugation. In the diversity of black bodies – with the myriad of languages, tribes, ethnicities, civilisational histories and faiths they encompassed – brought to the 'other bank' of the Atlantic in chains, Muslim civilisations and cultures were an essential part of those peoples. Historian of African diaspora, Sylviane Diouf's estimation of 30% or more seems to have become the shorthand of quantifying this. But it's not the numbers that matter, it's the enduring, resilient power of faith and culture that becomes an inseparable part of what the African experience in what becomes known as the Americas and the Caribbean is from the beginning and what it becomes.

Islam's enduring presence means that the Black Atlantic has always encompassed the Muslim Atlantic – in other words, it haunts its conceptualisation, present even when its mention is absent. That is why, before we even begin to look at the processes of cultural production and the emergence of cultural leadership in the Muslim Atlantic, we need to be clear what ground we stand on. The erasure of blackness from Muslim narratives and the exclusion of Muslims from some black narratives, doesn't change what we know to be germane to the emergence of this field and the way in which we theorise or understand this geography.

The Muslim Atlantic is an analytical lens, a discursive tool to sharpen the way in which we understand, observe, theorise and illuminate the Muslim presence – now and in the past – and how that presence has shaped the eco-system of Muslim culture and ideas and how it has shaped broader culture as well. As scholars like Suad Abdul Khabeer, Hisham Aidi and others have chronicled, we can't talk about Hip Hop without talking about Jazz, we can't talk about Jazz without talking about the Blues, we can't talk about the Blues without talking about the field hollers and the music of enslaved people and we can't understand the culture of plantation life without understanding the cultural manna that those who were enslaved brought with them – the griot traditions of Muslim West Africa, the recitation of Qur'an and qasidas, a rich corpus of poetry and language, sophisticated worldviews and theologies. Allah is in the Blues, Islamic personalities influence Jazz, Muslim movements and ideas are imbedded in Hip Hop. The most powerful cultural forces of our time have Islam's presence and Muslim creativity imbedded in them. This is the cultural reality of the Muslim Atlantic.

Culture should never be reduced to resilience or resistance, but culture is certainly the foundation on which resilience and resistance is built and created, expressed and enacted. The legal and institutional denial of humanity meant that those enslaved had to preserve their humanity in other ways. There are particular ways in which Islamic cultural and religious practices inspired and were employed during moments of sharp resistance to enslavement and violence. The Bahia Revolution of 1835 had Muslim identity and practice at its core. The Hispaniola uprising in 1522 was also led by Muslim slaves. The animus by some European powers to Muslims even within the institutions of slavery suggest an acknowledgement of a pervasive culture of resistance. The work by Khabeer and others to document and preserve the spirit and practices of the Gullah Geechee peoples of Georgia and the Carolinas who incorporated Islam into the fabric of their unique culture again points to the resilience of Islamic cultural and religious forms. This spirit exists too in the oft-ignored experience of indentured labour in the Caribbean, the process whereby South Asian Muslims became deeply imbedded in the geographies of places like Guyana, Trinidad and Jamaica. This spirit of resistant, resilience and survival makes up the DNA of the Muslim Atlantic. Like Gilroy's idea of the Black Atlantic, the Muslim Atlantic too mitigated against narrow conceptions of citizenship and nation-state belonging.

The migration of peoples from Africa, South Asia, the Middle East and beyond to the 'other bank' – whether directly or via Europe or some other stopping point – enriches the Muslim Atlantic, and is in many ways deeply tied to the post-colonial reality. This has resulted in an erasure of existing Muslim Atlantic histories and privileging of immigrant narratives of Islam and Muslimness. It also opens the possibilities of an ever-widening field of exchange. Malcolm X's project of building a more purposeful political and cultural connection with Africa and the emergence of what scholar and cultural critic Sohail Daulatzai theorises as the Muslim International gives us a way of imagining a (messy) space of intersecting racial, ethnic, linguistic, national, cultural and religious expressions. In many ways, my own father was a product of this Muslim International – though he may never have used that term. Born in India before Partition, raised in both Saudi Arabia and then Pakistan, pursued higher education in England (a natural place of post-colonial orientation), backpacked through Europe and ended up an economic immigrant to Canada, welcomed as part of a much needed new workforce. Travel through the Commonwealth and across the Atlantic was a natural part of living between nations. My great-great grandfather worked with the Royal Engineers for a time and his service received a commendation from a Scottish officer. Almost every family from our part of Punjab had served in some capacity the occupying Raj. My father's own political consciousness arising out of an engagement with political Islam was deeply affected by both personal and national history, as well as by a reading of the Muslim past and the culture that it produced. This was a migrating generation of global souls (to invoke Pico Iyer). Home was not just Canada or the United States or the United Kingdom, or Pakistan or Egypt. It was many places and with that comes a constant sense that the cultural ground is always shifting. This generation participates in the processes of Du Boisian double consciousness – and code switching – constantly. The Muslim Atlantic is space to imagine identities anew. It is a field in which Rushdie's imaginary homelands emerge, which are not faced with fear, as Rushdie suggests, but by cultural creation and co-creation.

I would conceptualise the Muslims Atlantic as a cultural eco-system. An organic, messy space where complex networks of cultural production, creation, co-creation, curation and ideas exist in relationship with each other and cannot ultimately be controlled or directed by any particular authority, but rather are open or vulnerable to influence and adaptation synthesis and conflict. My own understanding and theorisation of this idea has emerged from the work of cultural organising and from a series of gatherings of cultural producers, curators and thinkers which were convened by Asad Ali Jafri, former Curator of Programs for the Shangri-La Museum of Islamic Art, Culture and Design and now Executive Director of the South Asia Institute and myself.

Cultural producers, thinkers and curators are producing new work and knowledge, influencing each other, seeding new ideas, cross pollinating approaches, creating new boundaries and definitions, and synthesising wider circles of art forms. This Muslim Atlantic cultural eco-system exists within and across geographies with culture crossing from Africa to the Caribbean to the UK to Canada to the United States back to Africa. It is a dynamic cultural space and that dynamism has only grown as new forms of 'connectivity' have grown.

Where then are the nodes – the centres – of cultural change that are the engines of this dynamism? Thinking about the period following the liberation movements in Africa and beyond, as well as the emergence of a post Malcolm X Muslim International, we need to think about the way in which ideas and culture was emerging particularly in the context of the Atlantic. The anti-imperial and anti-colonial movements themselves were 'global' in the sense that they harnessed the energies of young people, cultural producers and thinkers in many geographies of the Atlantic simultaneously. The diasporas present in places like London, Paris, New York, Accra and Dakar were engaged in liberation struggles, in shaping them and amplifying them.

You can see this through the music of liberation and the emergence of jazz as a global medium for emancipation. The development of hip hop and its close connection to and adoption by cultural producers in Africa and the Caribbean results in the creation of new cultural languages. Music in particular is often theorised as means for resistance, dissent, the expression of discontent. It is also a music which affirms. It affirms new cultural identities, affirms cultural agency and creates cultural leaders. These vibrant Muslim musical cultural eco-systems are seen more clearly in the ways in which music criss-crosses the *maydan* of the Muslim Atlantic.

My own work over the past twenty-five years has wrestled and contended with the question of what constitutes relevant and credible Muslim leadership. Like others, I have sought to find such personalities in the category of religious leadership. As scholar Peter Mandaville often asks, who speaks for 'Islam' in the absence of centralised, formal and universally accepted religious institutions and structures? Indeed, some Muslim religious figures have laid claim to some kind of authority because they travel and circulate on both sides of the Atlantic, creating following and 'influence'. The lens of the Muslim Atlantic allows us to expand the idea of what Muslim leadership is.

Religious, political, civic and thought leadership are all an important part of the web of influences on and flowing from Muslim communities. Cultural leadership is often ignored or undermined. Yet if culture is the water in which we swim and, if we follow cultural historian Jeff Chang's mantra, that cultural change precedes political change, then I would suggest that the Muslim Atlantic needs to privilege cultural leadership in its understanding of power and influence. It is cultural leaders, those who are shaping culture through cultural production, through curation, through creating spaces and opportunities for exhibition and through funding that are facilitating the narratives and stories that the Muslim Atlantic tells about themselves. We are all producers and consumer of culture, of course. Cultural leaders are those who are able to harness cultural energies and make sense of what results from those energies.

When I think of a cultural leader, I think of someone like Imruh Caesar Bakari. Born in St Kitts, Bakari was among a small group of genre-breaking filmmakers and cultural visionaries who redefined Black British Cinema in the early 1980s (he worked alongside Menelik Shabazz) with films like the 1981 *Riots and Rumours of Riots*, *Burning an Illusion* which came out the following year and the celebrated *Mark of the Hand*, a 1986 profile of Guyanese painter Aubrey Williams. In one conversation I had with Bakari, he recalled the vibe in the Portobello Road cafes where he and other artists, writers and filmmakers from the African diaspora would sit with visiting legends like Senegalese auteur Ousmane Sembene. This is where the craft became idea, where new ways of producing and seeing art were formed and where cultural synthesis happened. London became a centre for cultural and knowledge exchange and production in the Muslim Atlantic. Ideas cross borders with ease. Bakari became one of the important theorists of African Cinema. Even the audacity of creating such fields – Africa is after all a dizzyingly diverse, complex, culturally rich continent – is only possible when we are culturally confident. We can have an African cinema because of the transnational exchange, conversation and gathering. We can create our own lenses to view the world, our own frameworks because the Muslim Atlantic and the larger Black Atlantic give us the agency. In the works of political revolutionaries like Guyana's Walter Rodney, there is a call to his brothers – those seeking similar political, social and economic liberation. These brothers are black, brown, African, Caribbean and in many cases Muslim. For those that claim the Muslim identity, they are certainly shaped by their particular experience but also connect to the universal ideas of the struggle shared by others. The shared language of Muslimness is part of what the Muslim Atlantic creates, yet the results of the thinking that arises from those identities is universal, accessible and part of larger cultural eco-systems.

As a child I grew up embedded in the Muslim Atlantic, even if I may not have called it that. My father was a product of his time in Britain where he convened with political activists from Africa and the Global South, followed anti-colonial liberation struggles and was in Paris during the May 1968 uprisings. When he finally settled in Canada, our mailbox was filled with journals and newspapers like *Afkar Inquiry*, *Arabia: Islamic World Review*, *South*, *Crescent International* and *Impact International*, which reported – from London – the news of the post-colonial world's difficult birth into political freedom and the continuing liberation struggles in places like South Africa, Kashmir and Palestine. He was exposed to the literature of Africa, Southeast Asia and the Americas during his student days and those books ended up on our shelf. I always felt London was close and the liberation movements which were celebrated in our home were tied to my even young sense of the world. Later, it would be my beloved mentor, friend and colleague the late Fuad Nahdi, who worked as an editor at *Africa Events* in London, and later established *Q News*, who gave me an inside look at the mechanics of what I can now call the Muslim Atlantic. The constant exchange of ideas, the positing of new ways of thinking and most importantly of Muslim being an expansive identity, not just a tribal one. He would often say the most compelling reporting on what was then called the 'Third World' came from London during that time. The space to think broadly, across old fault lines and borders was only possible when those borders were challenged – as Gilroy's formulation of the Black Atlantic challenged us to do. It is cities, place of intersection and prosaic encounter where the Muslim Atlantic finds its cultural manna. Cities become cultural engines more powerful than nation states. They are the energetic nodes in the network of transnational cultural exchange and production. They are the places where the Muslim Atlantic comes alive.

Sukina Abdul Noor Douglas and Tanya Muneera Williams, together known as Poetic Pilgrimage, hail from Bristol's Afro-Caribbean community and its vibrant cultural milieu. After accepting Islam and making their faith central to their cultural expression, they began to emerge as not only the voice of the Muslim street, but as cultural ambassadors and translators criss-crossing from the UK to Sudan and Senegal to Europe and the United States, never losing their Jamaican heritage or musical DNA, but developing a sound and a poetry and cultural approach that is emblematic of the Muslim Atlantic. Hip Hop is of course a global language, and I would suggest a pre-eminent language of the Muslim Atlantic, but Sukina and Muneera are themselves leaders able to exert cultural, spiritual and even political influence through their music and to have that influence felt in mainstream Hip Hop spaces as well as within spaces more closely defined as Muslim. Sukina and Muneera are themselves part of a tradition that includes Yasiin Bey (Mos Def), the influential, ocean-hopping MC whose work is not only iconic but pushes the boundaries of collaboration. Note his track 'R.E.D': beginning with Bismillah, shot in Africa, composed with three indigenous DJs who grew up on reservations in Canada, R.E.D. is a product of the expansive cultural sensibility emblematic of the Muslim Atlantic. Bey is a cultural producer who is first a cultural cross-pollinator.

The so-called genre of 'World Music' itself celebrates some of the most important and influential artists of the Muslim Atlantic: Youssou N'Dour whose ground-breaking Senegalese-Egyptian co-production after 9/11 finds audiences first in London, Paris, New York (home to a large Senegalese and Egyptian diaspora) and Berlin. Mali's Ali Farka Toure became the aural proof that the roots of the Blues are squarely in the Niger River Delta. Khaira Arby led the campaign to free Timbuktu organising concerts in places like Chicago's Millennium Park where crowds shouted 'Allah, Allah!' at Arby's frenzied rhythms, a testimony to the culture of her fallen city. The most celebrated 'World Music' in Muslim culture obscured by insufficient labels – Muslim culture borne on the banks of the Muslim Atlantic.

Digital influencers, creators and curators like Nadir Nahdi and his BENI platform are demonstrating how quickly cultural leadership can emerge, influence and mobilise support, interest and participation. By highlighting his own unique story as a child of many cultures and showcasing his network of creatives (through YouTube and Instagram), Nadir is showing us how to build actual and virtual communities of culture around ideas of shared experience, sensibilities and aspiration. That's why he can turn a running club into cultural convening, a yoga session into a cultural conversation.

Listening to MC, actor, poet, writer and cultural producer Riz Ahmed's latest album, 'The Long Goodbye', is to hear the work of someone who has decided to live in the fault lines of today's toxic political culture and fragmented social, political and economic realities. Not only does it contend with what it means to be Brown, British and Muslim, it signs the divorce papers on some kind of easy reconciliation with ideas of empire, colonisation, racism, Islamophobia and the ghosts of the middle passage and other large-scale acts of organised violence undertaken in the name of trade, commerce and Christendom. This new work isn't talking so much about representation as it is about assertion. It stakes claim to cultural agency, to producing culture on our own terms, to saying goodbye to toxic relationships and to being true to our history and our present.

MC, poet and educator Amir Sulaiman's iconic poem 'Danger' is an incendiary and discomforting cry from the margins to be heard, to be recognised and to be free. The words make our skin crawl and lights a fire in the belly. 'Freedom,' Sulaiman writes/intones, 'is between the mind and the soul'.

The possibility of the Muslim Atlantic is a dangerous idea: freedom. Freedom from white supremacy, xenophobia, racism, and Islamophobia. Freedom from constraints of national borders and from brittle dogmas. It embodies the resistance of those who found ways to resist the middle passage and the resilience of those who survived it. The very idea of an emerging – albeit messy, confusing and evolving – cultural leadership which helps push the boundaries of Muslim possibilities is dangerous to existing religious and political institutions. It upends the applecart of power within Muslim communities. It's of course not so simple, but the idea itself is tantalising and compelling enough. Cultural producers and leaders have many *maydans* to play in, the Muslim Atlantic is one of them – a potent and powerful field of interconnections and intersections that are only just beginning to be explored. Cultural change will continue to precede political and social change. Cultural leaders have an opportunity to nudge that change forward, creating spaces for intercultural, intergenerational, intersectional, interdisciplinary gathering and conversation. In the process, they have the opportunity to write the next chapter of not just the Muslim Atlantic, but what it means to be Muslim in the world now.

BLACK RADICALISM

Rasul Miller

In conceptualising the Muslim Atlantic, it is perhaps best to begin by considering the origins of the Atlantic world itself as a historical and political-economic unit. Muslims and people of African descent – two overlapping groups of non-white people who have been racialised in various ways – have been at the heart of that construction from its very beginning.

When we look at the beginning of the Atlantic world economy in the late fifteenth and early sixteenth centuries, we observe an increasing antipathy toward Muslims and people of African descent among European religious, cultural, and economic actors. I think it's important to put the relationship between that history and the origins of our modern notions of race and racialisation in historical context. Before that time in history, in ancient Rome or ancient Greece, if you would have started talking about people as being black and brown and white the way we do today, people would not have even the slightest idea of what you were talking about. So, in many ways, these are modern notions of race that became global in the subsequent centuries, and the Atlantic world economy has largely facilitated that transition.

The beginning of this prevailing racial regime involved the conflation and vilification of Muslims, Arabs, Saracens, Africans, Moors, and Blackamoors from Senegambia. All of that became the raw material out of which our modern racial hierarchies emerged, initially prompting an association of sub-Saharan Africa with Islam and, later, the conception of its inhabitants as people without history. As Portuguese Christians travelled to West and Central Africa during the late fifteenth and early sixteenth centuries in search of resources to exploit and routes to the land of the legendary Christian patriarch, Prester John, discourses emerged that rendered people of African descent appropriate for enslavement. This enabled representatives of various European states including, among others, the Portuguese, the

British, the French, and the architects of what became the Americas to justify their participation in this inhuman institution.

In theorising the Muslim Atlantic, this history unites the various racial groups that make up the bulk of the Muslim communities in the UK, the Americas, the Caribbean, and West Africa. This reality becomes clear when we consider that the same structures are at work in the Atlantic Ocean world and the Indian Ocean world during the era of European colonisation and subsequent neo-colonial exploitation. That is to say, the same processes that led to the extraction of innumerable resources, both natural and human via the transatlantic slave trade, from Africa in the Atlantic Ocean world, similarly siphoned untold resources from colonised areas in the region surrounding the Indian Ocean. Similarly, people from that region were forced by Europeans to relocate to Africa and the Americas through various forms of coerced labour – as indentured servants and the like. So that is where our presence in these lands begins.

In the case of the Americas – specifically the US and the Caribbean – the twentieth century witnessed the emergence, or more accurately the re-emergence, of various efforts by people of African descent to connect with the histories of Islam in the Atlantic world. Of course, these connections were largely severed through the violent, abusive, tumultuous institution of transatlantic slavery. Currently, historians are estimating that maybe a third of the enslaved African captives brought to the Americas were Muslim. It could have been much more, but we are still learning about the identities of these enslaved Africans whose histories were intentionally and violently erased. But we do know that a considerable amount of them had Muslim ancestors. To some extent, by the end of the nineteenth century, the memory of the relationship between Islam and people of African descent in the Atlantic world context had been largely forgotten. During the early twentieth century, that memory was revived through the emergence of various organisations that promoted Islam's Atlantic world legacy and popularised it in Black communities in the US – prompting more and more people of African descent in the West to embrace Islam.

In historicising the securitisation of Muslims, we might well begin by recounting that enslaved African Muslims were often prevented from practicing or openly identifying with their religion under the threat of torture or death. In the modern context, we might start by discussing the career of

Marcus Garvey. The Garvey movement served as an important institution for reconnecting Black people in the West with the historical legacy of Atlantic world Islam. In fact, it is among members of Garvey's Universal Negro Improvement Association (UNIA) that we find some of the first recorded twentieth century examples of Black American and Afro-Caribbean people embracing Islam. The Garvey movement also holds the important distinction of being the organisation on which J. Edgar Hoover – who went on to become the director of the FBI – cut his teeth. Hoover had the dubious distinction of being the architect of our modern regimes of illegal surveillance and targeting of both Muslim and Black communities in the US.

Hoover orchestrated an elaborate legal strategy to neutralise Marcus Garvey on charges of mail fraud. But in the wake of the Garvey movement, another important institution emerged in the US called the Moorish Science Temple of America (MSTA). Although smaller than the UNIA, the MSTA was even more successful in popularising the history of Islam in the Atlantic world. The MSTA was also highly surveilled, infiltrated, and targeted for a couple of reasons that I think are particularly important for our conversation here. One reason was its emphasis on building political and economic autonomy for Black people in the US. Another was the fact that, much like the Garvey movement, it succeeded in fostering an internationalist consciousness among working-class Black people. These become essential reasons why the MSTA was targeted by law enforcement in general and the FBI in particular. Members of the organisation were proponents of Third World internationalism. They critiqued US imperialism and promoted Black American solidarity with Japan during the 1930s.

By the 1930s, the MSTA had been weakened by factional disputes and sectarian violence. But from its ashes rose two important, concurrent streams that constitute the origins of the most popular iterations of Islam in the US during the twentieth century – the Black American orthodox Muslim tradition and the Nation of Islam. One of the earliest national Black American orthodox Muslim organisations was the Adden Allahe Universal Arabic Association (AAUAA). It was founded by Muhammad Ezaldeen, who previously served as a leader of the MSTA in Detroit. In 1929, he left the MSTA, travelled to Turkey and lobbied the Turkish government to provide land for Black American Muslims who wished to relocate to the Muslim world. As this occurred during the reign of Kamal

Ataturk and his secularisation project, Ezaldeen's plan was less than well-received. Subsequently, Ezaldeen moved to Cairo, Egypt, where he spent about five years formally studying Islam and the Arabic language. When he returned to the US, he created an umbrella organisation connecting orthodox Muslims throughout the country. Ezaldeen was deeply influenced by the discourses of Islamic and Arab nationalism that he encountered in Cairo in the 1930s, but he selectively appropriated aspects of these discourses specifically for a Black American context. He was highly surveilled by law enforcement, in part because of his organisation's espousal of Afro-Asian solidarity and Black American support of Japan – a growing symbol of non-European political power and military might. In the context of the Second World War, some Black radical intellectuals and activists around the country, including Black Muslims like Ezaldeen, encouraged Black radicals to see Japan not as their enemy, but as a natural ally.

The other stream of Islam in the early twentieth century US, one with which more people will be familiar, is that of the Nation of Islam. The Nation began in 1930 and, during the 1950s, grew to become the most visible Muslim community in the country. The Nation's espousal of Black Nationalism and critiques of white supremacy and US imperialism similarly made it a target of US law enforcement. The Nation was subjected to various schemes of surveillance and infiltration, as well as incidents of profiling and police violence. All of this gives us a historical perspective on the emergence of the notion that Muslims constitute a sort of fifth column in America – that because of their religion, it is somehow reasonable to suspect them of sympathising with hostile foreign nations and violent, anti-American conspiracies.

One of the important distinctions and implicit conversations between adherents of these two branches of Islam in the US revolves around the question of internationalism. On some level, both Black American orthodox Muslims and members of the Nation of Islam simultaneously devoted themselves to the task of building political economic power to transform majority Black and Brown communities in the US and demonstrated an internationalist political orientation. The two differed, however, on emphasis. Black orthodox Muslims were often characterised by their internationalism perhaps more than any other quality. They sought to build relationships and solidarities with Muslims and Muslim institutions around the world. For the Nation, the emphasis was on building Black political economic independence – something for which the Nation became known in cities around the country.

In 1954, Malcolm X began serving as the minister of the Nation's Mosque Number Seven, and shortly thereafter, he became the national representative of the organisation's leader, the Honourable Elijah Muhammad. Malcolm contributed to the Nation's surge in popularity throughout the US during the 1950s and 60s. During this period, the Nation experienced an unprecedented degree of visibility and success in promoting Islam and organising communities throughout the US, particularly in the urban north. It is also worth noting that the Nation was crawling with informants and was probably the most surveilled organisation of the period. In fact, Elijah Muhammad has been referred to as the most heavily surveilled figure during the civil rights era.

But then something interesting happened in 1964, when Malcolm X was forced out of the Nation of Islam. At that point, Malcolm also started to focus on the imperative for Black people in the West to embrace a more internationalist political orientation, while at the same time maintaining a concurrent emphasis on fostering Black political economic power locally in US cities. As an orthodox Muslim, Malcolm advocated armed self-defence in the tradition of Black organisers and freedom fighters like Robert F. Williams. This dual emphasis on internationalism and armed self-defence had long been a feature of certain strains of Black radicalism in the US. In the decade following Malcolm X's martyrdom, it became a hallmark of Black orthodox Muslim community organising throughout the Americas.

Black Muslim communities' advocacy of armed self-defence rendered them even more susceptible to propagandistic rhetoric that fuelled their increased securitisation in the US. One pertinent example of how Black American Muslims actualised this stance can be found in the Dar-ul-Islam movement. Founded in 1962 and deeply impacted by both Malcolm's embrace of orthodox Islam and the radical turn of Black political organising during the late 1960s, the Dar-ul-Islam movement became the largest network of Black orthodox Muslim communities in the US by the early 1970s, with affiliated mosques in the Caribbean and Canada as well. For members of the Dar-ul-Islam movement in cities like New York, Philadelphia, Detroit, Cleveland, Washington D.C., and elsewhere, community policing was an important component of a more comprehensive strategy to build robust Black Muslim political economies. Like the Nation of Islam before it, the Dar-ul-Islam movement focused on building strong, community-oriented institutions including businesses, schools, and a nationally distributed newspaper. Also like the Nation of Islam, mosques affiliated with the Dar-ul-Islam movement crafted community policing strategies to create safe zones around their houses of worship and their community institutions. The Nation of Islam did this by requiring its male members to serve as part of the Fruit of Islam, a well-organised and well-trained force that worked to ensure the safety of the mosque and surrounding residents. The Dar-ul-Islam's answer to the Fruit of Islam was called Ra'd (Thunder), which similarly soldiered to make both its mosques and nearby areas safe. However, whereas the Nation did not officially allow its members to carry weapons, it was not at all uncommon for members of Ra'd to stay armed.

One of the most prominent figures attracted to the Dar ul-Islam movement was H. Rap Brown, a Black Power organiser who served as the head of the Student Nonviolent Coordinating Committee (SNCC) for a time and also the Minister of Justice for the Black Panther Party. After being incarcerated in connection with his activism, Brown became Muslim while in prison and adopted the name Jamil Abdullah Al-Amin. After his release, he emerged as the imam of a national, Islamic community that we might refer to as a successor to the Dar ul-Islam movement. Imam Jamil established a mosque in Atlanta, GA, where he implemented some of the same strategies that characterised both his own radical activism and the work of the Dar-ul-Islam movement in places like New York and Detroit. In Atlanta's West End, an impoverished area where the police had failed to provide adequate safety to community members, Imam Jamil organised local Black orthodox Muslims to rid the neighbourhood of drugs and crime – thus rehabilitating the area through community policing.

A commitment to armed self-defence – whether in the face of white vigilante violence, police brutality, or the lack of safety caused by systemic poverty and the state's criminal neglect of urban Black communities – also characterised many of the Black political organisations that emerged in this period. These include groups like the Black Panther Party for Self Defense, Maulana Karenga's US Organisation, and the Black Liberation Army

(BLA). The BLA is particularly interesting for the purposes of our discussion. The BLA was a radical wing of the East Coast Black Panther Party. It was greatly impacted by the rising popularity of Islam in cities like New York and Philadelphia, and many of its members were Muslims. Some of these Black Muslims associated with the BLA liberated the political prisoner and Black freedom fighter Assata Shakur, who lives free to this day with political asylum in Cuba.

Against this backdrop, the vilification and securitisation of Black and Muslim communities rose to new heights as law enforcement officials utilised illegal methods of surveillance and infiltration, like those associated with the FBI's infamous COINTELPRO program to destroy organisations and even assassinate young activists. From this history, we can observe continuity as the same legal apparatus and the same kinds of strategies used to neutralise Marcus Garvey in the early twentieth century were further developed and deployed against the Nation of Islam and, eventually, virtually every organisation associated with Black Power. This also served as a precedent for the persisting surveillance of Black Muslim communities up to the present.

Beginning in the neoliberal era of the 1980s, the possibilities for grassroots organising became straitjacketed. In that moment, Black, Brown, and Muslim communities were subject to greater surveillance and criminalisation. Earlier strategies for community policing and armed self-defence became almost impossible to pursue in an era marked by heightened suspicion of Black and Brown communities and increased militarisation of the police, and this continues to be the case today. For instance, just imagine if someone today advocated for Black Muslims to police their own neighbourhoods – armed with their own weapons at that! Imagine the level of fear that would evoke and how the government and law enforcement officials might respond. But this is exactly what communities were doing during the 1960s and 70s. The limitations placed on Black and Muslim communities' ability to organise for self-determination, due to heightened fears and increased securitisation, was part of a broader shift in US politics. The preceding decades witnessed a broader climate of widespread political dissent related to the anti-war movement, the Civil Rights Movement, the Black Power Movement, and other expressions of political radicalism. However, from the 1980s onward, the space for radicalism and political dissent shrank significantly.

In the closing decade of the Cold War, this also meant that the kinds of Third World internationalism that previously characterised these communities were further suppressed.

From the 1970s onward, new Muslim communities began to emerge as greater numbers of immigrant Muslims moved to the US with a very different economic and political orientation than their predecessors. Muslim immigrants who come to the US before 1965 were primarily single men who worked as unskilled labourers. Due to segregation, they were often forced to live in majority-Black neighbourhoods. There, they collaborated with Black orthodox Muslims to build multi-racial religious communities.

But that trend changed with the passage of the Immigration and Nationality Act of 1965, which abolished the earlier quota-based system and sought to recruit highly skilled labourers.

Thus, many of the Muslims who immigrated to the US after 1965 had professional backgrounds, and relocated there to work as doctors and engineers. The circumstances in the UK were, of course, very different. This speaks to the great potential that our transatlantic conversation presents. In the UK, Muslims have a kind of class solidarity that is, ostensibly, less common in the US today. What does that class solidarity make possible? The professional opportunities and resulting upward mobility afforded to many Muslim immigrants in the US served, for a time, as a kind of veil or shroud from the realities of American racial capitalism. Many immigrant Muslims naively imagined the US to be a meritocracy, where, through hard work, the American Dream was attainable by all.

While Islamophobia is widespread in the US, it is arguably less pervasive within Black communities. This is largely because there is a very real memory among Black Americans of the positive impact that Black Muslims had on Black and Brown neighbourhoods during the 1950s, 60s, 70s, and 80s. This was especially true of the Nation of Islam, but was very much true of Black orthodox Muslim communities as well. There are cases in New York City, for instance, where various Black Muslim communities were targeted by law enforcement, and Black non-Muslims rallied to defend them against the police. In one instance, when a Harlem mosque was under siege by the New York City Police Department, local residents surrounded the police and started to throw bricks and bottles at members of the NYPD. The residents of Harlem said, 'We will not allow you to harm these Muslims who are part of our communities and who make our communities better.'

This emphasis on serving and benefiting the broader community is one of the critical sources of the power that twentieth century Black Muslim communities were able to amass. This, coupled with a concerted effort to reinvigorate an internationalist consciousness among aggrieved populations in the West, could reveal a pathway forward for resisting and combating the structures that undergird both Islamophobia and white supremacy. These structures – neoliberalism, capitalism, and neo-imperialism – are inherently transnational. Therefore, any attempt to oppose them must be transnational as well.

Part of what I find generative in facilitating a transatlantic conversation between Muslims of colour through the notion of a Muslim Atlantic is the potential it holds to help us rediscover a rich tradition of internationalism that, while based on shared notions of spirituality and morality, has the potential to bring about major political and social transformation as well. Perhaps we might discover a way to reopen the imaginative space for people to conceive of pursuing radical strategies to empower their communities, like those developed by our Black Muslim foremothers and forefathers, rather than settling for limited reforms or seeking inclusion from states and economies that are fundamentally based on white supremacy and inequality. How might we forge new strategies, based on old lessons, to empower non-state entities that are actually accountable to our communities at a grassroots level? Such entities could, like the Nation of Islam, the Dar-ul-Islam movement, and so many others, adequately secure their own communities and provide benefit to the broader society – undermining the defective logic behind current regimes of state-sponsored securitisation.

SECURITY

Shirin Khan

The United States and the United Kingdom have enjoyed a close and mutually influential alliance for decades, one that leaders of both countries long considered their most important bilateral relationship. Currently, the two nations are in a remarkably similar state of affairs when it comes to security issues. Between lone wolf actors seemingly radicalised on the internet, the looming question of how to deal with foreign fighters returning from Syria, and the increasingly violent rhetoric of far-right and white nationalist extremists, the US and the UK have seen a shift from national security risks posed by international actors to a more pressing threat of domestic terrorism. One thing that has not changed in the wake of these evolving threats is the securitisation of Muslim communities, still believed by many to be a root cause of widespread instability. From something as significant as counterterrorism policies – both those explicitly as well as implicitly geared towards Muslims – to something so seemingly innocuous as the negative portrayal of Muslims on national security-themed television shows, it's clear that the 'special relationship' shared by the two nations also lends itself to a shared perspective on the securitisation of American and British Muslims.

Growing up in the US, I frequently travelled to Britain to visit family. My father and his sister are the only two of seven children to have left India and settle in the US and Wales, respectively. When visiting family in Wales, I don't remember thinking twice about our families being minorities until much later in life, but I did feel from a very young age that I could relate much more to my British cousins than to our family in India. A shared language, yes, but also a shared space within Western culture and civilisation. My cousin and I would watch episode after episode of *Friends*, and I would return to the US with Craig David's latest song stuck in my head. Even as a 10-year old I could recognise the name Tony Blair, but perhaps that has more to do with his very public and unwavering support of the United States after the 9/11 terrorist attacks than with my time spent in the United Kingdom. In thinking about the ways US and UK security policies and attitudes have developed over time with regard to Muslim communities, this is a key point to which we can trace back. Two allies on the brink of two endless wars abroad that would irrevocably change the way a significant subset of their populations at home would be perceived by fellow community members and security officials alike. The UK's response to 9/11 was immediate and mirrored that of the US, despite not being targeted on its own soil until the 2005 London bombings. As such, the administrations of President George W. Bush and Prime Minister Tony Blair simultaneously introduced increased security measures at home and made costly commitments to the wars in Afghanistan and Iraq, resulting in permanent damage to civil liberties as well as community cohesion.

On a recent trip to visit my cousin, who now lives in Birmingham, England, we spent an afternoon at the Bullring, a popular shopping centre in the heart of the city. As we exited the main building into the outdoor market area, it was a familiar scene: a woman selling Pikachu and Spiderman-shaped balloons to a queue of people amidst tempting aromas of fresh popcorn. Yet there was also a strange addition: a *kurta*-clad preacher standing on a crate speaking loudly into a microphone. I was surprised. I noticed the *taqiyah* perched on his head and the table behind him offering pamphlets about Islam. It was not lost on me that this man was able to adopt the very British tradition of soapbox oratory and use it to spread his version of the message of Islam in the middle of a busy town centre. It had me thinking about what a reaction to something like this would be at home in the US, the world's foremost bastion of free speech. One might see it to a lesser extent in big cities, but I struggled to imagine someone powerfully preaching about Islam while passersby carried on with their day all around him, especially in the Trump era. Upon seeing the preacher and reacting to him, my cousin remarked that it was amazing how freely Muslims are able to live and practise their faith in the UK, which struck me. I was used to hearing from subject-matter experts that Muslims are comparably much more assimilated in the US, and it goes without saying that Britain is dealing with its fair share of religious and cultural intolerance, but my cousin's experience was different. When she made the personal choice to wear a hijab after marriage several years ago, I would be lying if I said I wasn't slightly worried that something would happen to her. It comforted me to know that she felt safe, while I thought sadly of the pointed anti-Muslim rhetoric being peddled in my own country and the subsequent sharp increase in systematic discrimination and criminal incidents linked to it.

At the time I was working with the Muslim Diaspora Initiative at New America, a non-partisan think-tank in Washington, DC, researching this exact phenomenon for what would eventually turn into an interactive map detailing 'Anti-Muslim Activities in the United States'. As such, I was acutely aware not only of the lengths to which ordinary people go to harm Muslims, but also of how many state legislatures were — and still are — consistently debating anti-Muslim laws. A popular approach among local and state-level lawmakers has been to propose explicitly 'anti-Sharia' bills, or thinly veiled anti-'foreign law' resolutions, that claim to prevent traditional Islamic law from infiltrating US courts. We found that not only had at least 37 of the 50 state-level judiciaries considered such legislation, but that the language of the bills was nearly identical. It soon became apparent that the source of these copycat laws was primarily two organisations working in tandem: the Center for Security Policy, a far-right think-tank that alleges radical Muslims have infiltrated the government, and ACT for America, a non-profit that bills itself as a 'national security grassroots activist organisation', also widely considered the largest anti-Muslim group in the US. The legislators introducing and advocating for the bills known as 'American Laws for American Courts' argue that US citizens are at risk from potential acts of terrorism and from being subjected to foreign laws, specifically from refugees arriving from predominantly Muslim countries.

Someone who doesn't necessarily know that Sharia is more a set of religious guidelines, and more importantly, that any foreign laws are subservient to the US constitution anyway, might not understand why these anti-foreign laws are a bad thing, which is exactly their intended use: fear-mongering resulting in discriminatory policies. This idea that Islam is not compatible with democracy is shared by many across the Atlantic. According to a report published in early 2019 by the anti-fascist group Hope not Hate, more than a third of people in the UK believe that Islam is a threat to the British way of life. More specifically, nearly a third erroneously believe in the existence of so-called 'no-go zones' where Sharia law is fully implemented and non-Muslims are forbidden to enter.

Considering these completely false claims are being peddled by elected officials nation-wide, it became glaringly obvious that there was next to no Muslim representation at any level of American government at the time. Only twelve Muslims ran for office in the 2016 election cycle. Fast forward to the 2018 midterms, however, and that number jumped to over one hundred Muslims, a record fifty-five of whom were elected to offices ranging from city council to the US Congress. Call it the Trump effect. When considering trends in the UK government by comparison, British Muslims have also suffered from disproportionate under-representation, but they've had more success reaching high-level, highly visible offices: Mayor of London Sadiq Khan, for example, as well as Baroness Sayeeda Warsi, who held several prominent positions in Prime Minister David Cameron's cabinet. And that's not to say Muslims being elected or appointed to office is a guaranteed win for the overall community; of the nineteen Muslims who won seats in the 2019 parliamentary election, four are Conservatives belonging to the very party that is facing repeated calls for an inquiry into Islamophobia. Perhaps they hope to effect change from within?

It was during the same trip to Birmingham that I watched the first episode of the critically acclaimed BBC show *Bodyguard* in which a veteran suffering from PTSD is installed as the personal bodyguard for Britain's hawkish Home Secretary. In the first episode, said bodyguard thwarts a terrorist attack by talking down a trembling, hijab-wearing woman strapped into a suicide vest. Certain aspects of the show reminded me a lot of *Homeland,* the popular American television show that focuses on US counterterrorism and intelligence operations – namely that both were met with tough criticism for their portrayal of nearly all Muslim characters as violent extremists. I used to watch *Homeland* with my sister when I was in college, and she once teased me for saying I wanted to be like Carrie Mathison, the main character of the show. What I meant was that I wanted to be a gifted intelligence analyst who travelled around the world helping to thwart terrorist attacks. 'You want to hide the fact that you're bipolar from the CIA and make extremely questionable decisions when you decide to go off your meds?', she laughed. She had a point, Carrie was not an ideal role model, but I did eventually go on to pursue a Master's degree in Non-proliferation and Terrorism Studies with hopes of being an intelligence analyst.

This was not a degree that many in my extended family, or many outside of my family for that matter, understood very well. My dad's family in India is Muslim, and my siblings and I were raised as such for several years, though it began to wane quite early on. For me, it was around the time I was in elementary school. We had moved to a new city and never found the same sense of community that we felt at our prior mosque, and so we gradually stopped attending as a family until only my dad was going on Fridays. Eventually he stopped, too. Each of us had our own personal reasons for disengaging, but I can say with confidence that it had a lot more to do with organised religion as a whole, as well as adapting to a post-9/11 America, as opposed to issues with Islam specifically. When I took my first course on terrorism in college, I began to visualise how my background could be of use in the diplomacy or security field. I considered myself somewhat of a 'cultural Muslim', that is, a Muslim not in practice but rather in name and heritage, allowing me a unique combination of empathy and objectivity. Although I didn't identify as a Muslim myself, I felt the same desire as many Muslims across America in wanting to be the conduit through which my mostly white, conservative childhood friends and their parents would realise that Islam is not a monolith. Look to my loving father and his jovial, non-terrorist, Muslim Indian family, not Osama bin Laden and Abu Bakr al Baghdadi. And look to me, someone who doesn't practise and yet understands that the vast majority of Muslims interpret theirs as a religion of peace, to the point that I've pursued a career in deterring those who would instead use it to cause death and destruction.

In the scholarly study of terrorism, it is widely accepted that modern global terrorism is comprised of four overlapping waves beginning in the 1880s: Anarchist, Anti-Colonial, New Left, and Religious. Just a few years ago, when the Islamic State had reached its zenith, it was painfully clear that we were still riding the fourth wave and seemingly would be for some time. It made sense, then, that many of my graduate courses between 2015 and 2017 covered 'Jihadi' terrorism, the catch-all phrase for security threats posed by radicalised Muslims. I also enrolled in a course called The American Radical Right, for which the syllabus read 'certain violent far-right paramilitary organisations nowadays constitute the greatest terrorist threat to the US homeland (apart from foreign jihadist groups).' In fact, as I would come to learn, the FBI concluded in 2017 that 'white supremacist groups had already carried out more attacks than any other domestic extremist group over the past sixteen years' and were likely to carry out more attacks against minority groups. But these types of organisations and the closely related white nationalist movement was, and still is, completely absent from the national discussion about domestic terrorism.

I had all but decided that I wanted to focus my degree and my career on the threat of far-right domestic terrorism when my world was turned upside down by the election of Donald Trump. I immediately felt deflated, and that it would be a waste of time to focus my energy on countering a group of people that this president was actively courting. When I voiced my concerns about working for the Trump administration to peers and mentors, some understood and agreed, while others countered that people with my background – and my values – were needed there more than ever. And anyway, how much does policy really change from one administration to the next? Quite a lot, as it turns out, but this is no ordinary administration. As a new graduate embarking on the job hunt, I half-heartedly sent in a few applications for intelligence positions, but ultimately decided I could not stomach the thought of entering the government sector, especially in this capacity, at a time when I whole-heartedly disagreed with the direction it was taking.

While I was grateful that my institution was offering such a relevant and timely course about far-right movements despite the lack of national coverage, I was also cognisant that something was missing. One brief session of a broader Counterterrorism class aside, there was no course dedicated exclusively to the concept of Countering Violent Extremism (CVE), a central tenet of President Obama's counterterrorism policy, particularly in the domestic sphere. In fact, one simply cannot discuss the securitisation of Muslims in the West without discussing CVE, or its counterpart more often referenced in the UK, Prevent. While it has no agreed upon universal definition, much like the term 'terrorism' itself, CVE/Prevent focuses on cause rather than effect. Ideally, the concept is to counter the appeal of extremist ideologies and organisations by convening community groups, such as non-profits and universities, as a complement to law enforcement efforts. It sounds so promising in theory, and I think it could be, if only it didn't end up stigmatising Muslim communities and ultimately being used as a proxy for intelligence gathering.

A perfect case study is one of the US cities involved in the Department of Justice's 2015 pilot CVE programme, Minneapolis-St. Paul, chosen for its significant population of Somali-Americans. The Minneapolis programme was focused on preventing recruiters from both al-Shabaab, a terrorist group based in Somalia, as well as the Islamic State from reaching Somali-Americans. This effort brought together community-based organisations and local partners including public school systems, interfaith organisations, non-profits, NGOs, and governments on every level. Together, the organisations offered community-oriented programmes including after-school mentoring, scholarships, and job training in order to address several identifiable 'root causes of radicalisation'. The programme suggested intervention models both within the school system and in the wider community that would reach students and families before law enforcement was ever involved, ideally before a crime was ever committed. In reality, the framework faced tough criticism from the very Somali-American community it was supposedly trying to protect. For one, CVE is meant to tackle these issues using primarily a non-security approach, and frankly it's hard to separate a programme funded by the Department of Justice from the idea that it is simply another law enforcement measure. This left some feeling like the programme was merely a veiled means of government surveillance on the Muslim community. It also came under fire for relying on unfounded theories about radicalisation that assume there are consistent and predictable behavioural indicators of who will become a terrorist, despite admitting themselves that there is no such identifiable path. As a result, the communities where CVE efforts are focused – the overwhelming majority of which are Muslim – are considered inherently violent. In fact, some organisations identified by Department of Justice as key partners are avoiding participation in the framework altogether citing the stigmatising and discriminatory focus on Muslims.

President Obama's CVE pilot programme was directly influenced by the Prevent programme implemented in the UK as part of a wider counterterrorism strategy following the 2005 London Underground bombings, with the aim of preventing individuals from being radicalised or supporting terrorism. The Prevent policy faces much of the same criticism as CVE programmes in the US, namely that it disproportionately impacts people of the Muslim faith or background and is just another surveillance mechanism. Ever since the Prevent policy became a legal duty for public sector institutions in 2015, however, revelations about just how far the programme goes have led to increasing public mistrust. Schools and universities, for instance, are required to monitor students and report incidents they consider extreme, while many teachers are not only uncomfortable in this role but also say they haven't received adequate training that might help them differentiate an 'extreme' idea from an exploratory one. Unsurprisingly, this requirement has resulted in several highly discriminatory incidents: a thirteen-year-old boy using the term 'eco-terrorist' during a class discussion about environmental activists was subsequently being asked by Prevent if he was affiliated with ISIS. A graduate student of a Terrorism, Crime and Global Security masters programme – much like the one I was enrolled in myself – was questioned by Prevent after he was reported for reading an academic book entitled *Terrorism Studies* in the campus library. I may have opted not to bring my assigned reading from *Messages to the World: The Statements of Osama bin Laden* with me on the flight home when I was a grad student, but I certainly could not have imagined triggering a negative response in my own school library.

This is a point where we can see an interesting divergence between the UK and the US, especially considering their usually quite parallel counterterrorism policies. With the pilot programmes now stalled, the US hasn't done much in the realm of CVE other than awarding grants to non-profits committed to the cause. While the Obama administration funded organisations geared towards countering both Islamic extremism and white supremacism, any hopes for an all-encompassing CVE effort effectively died with the election of President Trump, whose administration fails to recognise the threat posed by the latter while continuing to fixate on the former. And it has become increasingly clear in Britain that government-led efforts are generally both unpopular and counterproductive – perhaps rendering Prevent an example for policymakers in the US of what *not* to do. It is doubtful that the US's CVE efforts will get a boost any time soon given the current political climate, however, there is no lack of well thought-out, research-driven suggestions on the table when the tide eventually turns, even if it means withdrawing the federal government from CVE-related partnership building entirely.

While the overall number of terrorist attacks in the US and Western Europe has decreased over the past few years, we are still grappling with huge security issues that disproportionately affect Muslims. Now that the Islamic State has lost its territory, one of the biggest dilemmas facing several countries is how to deal with their citizens who left home to join the terrorist group in Iraq and Syria. For months now, this issue has seemingly paralysed Western countries; some have outright refused to take back militants as well as their wives and children citing obvious security concerns. Many simply do not have a policy in place to handle this particular situation. But all will eventually be put to the test as Turkish President Recep Tayyip Erdogan has made it clear that he will deport all foreign fighters currently detained by Turkey. Here is an instance where the policy decisions of the US and the UK have diverged; while the US has already repatriated several of its own citizens, Britain has instead stripped dozens of former militants of their citizenship and refused to allow them into the country. It is of course easier for the US to make this judgement call given the comparably far lower number of American foreign fighters, and President Trump has walked back earlier comments about detaining thousands of militants in the wartime prison at Guantanamo Bay, Cuba. The US government is putting increasing pressure on allies to take back their foreign fighters, undoubtedly driven by the worsening security situation in the region after the abrupt pullout of American troops. It is true, however, that the Department of Justice has been able to charge several American citizens for their alleged involvement with the Islamic State.

Meanwhile, Prime Minister Boris Johnson has taken a case-by-case approach to the question of repatriation, and Britain has demonstrated a slight shift in policy with its recent decision to accept several orphans and unaccompanied children from former Islamic State territory. A controversial proposal to renew the Treason Act 1351, initially designed to punish anyone caught plotting the death of the monarch or 'adhering to the King's Enemies', has also gained traction since the idea was first put forth by the Policy Exchange think-tank in mid-2018. As the UK was weighing what to do with Shamima Begum, the 19-year-old who wishes to return after running away from her London home to join the Islamic State – and whose case is at the centre of the overall debate, the then Home Secretary Sajid Javid noted in early 2019 that the idea of updating the six-hundred-and-fifty-year-old treason legislation to apply to home-grown extremists was worth considering. Since then, Boris Johnson has also expressed support for reforming the law to better deal with transnational terrorist groups, while critics maintain that the offence of treason is outdated and that modern counterterrorism measures are better equipped to deal with today's problems. It remains to be seen how the UK might move forward in this regard, but the pressure is mounting at home and abroad as questions arise about the implications of citizenship, and the limits to which it offers protection.

Both the US and the UK are helmed by leaders who, despite having an unwavering contingent of supporters at home, are seen internationally as reckless and divisive, and both are in the midst of an inward turn: President Trump touts an 'America First' agenda while Prime Minister Boris Johnson is forging ahead with completing the Brexit process. In fact, for many Americans, the passage of Brexit served as a defining moment in 2016 as their presidential election grew nearer. Would the political revolution that had just transformed the UK extend across the Atlantic? I, for one, was firmly of the mindset that it could not possibly happen. As I would come to find out, a much larger portion of the country than I previously understood was emboldened to ensure that it would. But to the extent that there is a continued Atlantic approach to securitisation and counterterrorism policies under the leadership of such similar characters, there is also a burgeoning Atlantic response. Muslim actors, activists, comedians, authors, ordinary citizens – they are all carving out a space from which to forcefully challenge what has become the status quo. In this way, I think the resolve of British and American Muslims to not only remain but continue growing as a visible and active segment of society, and to advocate for fair treatment from fellow community members and security officials alike, is stronger than ever.

BACK TO BRISTOL

Tanya Muneera Williams

It is difficult to tell a story when the story spans hundreds of years. In reality, there are many more chapters to be written. I was born in Bristol. And now here I am in a crowd, every direction is jammed with people, we are trying to be together yet respectful of each other and giving space, social distancing as much as we can. Some are more successful than others. I am among the unsuccessful ones, although I have not touched anyone. I am overly cautious to the point that it must show on my face. I am assuming so because I have been asked by two people so far if I am okay. One even goes further and tries to direct me to a quiet space in case I need to sit down. It is too noisy to tell him, yes thank you, I am okay, and I know he wants to be helpful, so I let him continue. Just as he finishes, there is a gigantic jubilant roar. I don't know what is happening, but I cheer and roar too, the ecstatic feeling of happiness feels more contagious than the corona we are trying to avoid.

A man in front of me is pulling a speaker on wheels. This image looks like a flashback to my childhood, when my cousins and I made the trip from St Thomas Jamaica to Dunn's river falls, and on the way back, fishermen stood on the roadside selling steamed fish wrapped in silver foil. This could have easily been one of the fishermen. Though his frame may have been slender he had a cool confidence that made me think he knows exactly where he is going. There was something about him that warmed my belly, so I followed.

I don't remember what reggae song he was playing on his speaker, but it was something about redemption, liberation and the will of the people. Wherever he went there was a clear path as if he was Moses. He stops at a mass of people standing around, looking at something on the floor. I can't see what is happening so I make my way around the mass to find a gap where I can fit. There is a girl standing on a bench or something taking photos, so I hand her my camera and ask her to take pictures for me too. When she hands me back the camera I see a picture of the graffitied face of a statue that I know too well, on top of it lays an afro comb and a tropical drink juice box.

This statue once towered above us mere mortals, a symbol that Bristol was not ashamed of its slave history, a symbol that this was not even history because the legacy of slavery is alive and kicking now, a symbol celebrating those parts of Bristol where people are not welcomed and if you enter and you are triggered, then well, it's too bad, a symbol that in a few 100 feet, you will enter the space of old money, slave money, saturated wealth, old institutes and networks that serve the descendants of old money. This statue was pulled off its plinth, pushed down the road, and shoved into the water. The same waters that many African enslaved people died in as a result of Edward Colston, the man depicted in the statue.

They say Bristol is changing, I don't know but I hope so. I was born in Bristol in the 1980s, the youngest of four and the only girl. One of my earliest recollections is my family huddled together in the living room around my dad waiting for him to fix the aerial of our very first colour television. I spent a lot of my childhood sat way too close to the telly and was forever being told by someone to move back. This box allowed me to make sense of the wider world and I was glued to it. Saturday morning TV programmes, with hip young presenters talking to stuffed animals, music chart shows which introduced me to bands like Bros, Pet Shop Boys and Lisa Stansfield, as well as sitcoms like *Only Fools and Horses* and American series like *Dallas*, a glittery dramatisation, but the age-old story of clans fighting for power and resources.

Power and resources became a regular feature on this family box. It was replicated often but particularly on the various news programmes, a fight I watched just as intently as I watched everything else. These news programmes made me realise my fragility; I was exposed to the threat of nuclear war, the threat of paedophilia, the threat of AIDS, the threat of terrorist attacks. This was back in the days when the word terrorist was not a synonym for Muslims alone, there were a few others who bore that label before we were handed the baton. Like most people's childhood, I had an assorted bag of ups and downs, like most people's childhood I learnt the life-long lesson of how to walk and balance the feeling of uncertainty and fear against the backdrop of general life things for a kid of my age, such as riding bikes and playing football, pulling off the arms and poking out the eyes of my dolls. But these threats led to a clear fear, an omnipresent sense lingering in the background of an invisible foe that was closer to me than I was to the family colour TV. This foe followed me everywhere, and not even I could tell it to move back.

During the early noughties, I moved from Bristol to London, the big city, the place we all moved to or at least dreamed of moving to. That's how it felt, London for me was this place I had to go, I had to find myself, explore my narrative and create my own story, my own adventure. I imagined moving to London would allow me the freedom to etcher sketch my bold chronicles with all the colours of the sun reflecting from a broken shard of glass against a white wall. And I did just that, I did that and more. I travelled further than I had imagined, and contributed to culture in more ways than I could fathom, back then on the verge of my move I was an awkward black girl leaving her city because she thought it did not love her the way that she loved it.

Now, eighteen years later, moving back to Bristol, I have been thinking a lot about this city, my city and my experiences growing up. What led me to leave, just what was it that made me feel unloved by Bristol. I have been thinking about the context into which I was born and the context of the city which I now see before me. All around you can see the legacy of slavery. In the names of buildings and street names such as Colston Hall, Brunel Rooms, White Ladies Road, Cabot Circus, Portland Square, Jamaica Street, Blackbody Hill, the names go on. You can see the legacy of slavery in the distribution of wealth across the city and in just how segregated it is. You can see it in statues, the architecture, museums, schools and universities. You can see it on the tips of tongues like a forgotten word screaming to be remembered, and maybe even psychologically and subconsciously you can see this in the minds of people.

But we don't have to go back as far as slavery to think about the city of Bristol and the context in which I was born. You can go back to the 1950s and 1960s the bloom of post-war Britain where many people from the Caribbean entered the country to rebuild its mother country. Black book in hand they were citizens too. Both my parents entered Britain from Jamaica and ironically lived just minutes away from Jamaica Street. This was before they met, but they joked that they may have been far away from Jamaica, but were still close to the sunny island as a result of their proximity to this street. Their closeness to Jamaica was more accurate than they knew as they were unaware of the extent that the many mansions, grand buildings, and the infrastructure of the city had come about as a result of forced labour and cane plantations. They were unaware that Britain's addiction to sugar and bad teeth was cultivated here.

We can look at the bus boycott of 1963 to help us to understand the context of modern-day Bristol. We can look at the contention of the sus laws in the 1970s and just how impactful it was in setting communities up in direct opposition to anything institutional; the police, physical and mental health organisations, local councils, housing associations, educational institutes, employment bureaus. Yes, they were a means of hope, a means to dignity; but it was also these institutions which had been used as tools to systematically strip away our dignity in the first place. The double-edged sword which cut deep into old scars that were never given the time to heal.

And then, of course, there were the 1980s. In April 2020 in parts of Bristol, we commemorated the fortieth anniversary of the St Paul's riots, or as it is now being called, the St Paul's Uprising. At the heart of the action was The Black and White Cafe, the most raided building in the country. The gloomy mist of the uprising can still be felt in Bristol. The demonisation of the majority Caribbean community can still be felt in Bristol. Newspapers, radio and television demonised these people, my people. We were an example for other migrants entering and already living in the city, of what not to be. It was excusable to beat us, to exclude us, to fire us, to not employ us, to not buy, sell nor rent to us, to not educate us. We were under the underdog.

Up until my late 20s, I thought I remembered the uprising and the fear that my parents felt due to the violence taking place at the time, but also because of police retaliation. I thought I remembered the worry that my parents had for my older brothers. I thought I heard conversations being had by elder family members about whose son or daughter may have been involved. I thought I saw scary images of what looked like thousands of police officers lined up further than my line of sight. I thought I remembered the day that I learnt that the police did not like those who looked like me.

But my mum said 'stop being silly, there is no way you can remember that you were not even born yet'. I was getting confused, you see, I thought I saw the St Paul's Uprising. It was not until years later that I realised what I actually witnessed.

In 1986, in the same area of St Paul's something by the name of Operation Delivery took place. The Black and White Cafe was once again at the heart of this. An area the size of two or three main roads and a handful of blocks had six hundred police and other hired men descend upon it as part of drug raids. Imagine the scene – rows of police as far as the eye can see with batons, shields, riot gear, vans, controlled by menacing-looking men.

Beyond anything, any fear, any threat that I had witnessed on the family colour TV, this act of state securitisation scared me the most. This was my bogey man, the thing that went bump in the night, that kept me up and there was no glass screen that separated me from it. Uprising, race riot, or blacks acting up? Criminal blacks being dealt with in the way they deserve. Working-class people acting up, 'they are lazy and don't work hard so now they are bitter, have a propensity to rob, steal and complain'. That was the story that was told. Yet if you were to blur the scene and tell me this image was in any warring country, any civil unrest, any country with extreme security that is hostile to it citizens, I would believe you.

It's interesting that Operation Delivery is just a footnote in history and that's if we are lucky. It's interesting that Avon and Somerset Police has been identified as the most institutionally racist police force in the UK today. I wonder if they are proud, I wonder what would happen if they just talked about it. Acknowledged it, and their complicity in the wrongs of that era. Do they know that when they ignore it, they gaslight us which is traumatising within itself. The young officer just joining the forces I wonder if he even knows just how frightening he is and why his uniform is a trigger and a reminder of how they see us. To the non-black Muslim communities, who bought into the demonisation of black folk and who are now experiencing this scrutiny, and demonisation. Do you still believe them? Are we still who you strive not to be?

First comes scrutiny, then fear, and then all of a sudden a security threat is born. Justified securitisation is born. Fractured communities are born. Citizenship is lost. Belonging is lost. We are lost. What will it take for us to be found?

ECHOES ACROSS THE POND

C Scott Jordan

It is difficult to imagine the now alternate universe where our lives proceeded uninterrupted by Covid-19. Consider Thursday 7 May 2020. It was supposed to be a rather special day. Londoners were to break from their busy, quick footed trots. Momentarily tearing their eyes from glowing screens or distant, sightless stares to take note of names upon paper. To place their mark before one. They would have cast their vote to determine whom thereafter should have been the Mayor of London. Brexit, transubstantiated via newly elected Prime Minister Boris Johnson's magic this past winter, would have no doubt weighed heavy upon the mayor's head. Increased knife and acid-based violence was to be top of the list of campaign issues alongside the infinite need for affordable housing, and the merits of a 'green city', not to mention the decriminalisation of cannabis. Could the most surveilled city on the planet use another CCTV camera and might Heathrow look good with an extra runway? All this and more would have floated about mental bubbles over the heads of Londoners from Enfield to Croydon.

But this didn't happen.

Brexit has been usurped as the main, and often only, talking point in 24-hour news and public discourse. This usurper has even forced public discourse to seek the safety of cyberspace. We huddle away in our homes, keeping our distance from those closest to us. Masks and rubber gloves accompany the usual fashion accessories of a coat and brolly before venturing out the front door. A new threat is being slung around out there, commandeering our attention from the threats of acid and knife violence. No doubt, the minds of the electorate were more than preoccupied with the new concerns of our covidy times, and so delaying the election for a year is about as good an idea as what will come out of decisions made during the panicky pandemic. But the question is, can the old issues sit back idly, waiting for us to wade out this storm?

After all, before the civilisational halt ordered by Covid-19, there were indeed various issues of varying degrees of urgency that will require tending to. But, not only has this garden been allowed to run rampant, it has been as shaped by the pandemic as any other element of everyday life. Perhaps the best solution for such a wild garden may be to tear it all up and begin again. Yet, I believe we find that even the soil has been contaminated with the revelations of how unprepared we were that came to light during this nearly global lockdown. Our systems, especially democracy, that supposed perfect realisation of humanity's ability to govern itself, shines a little less bright, all things considered.

Democracy seems to have a particular problem with minorities. What is represented by the people's democracy has largely been the interests of white, male, landowners. Later in history, the list of what was to be represented had grown, but only very recently has the representatives elected to represent come from an expanded pool of citizenry. With the rise of female and non-white elected leaders, a new challenge has presented itself. A female leader is not only to represent their constituency, whether or not it is spoken, there is an expectation that they especially represent the women of the constituency and to a certain extent all of femininity in making up for the centuries of repression under the patriarchy. This situation is similar for any elected official from another minority community. And may God have mercy on the poor souls who represent two or more minority communities.

For the incumbent Mayor of London, Sadiq Khan, a man notably labelled by a fellow candidate as the 'mad mullah Khan of Londonistan,' is caught between Scylla and Charybdis. As this election-that-could-not-be was ramping up questions demanded what Khan was doing for the British Muslim population (as if that community was as united and simply demarcated as the term might suggest). While it is not a new challenge for an elected official to represent their various constituents, especially those of different genders, sexuality, religious identity, nationality, education level, and so on, does a minority leader owe a greater duty to give back to their particular community? And what can we learn from the cruel nature of democracy in attempting this tight rope stunt?

To tease at this particular wickedness of representative democracy it helps if one turns the clock back four years. Khan's election was a much-needed reprieve from other bewildering electoral phenomena occurring in 2016. Despite the historic milestone of being London's first Muslim mayor or the son of a London bus driver, supporters were quick to note it was not his appeal to diversity, either ethnic or socioeconomic, but his political promises that saw to his victory. After all, only one eighth of London was Muslim, hardly the force to capture London's chief office. Yet, many hoped he would reveal the open and accepting nature of the truly international city in the heat of xenophobic accusations following Europe's response to the refugee crisis spewing out from the civil war in Syria. Khan's language emphasised the word 'all' in reference to those who's futures he we seeking to better as Mayor of London.

This message of unity would be the stake upon which his opponents sought to burn his career. Whether embarking on dramatically symbolic feats as walking by foot from India to Pakistan or taking to the mosh pit of popular opinion known as Twitter, daring to tweet the word 'islamophobia', a cacophony of praise and condemnation would surely follow. In fact, in Tweeting on islamophobia, Khan sought to reassure British Muslims following the tragic attack on the mosque in Christchurch, New Zealand. Following his tweet, which critics claimed should have reassured *all* Brits, not just one particular group, he went on to write a letter to then Prime Minister Theresa May, pleading that the Tory's adopt a new definition to islamophobia. Following the Christchurch shooting, anti-Muslim hate crimes rose by 593% in the UK. Yet, if Khan did not speak for all of London, he was being less than what his post demanded. If he apologised, or refused to make a statement, he would be accused of being a sell-out, a traitor, or something worse by the minorities for which he stood as exemplar to.

Compounded contradictions. Lose-Lose. What could honestly be expected?

In reviewing Sadiq Khan's strange conundrum, another example echoes from across the pond. An echo that could not have imagined the narcissistic quality of the United States' forty-fifth president that would follow. As it was the forty-fourth president, Barack Obama, who faced Khan's dilemma, but from the black community in the United States.

Similar to Khan, Obama's first speeches after being elected to the Presidency rang to the tune of unity and healing divides within the country, a typical desire after the traumatic event that US elections had become over the last couple of decades. He set himself up as a creation of the romanticised notion of the American ideal. A mixed-race child with a funny name who was not of the establishment, who came from humble beginnings and wanted to see America give opportunity out to others as he was given in his life. Khan also wanted the opportunities afforded to him in London to continue and be able to reach more and more. It is the greatest possible ending to a story of success, when the successor turns around and gives the opportunity he took back to the future, so that others may also succeed. Barack Obama was seemingly plucked from obscurity when he was asked to deliver the keynote speech at the 2004 Democratic National Convention. Four years before taking the reins of power in the US, Obama said 'there is not a liberal and a conservative America, there is the United States of America. There is not a black America and a white America and Latino America and Asian America, there's the United States of America!' Then in 2008 he became president and racism officially ended and we all rode off into the sunset. This is the story we wish could be told, but, once again, this was not the timeline we embarked upon.

'Change we can believe in.' This was Obama's campaign slogan in 2008. Change, something so long overdue, especially in an America that had had an eight-year Republican regime driven by two foreign conflicts with no end in sight and an economic catastrophe over a decade in the making with no clear resolution upon the horizon. What members of Obama's first presidential campaign team didn't take to mind is that change must come slowly because humans by our nature do not like change, even when we long for it. We are creatures of habit. Creatures of routine. And now a man stood in the White House. A black man. And every day, the 24/7 news media machine reminded millions of Americans that change had happened. Change was the name of the game from the moment Obama hit the ground running. His inauguration, coinciding with Martin Luther King, Jr. Day was seen as King's dream having been realised. The future had arrived. Even the inaugural ball, a typical lovefest of tradition and high-class society, was instead a 'Neighborhood Inaugural Ball' that was open to the public. The affair gave off the feel of a block party common in low income neighbourhoods all across the country. Beyonce Knowles and Jay-Z performed as the new President shared his first dance with the new First Lady. Black culture was seeing its way into the highest office of the land. Many middle-class white Americans, recently evicted from their homes and finding it hard to get a good job watched the celebration and the continued bail out of Wall Street fat cats. The change that had landed in America for these individuals was not all bread and roses.

On another side of the spectrum, several prominent black thinkers begged a different question. Was Barack Obama black enough to be the first black president. Aside from coming from a mixed family, other elements called into question his credentials as a heroic figure for disenfranchised black Americans. First off, he was raised in Hawaii, a place unlike any other in the US for multiculturalism and in the pursuit of plurality. Then went on to Columbia University, Harvard, and Chicago School of Law. All institutions of prestige and privilege. Despite residing next door to some of the greatest examples of poverty and race/class divide in the country, his degrees gave him the appearance to many as another member of the establishment, primed for the position he would soon take by the powers at be. One did not just rise to influence in a city like Chicago or a state like Illinois. Corruption is more guaranteed than gravity in the Windy City. Then there was the way he talked, the way he walked. The way he held himself. Who was this man really representing? From the first day of his campaign even unto today, he must fight a battle between being both a black man and the representative of the United States, a country whose history has more than once flirted, even bathed in the toxic waste ridden springs of white supremacy. A country so diverse and large and powerful cannot conceivably be properly represented by one man or woman. And for the first time in its over two-hundred-year history, the man in its highest office was asked to do the impossible. To juggle self and nation. To represent the one and the many. The jury of history, if it is wise, will be hung on this issue for many years to come.

Yet, less than a year into his Presidency, Obama faced his first major trial. On 16 July 2009. A black, Harvard professor, Henry Louis Gates Jr., had just returned home to Cambridge, Massachusetts after a research trip to China. When his taxi dropped him off at his home from the airport, his door was jammed and he was unable to open it. So, Gates, with the assistance of the taxi driver, struggled and eventually opened the door. Neighbours would call the police when seeing two men struggle to open the front door. After the professor had gained entry to his home, Sgt. James Crowley, a white man, of the Cambridge Police Department would arrest Professor Gates for breaking and entering into his own home. In response to this event, Obama made a seemingly innocuous, off the cuff remark, calling members of the Police department involved 'stupid'. Quickly, the opposition labelled him a cop hater. Worse yet, the Republicans would begin to spin the idea that Obama used his race to weave division into the American psyche. As if he were an evil genius hellbent on a 'watching the world burn' type masquerade. Protestors even began wielding signs portraying Obama with the face paint of the Joker from Christopher Nolan's *The Dark Knight*. Yet, the night was only to get darker. Obama attempted to quell the scandal by inviting both Professor Gates and Sgt. Crowley to the White House to share a beer. The press dumbed this the 'Beer Summit' and made Obama's prospect of being able to tackle other diplomatic feats such as peace in the Middle East, Iran, or North Korea as way out of his league. The whole affair went down as a major embarrassment for President Obama and quickly sealed the fate of his new policy on race issues. The controversy and scandal would be much too much and 'no comment' was to be the official position. The First Black President simply could not speak on race issues.

This contradiction would number among the scores that occurred during the Obama presidency. The whole Professor Henry Louis Gates controversy was a silly example of something that should not be happening in what was dubbed the 'post-race America' that was supposed to have been ushered in with Obama's election. What analysts failed to see and many of us would not notice until the election of one Donald J. Trump was that America was far far away from post-race, and rather was sprinting headlong into a hyper-racist America. The first black president was too much for a country that was still deeply entrenched in racist tendencies. So much so that a violent backlash was the only result possible. A match had been lit and no one cared to note that we were all standing in a pressurised oil barrel. What could have been expected? Not to mention this fire was given fodder, willingly by a Republican Party who, while licking its wounds following Obama's election, prepared to engage in one of the most unforgivable sin of contemporary politics. That unforgiveable sins was to use division and lies as a weapon to breathe life into a new age of hate. And, like what one can expect when committing such a vile and accursed act, they had to make a great sacrifice. This sacrifice put the very future of the Republican Party into question. It would be a blood sacrifice.

Enter Sarah Palin, the perfect candidate to perpetrate this despicable act. That cantankerous and loathsome person had just been jettisoned into the historical permanence of parody by Tina Fey of *Saturday Night Live*. And she used her popularity to great effect. Her somewhat modest demeanour and acceptance of the perception her 'simpleton' accent would give her, allowed her to wage a quiet revolution. She too was not an insider. She began condemning the establishment for their failure made proof positive in the election of Barack Obama. Add a few lies, and before you know it a daft mob of Americans were ready to start pouring tea into the nearest harbour. Obama must have been born somewhere else, look how different he looks. The birther controversy continued all the way through the 2016 presidential election and I'd bet dollars to donuts it will come up again in 2020, despite the fact that Obama had handed over his birth certificate in the run up to his election in 2008 in accordance with regulations. Joining the ranks of Sarah Palin to spearhead the birther debate was none other than Donald J. Trump. And then as Obama staked his legacy on comprehensive healthcare reform, a dream of the democrats since time in memorial, Sarah Palin spewed forth the rhetorical regurgitation of 'death panels'. Supposed panels of medical professionals who would hold trial over who was to be granted healthcare or who was to take a hike or be sentenced to death. Suddenly, millions of Americans feared Obama's death panels issuing death warrants to the elderly, those infirmed, or those of special needs. Yet, all along the whole thing was utter nonsense, not at all supported by the text of the legislation. I recall being a student pouring through the text of what would become known as Obamacare. Its evolution and compromise that eventual led to it being the semi-failure we see today in America. Yet, all along, I wondered if 24/7 news pundits had even read one word of the original text, but rather just bought into the lies that gave the impression that America would become a socialist republic, sending doctors to labour camps and giving free drugs to illegal immigrants. Sarah Palin didn't need Fox News, for she was clever enough to see the early power of social media, taking to Facebook to spread her hate speech. The Tea Party would form as an off shoot of the Republican Party, that eventually, like a cancer has all but overtaken the once, at least somewhat respectable, GOP. Breitbart rose up and went to the depths of depravity which even Fox News would dare not tread to destroy Obama and the, in their eyes, fascist liberal powers that be.

'If I said the sky was blue, they said no!' Obama's campaign of unity and hope from 2008 was anything but as he literally had to fight for survival four years later. There would be no unity in 2012, only bitter descent and abhorrent unacceptance. Change, the oxygen everyone was euphorically breathing had become a poison on which America began choking. The US had always prided itself on freedom of speech and especially of that against its own political leaders. Parody and satire have always had a warm home in American entertainment. And because of that, when it came to Obama, it would appear, the mild racist undertones could be forgiven. But perhaps they should not have been. Obama was often depicted as Hitler. Okay, and so has every president since World War II. While the message is almost always a bit extreme, it was accepted. Yet during his administration, protestors held signs depicting Obama as a monkey or an ape and in a pretty grotesque display of call backs to Jim Crow era insignia. Vehement denial of his citizenship, claims that racism was to be his iron rod, and death camps resided at the heart of the mucky speech of the day. Obama's middle name, Hussein, fed the lie that he was secretly a Muslim savoir sent to enslave the Christians. But I assure you there is quite a healthy constituency of people in Pakistan whose houses had been drone struck to kingdom come by Obama's order that would beg to differ. Lies about immigrants, lies about taxes, and lies carried over from the past all swirled together. Any historical analysis of the Obama Administration should begin with a parsing out of the lies surrounding the news which will prove considerably more difficult than sorting the wheat from the chaff. And the result will be something far from unity and a lifting of the race issue in America to a new level.

Yet, one more nail was needed to seal the coffin for a hope of America ever transcending racism. In the lead up to a long campaign in 2012, a shooting took place in the 'armpit of America', Florida. Seventeen-year-old Treyvon Martin was walking home through a gated community where his relatives lived when he crossed paths with George Zimmerman, a neighbourhood watch coordinator. The unarmed black teenager was shot and killed during an altercation that arose between him and the mixed-race Zimmerman. Zimmerman was initially charged with murder of the boy, yet was acquitted claiming self-defence. Racial tensions were again ignited within the country, a debate over the wearing of hoodies turned up old debates of female dress protocols and intent. The black community needed a leader to say something about this grave injustice. Yet, Obama had learned his lesson. He could not win if he dared to engage. So quiet he remained. That is until a throw away question was posed at a press conference. What of Treyvon Martin? 'If I had a son, he would have looked like Treyvon Martin.' He said this and expressed his condolences to the family, the shame of a life lost. And once again, the hate machine sprung back to work. Obama the racist, using racism to divide. What of all the other unjust shootings that occur in spite of race or class? Obama doesn't understand the full story? Obama's son would wear a preppy school uniform, not a hoodie? He is a racist who knows nothing of race! He doesn't even know what it means to really be black. And on and on the chorus sings its buzzing buzz. Obama was doomed to fail on launch at any attempt to unite the United States, even for the sake of justice. Especially if race was involved. Even the Sandy Hook School shooting, a case with no easy ties to race, could not work as a tragedy which could unite the United States as 9/11 had but a decade earlier.

No, for the opposition that had to be opposed and oppose they did. To the nth degree! Now Obama wanted to take your guns. How dare he use the death of children to spread his fascist liberal agenda. One pundit even claimed that the Sandy Hook shooting was an elaborate hoax, set up to win Obama approval points, points he no longer needed as he had already won the election to his second and final term. Absurdity, obliviousness, asinine, ludicrous and all other such states of being were cast to the wind. The sky was the limit, lie until you make it. Lie until you die. Obama, a man of hope, of good change, the realisation of a dream was cast in shackles unable to be the mythical figure the 'rest' of America wanted. So, he became the monster we created. Where those who remember the horrors of the Bush Administration (ah another contradiction, for now in the age of Trump, we long for the comfort of the Bush era!), what was needed in its follow up was drastic reform and the diminishing of the powers held by the executive. Yet, with the hate machine running at full force, all Obama could do was use the powers the office had garnered over its last sixty odd years. Obama was mad as hell and he wasn't going to take it anymore. The imperial presidency reborn. Executive order after executive order. If a cancer ridden Congress was in deadlock, he would let his pen do the walking. Drone strikes, healthcare reform, gun legislation, and much much more. With each stroke, he only made the office more and more powerful. Let us hope we don't give all that power to someone who might abuse it...

The destruction of Barack Obama and the hope of progress for black America was put to image by the most unlikely of individuals. Michael Moore is a documentarian who has never gone far without provoking a bit of controversy. Yet his greatest enemies in the past have remained George W. Bush, whom you might remember he yelled 'Shame on you' during his Oscar acceptance speech in 2003, the NRA, and the Republican Party. Yet, his love for his home, the State of Michigan, which he has acknowledged as a breeding ground for the insane and the dangerous, has revealed a new enemy beside that of Donald Trump. The most unlikely opponent of Barack Obama. In his 2018 film, *Fahrenheit 11/9*, Moore takes the audience to Flint, Michigan. The town of over ninety-six thousand people, predominantly of African American ethnicity, made destitute from the decay of the American automotive industry and now suffering from an official water emergency since 2014. The water of Flint was toxic and undrinkable and no one in power had any desire to change this state of affairs. Moore lambasted the Governor of Michigan at the time, the less than charming Rick Snyder before putting to screen the disappointment of the nation's top executive. Flint had invited President Obama to visit in hopes that he would personally see to the resolution of the crisis. He was welcomed with jubilation by a predominantly African American community, many of them representing the record number of black voters that turned up during both of his presidential elections. Yet few other collective jaw drops have ever been set to film like that of the town of Flint when Obama took to the stage with a small glass, filled barely halfway with a clear liquid. Into the microphone, Obama declared that in that cup was water from Flint's tap. He then took the most pitiful sip from the cup, throwing back the mostly backwashed dripple before forcing a smile to his face before the dumbfounded crowd. He assured them that all was well and that the water was safe, when, in fact, it was anything but. Obama lost his greatest approval percentage over the Beer Summit scandal, yet I can assure you that every hopeful Flint resident in that room would take back both of their ballots if they could in response to that categorical denial of his own community. Treachery does little justice in the face of such a callused slap to the face.

Can we blame him? Have we not seen the monster? Is it not us, ourselves? If but a modicum of solace can be distilled from this tragic tale, is it not something more than the madness of politics? Are our heroes doomed to become villains of another shade? Is hope, as Colonel Mackenzie puts in in the 2019 film *1917*, 'a dangerous thing'? Is this the fate of minority leaders? Must they conform to the fold of normality, lest the opposition haunt their every day and night? The mind boggles when one tries to take social media and fake news into account. Are we all doomed to a horrible cyclical fate? Is this Einsteinian insanity escapable?

Can we blame Sadiq Khan for not having done more for British Muslims. Going out of one's way, to take power for a community that has not been without its own controversy and corruption in the last few decades. What would a Brexit fuelled fearful-of-becoming-a-minority white British population make of Khan? Heaven forbid Khan be falsely labelled an anti-Semite. If the real powers of opposition can make Brexit happen as it did, then what could become of Khan would render Obama's dilemma as little more than a minor inconvenience. Perhaps we are forced to conclude that this is simply the way of democracies. Plato's tyranny of the majority may be more real than even the thinkers in *Republic* could have imagined. So tyrannical, that it even holds power when the majority isn't in the seat of power. So, for two hundred years of one white guy after another being President of the United States and over eight hundred years' worth of mostly white Mayors of London to suddenly be handed over to someone of a darker hue, it was almost foolish to think there wouldn't be at least a little whiplash.

This arc of the pendulum is the great fear of all the Khans and Obamas of the world. It is perhaps why Khan remains as neutral in directly reaching out to his community as when Obama made his few forays into political issues bearing racial undertones, even in their sparing occurrence, the opposition jumped upon him with the fire and brimstone of a woman scorned. And then rose Trump and the Alt-right army. How much fodder does the National Front need? What monsters might the Tories awake in the darkness of nationalistic fear and identity crisis? Lest we forget about British Values!

It should be noted that neither Khan nor Obama desired to be the first of their particular circumstance. They just wish to be great leaders. Along such journeys, where it can help, the use of one's identity for the sake of upholding diversity of their constituencies can be attractive. Yet, politics is like a medicine. We run to the chemist in hopes of curing our ailments. But, as so often, no one knows the correct dosage and in the chase for a miracle, we over indulge and in our glut we have turned a medicine into a poison. And like all solutions with half-lives, they must run their course through the system before another round could be administered or another treatment attempted. We want change as though it's something that can be packaged and bought over the counter, completely disregarding the chaos that comes as a side effect in the fine print of the advert, just before 'bleeding and possible death may result'.

The unfair burden of being a minority representative is played out to comic book proportions in the battle between Donald Trump and a group of under fifty, lefty minority congresswomen dubbed 'the Squad'. Trump berates the Squad, comprised of Alexandria Ocasio-Cortez from New York, Ayanna Pressley from Massachusetts, Rashida Tlaib from Michigan, and Ilhan Omar from Minnesota in a mix of sexist, ageist, and an asinine tonic of socially acceptable racism, often on his favourite battlefield: dearest Twitter. He paints them naïve 'little girls' incapable of understanding real, adult politics because they hold views different than his or refuse to tow the misogynist, hateful line. All of these women came to power, having to fight at an unfair disadvantage in Donald Trump's America, in the 2018 midterm elections. He holds them to fixing the level of crimes in their own constituency before they can criticise him on his policies and goes to school house bullying levels to draw claims on their ignorance on global affairs because, again, they come in conflict with his own.

The already difficult calibration of the scales of representation that minority elects must manage is thrown a curve ball by rampant hate, such as islamophobia. Because of this Congresswomen Tlaib and Omar almost get it the worst. Holding anti-Israeli views, especially concerning the US financial role in Israeli politics, has earned them both the label, as per the parlance of American politics, of being anti-Semites. Labour Party, MP for Bradford West, Naz Shah has had to battle mirrored political gymnastics after a series of Twitter faux pas. Shah has even been held to disciplinary action and made to apologise. Congresswoman Omar faces the full Islamophobic gantlet. Donning the hijab, although an American citizen, she was a refugee of Somali origin, she is young, and she is very vocal in her opposition to the US's Israeli policy. The Republican party propagated false rumours of her ties to 9/11 while Trump evoked imagery of the destruction that occurred that day to make the point that she can't possibly understand what 9/11 means to 'real' Americans. Whatever that is supposed to mean when all supposed 'Americans' trace their own lineages to one refugee community or another. Except, of course, the Native Americans, but they, in the ultimate irony, are not give a voice at the table.

We can often get lost in trying to simplify contemporary politics. But politics of this age has no room for simplicity. It is complex; and assumptions cannot be made that the only place a minority representative has resides within the ranks of more liberal or lefty parties. A real struggle is lived everyday by the minorities who find themselves more politically in line with conservative parties the world over. This is made even more problematic when these very parties have reams of accusations of xenophobia and often draw party lines in direct contradiction with the existential values of their more easily marginalised party members especially as they trend towards the alt-right. Sajid Javid could easily have been the leader of the UK Conservative Party and thus the UK Prime Minister. After losing the leadership election to Boris Johnson in 2019, he fell into the Chancellor of the Exchequer position and was poised to lead the UK Treasury through its transition out of the EU. Javid is an interesting case in representation. While he was raised a British Muslim, he has noted that today he practices no religion and is married to a Christian woman. He has even gone so far as to criticise the British Muslim community for having a hand in, if not just allowing, a rise in terrorism in the last two decades. Meanwhile, he shares the commonality of receiving anti-Muslim hate mail and death threats along with other member of Parliament from Muslim origins. During the 2020 cabinet reshuffle, whatever niche minority specialised community a member of the Conservative Party might hope to represent, Johnson only cared about one demographic. Him. You either prove your loyalty to Boris Johnson, or its good day to you sir. Javid was already on thin ice with 10 Downing Street after Dominic Cummings sacked one of Javid's aids without his approval. The night before the reshuffle, Javid handed over his resignation when he was faced with the ultimatum stating that in order to maintain his post, he had to sack all his underlings to make way for only proven Pro-Johnson minions. After a decade of ideological and identity negotiating as he rose up the Conservative ranks, his tale resides in the realm of tragedy as he returns to the back bench.

While perhaps less a tragedy, the struggle put on by the Baroness Sayeeda Warsi begs numerous questions concerning the limitations that seem requisite to being a minority representative in a contemporary democracy. The Baroness Warsi rose up quickly in the UK's Conservative Party to eventually become its chairperson. Under the former Prime Minister, David Cameron, she also became the first female Muslim to sit as a member of the cabinet. Now she resides within the House of Lords and is a member of the Privy Council. She has faced all the same problems alongside her contemporaries. Diverging slightly, she faced the contradictions perceived between her party, her constituents, and her personal views with a sort of grace. She navigated touchy issues as exemplified by her approach to immigration by weighing both sides. She gave credence to the need for upholding law and order on one side while also being considerate of human rights to abide the other. Like Javid, there was bound to be the final straw, a point of no return, where loyalty to party and self could not be reconciled. For the Baroness Warsi, this was Cameron's stance on Israel and Palestine. She resigned from his government in 2014. She regretted not taking more of a stand on the Palestine question, but would the structures of the UK's constitutional monarchy have allowed her to represent the views she held to any satisfaction? Most interesting, it was once she was free from the conundrums of representative democracy when she could actually represent her views in British society. Since leaving government she has used her influence in the House of Lords to push for the interests of her fellow British Muslims, most notably in her continued pursuit of a formally recognised definition of islamophobia from the UK government. While this chapter lingers with the anticipation of hope for a happy fairy-tale ending, it still seems like this is incompatible with Western representative democratic systems.

Must the situation be so bleak for representative democracies? Does democracy have a built-in flaw, incapable of being transcended? Must our politicians be damned to the fate of 'the Sisyphean dreamer' in Jack White's song *Over and Over and Over*? Attempting to be Vitruvian men and women, divided in identity as per the census data of their constituency, spending precise percentages of time pandering to various communities never able to fully satisfy anyone? From one framing of thought: yes, this is the fate of our representatives in this world of extremes we find ourselves in. The age of discontent cannot be satisfied. A look at any comment section on the internet reaffirms this pessimistic notion. So, perhaps the problem lies in the framing. The way we have been asked to think about things brings us to this foxhole of despair. So, it needs to change. But we humans oh so hate change. Despite how we feel about it, there is a brilliant example of when one man changed his mind. He very nearly changed the world.

Compromise and open-mindedness are not the first attributes one would pin to El-Hajj Malik Shabazz, Malcolm X. In some circles, he remains as divisive a character today as he was the day he died half a century ago. But there seems to be so little focus on the last chapter of his life. He was stubborn, no doubt, but if a convincing argument could be made, he admitted, he would change his mind. He was, since his days in Charlestown State Prison, an avid reader and therefore a devoted student, always open to whatever lessons life would throw his way. No doubt, what life had thrown him up to that point only made it appear that there was one way to conduct himself. Black was familiar and white was evil. This permeated his thought and the language he chose to use. It was cut and dry for Malcolm X. He was fighting a war against racism in America. And his only allies were the American black community. Even sympathetic white people were turned away, they would have to work on their own. He was the antithesis of white supremacy in America. Its equal, yet opposite. And so, the two forces would appear entrenched in titanic combat until judgement. As many of my more worldly friends would agree, the only cure for this oh so American mental block is for an American to go to a place beyond the borders of that misguided country.

And what better a place for Malcolm to learn of life outside America than on one of the greatest journeys a human can embark upon. *Hajj.* When Malcolm X went to Mecca in 1964, he was already a global celebrity but he humbled himself as he stumbled through the various steps along the *hajj.* As many things are done differently in America, Islam was no exception. Aware of this, he followed one step behind his guide, trying his hardest to follow the strictest adherence to ritual and tradition. While many embark on *hajj* ready for a truly religious experience, Malcolm had not expected the form his eye-opening moment would come in. 'I have eaten from the same plate, drunk from the same glass, and slept on the same bed (or on the same rug) – praying to the same *God* – with fellow Muslims, whose eyes were the bluest of blue and whose hair was the blondest of blonde and whose skin was the whitest of white.' In the dry heat of the sacred city, Malcolm put it all together, it would be through unity that the change he desired could be accomplished. In their mutual brotherhood, endowed by Allah, their 'whiteness', a term Malcolm X equated with 'evil' was removed. 'I have never before seen sincere and true brotherhood practiced by all colours together, irrespective of their colour.'

An enlightened man, Malcolm X flew back across the Atlantic on a new mission from God. He would return to America and make his peace with the Nation of Islam. He would partner with Martin Luther King, Jr. and form a strong alliance with other God-fearing black Americans. Their ranks would partner with Robert F. Kennedy's and his quiet band of black artists. It would have been one of the greatest political movements in history. Racism would be exposed and fought, and relations amongst all Americans would be completely restructured. These powerful leaders would pass laws and shift policy to build an America that was truly of the people and for the people.

But this didn't happen.

Less than a year after his latest awakening, sixteen shots would pierce his body and end his life. Hate would win the day and the battle would continue. And as per the equal and opposite force, the white grave diggers were not even be allowed to bury Malcolm X at his final resting place. Yet, what was does not have to always be.

We often expect of our politicians what we expect of our celebrities. That they be anything but human, complete with its constitutive limits and flaws. We ask them to tackle unrealistic feats. To change the world, but not too much. And we neglect what is not 'us' and cast caution to the wind in pursuing our agendas. If what we are doing is right and true, how can it be anything but good. But the extreme opinions we must hold have their poles and in an age of discontent, how could one even consider 'going along with it'. Hopefully, there is a silver lining to all the tumult brought on by Covid-19. Have we not had our eyes opened? Even just a bit? Are we not looking at community differently? At humanity and society? Are we not changing the way we live our lives? Concessions and compromise for a greater good is what is taking place, even though that sounds like defeat according to how we thought of things only a few months ago. It hasn't been easy and it won't get any easier. We should also be careful as we return to improper, laxed hygienic practices and overuse of hand sanitiser as the miracle fix-all, where, in fact, that may be brewing super bugs for later, when social distancing and quarantine may not be an effective combat strategy. There is no simple solution. And it really needs to be an all for one and one for all effort. But at this moment we have a great deal of potential pathways before us. I just hope the next time we don't have to say: 'but that didn't happen.'

ARTS AND LETTERS

BLACK FEMALE MUSLIM EMCEES

Aina Khan

'If hip-hop has an official religion, it is Islam.'
Harry Allen, Public Enemy's 'Media Assassin'

It began with the 'First Lady' of Islamic hip-hop, Miss Undastood. A social worker by day who moonlights as an emcee, the New York-based rapper, described as the Muslim answer to Eve and Foxy Brown, was perhaps the only well-known female Muslim rapper at the turn of the millennium. With her slick lyricism in underground rap battles, community gatherings and more recently on Instagram, Miss Undastood has boldly rapped about domestic violence, the struggles of single parenthood, her lived experiences as a Black woman, and quarantining in the age of the coronavirus.

However, when Syrian-American rapper Mona Haydar released her superb debut single, 'Wrap My Hijab' in 2017, mainstream media and some sections of the Muslim community celebrated her as the 'first' female Muslim emcee. It was a dismissal of the legacy of a genre born from the Afro-diasporic experience in the 1970s as a defiant riposte to crippling social inequalities and white supremacy in the United States. A long history of anti-Black racism within the non-Black Muslim community prompted the erasure not just of Miss Undastood's formidable contribution, but also other Black female artists across the Muslim Atlantic in the United Kingdom where Sukina Douglas and Tanya Muneera Williams, formerly known as Poetic Pilgrimage, were the first female Muslim emcees in Britain.

A new generation of female Muslim emcees, in the United States especially, have emerged in the last decade to carry the hip-hop mantle of their predecessors: Alia Sharrief, twin rap duo Ain't Afraid, Boshia-Rae Jean, Sister Keylani, Neelam Hakeem, and Mona Haydar, to name but a few. These veritable goddesses of hip-hop use their music to celebrate their womanhood, their racial identity, and their faith, offering unapologetic social and political lyrical commentary on the issues of our time from the Black Lives Matter movement, the erasure of Black Muslims from Islam, the hyper-sexualisation of women, and masculinity, to Donald Trump's anti-immigration policies. These women are cultural innovators and bridge builders reaching out not just to the Muslim community but the non-Muslim community as well.

Miss Undastood began rapping when she was eleven years old. Shortly after her conversion to Islam, following the footsteps of her Catholic father, it was in the school grounds of her 'strict Islamic school' where the First Lady of Islamic hip-hop came into sonic being. 'I was just trying to bring some light to the school lunch hour. It was very dry, very boring. So I started putting together lyrics. I found myself having to hide them, so certain girlfriends would meet me in the bathroom, and I might share my raps. It was mainly just a bunch of rhyming words. No themes', she says. The earliest song she wrote about her journey to Islam, One World, in which she raps, 'I was born Muslim, baptised Catholic'; nods to her early Catholic upbringing and the idea that all of humanity are born Muslim, thus any 'conversion' to Islam is a reversion. Growing up, her inspirations were female emcees like Salt-N-Pepa, Queen Latifah, Yo-Yo, and Heavy D. When she was a teenager, her attention shifted to Lil' Kim, Foxy Brown, The Fugees, and Nas; the former Fugees frontwoman, Lauryn Hill, was her favourite.

At the time Miss Undastood began performing publicly in the early 2000s in talent shows, bloc parties, jails, *walimahs* (Islamic wedding receptions), and college shows, there were no other Muslim women emcees. The question of whether Muslim women could perform in public was then and still is somewhat controversial within certain sections of the Muslim community who hold the opinion that a Muslim woman's voice is *awrah*, something that should be reserved in private for members of her family. Her stage name came from the frustration that her intentions were being misconstrued:

> Whenever I wanted to talk on political topics or stuff that's taboo, people were taking things out of context, twisting a lot of the words and making my

intentions look negative. I was just being a 'feminist', or a 'man-hater'. Being a Black Muslim woman in hip-hop, it's not easy. For starters, it's a male domi-nated industry. But then you add the component that you're Black, when you bring the Muslim element, you always have the problem of what people think our religion says. 'You should be seen not heard', 'You shouldn't be on stage', 'You shouldn't be on display'. It's difficult with all those three things com-bined to try to do hip-hop. Then we have the *haraam* police. When I first started, they used to say things like I was hip-hopping my way to the hell fire. Sometimes people would send their kids to the stage to tell me to shut up. The fact that I rap makes men feel like I'm not religious enough, that I'm not pious enough. 'Oh, you're doing that? You can't be on your religion. You can't be on your deen (faith)'.

Hip-Hop and Misogyny

Across the Muslim Atlantic in the United Kingdom, Tanya Muneera Williams and Sukina Douglas, who met at a high school choir in Bristol, formed Poetic Pilgrimage in 2002. Though they became the first British female hip-hop group after they converted to Islam in 2005, the name of their group captured their own spiritual odyssey for meaning and knowledge before their conversion and their desire to elevate the voices of Black British women. Sukina recalled the early days when the reaction to their music within the Muslim community was so visceral, they were kicked off tours and accused of leading Muslims to hell by promoting *haraam* (forbidden) music. 'Our biggest issue', Sukhina said

> was being Muslim women performers within the Muslim community. People were not used to having women speaking so courageously and so fiercely about what they believed, in the context of the Muslim community in Britain. As much as there were many people who loved us, we had a lot of people who disliked what we were doing.

Another early female Muslim rapper braving crowds and community halls still ambivalent about Islamic hip-hop and female emcees, was Alia Sharrief, a California-based emcee, human rights activist and hip-hop teacher. Sharrief is the founder of The Hijabi Chronicles, a collective which provides a creative sanctuary for Muslim women and teens, that hosted the first all-female concert showcasing the talent of Muslimah emcees in Oakland. She began performing from the age of four when she created a rap duo with her sister. After several scuffles with school bullies, it was her grandmother, the prominent civil rights activist, Margaret Stroud Block, who inspired her to write instead of fight. 'I was a little kid with a hijab', she said. 'My school peers were trying to test my gangsta,

Alia Sharrief stands in front of a mural of herself and other female activists in Oakland, California. Credit: Aina J Khan

but I had a little smart mouth. One day my grandma was like, "Girl you got to pencil-whoop them. Use your words." So instead of whooping them, I started writing everything out.'

The objection towards Islamic hip-hop goes beyond the interpretation that all music except for percussion instruments are prohibited according to a well-known ruling. Hip-hop, in particular, elicits an incendiary response from some sections of the Muslim community because of the idea that the practices of Black and Latino communities where hip-hop sprung from are 'un-Islamic'. In the American context, the cultural practices of immigrant Muslims from South Asia, what American scholar of Islam, Sherman Jackson terms 'Immigrant Islam', has surreptitiously been presented as 'authentically' Islamic. It's this assumption that led many to dismiss Sharrief, Miss Undastood and Poetic Pilgrimage's artistry as haram. The Muslim community, Sharrief says, 'would reject us. They said we were "too strong", "too Black", "too much like Malcolm X". The first time I got called a nigger was at the mosque'.

Muslim community's rejection was also a product of the fact that the commercial ascent of hip-hop in the 1990s was characterised by Notorious B.I.G.'s lyrical salvo of 'tits and bras, ménage à trois, sex in expensive cars', and the sex-positive lyricism of female artists like Lil' Kim and Foxy Brown. Much of the commercial hip-hop that emerged from that decade cast an aesthetic of shimmering hedonism, misogyny, and the objectification of women over a music genre that was once a sentient response to urban deprivation and trenchant police brutality in America. It wasn't that hip-hop was from its inception, patriarchal. As Saud Abdul Kabeer, Michigan-based hip-hop scholar and author of *Muslim Cool: Race, Religion, and Hip-Hop in the United States*, explains, hip-hop was a product of its environment where patriarchy had diffused itself into the way it was narrated historically, such that the birth of hip-hop begins with the masculine origin story of the Bronx Big Three: 'When people talk about the history of hip-hop, they talk about the godfathers, the forefathers. There's acknowledgement of male DJs like Grandmaster Flash, Afrika Bambaataa, and DJ Kool Herc. But there are no women in that story.'

In the mid 1980s, Queen Latifah was one of the first female emcees to normalise Afrocentric hip-hop aesthetic in the form of head wraps and kente prints. Carolyn Rouse's research on American Black Muslim female converts builds a picture of the alignment of these Afrocentric practices with Black Muslim practices. Rouse suggested Black Muslim women whose identities sat at the intersections of their Blackness, their womanhood, and their Americanness, chose to cover their hair and bodies as Muslims not just to embrace their spiritual identity but also to reject feminine beauty standards of white supremacy and internalised self-loathing the writer Toni Morrison admonished so poignantly in her novel, *The Bluest Eye*. Whilst 'Immigrant Islam' dictated that modesty for Muslim women could be exhibited only through Arab and South Asian inspired hijabs and *chaadars*, Muslimah rappers like Alia Sharrief and Neelam Hakeem, notes Khabeer, observe modesty and salute their African heritage by, 'reclaiming Afrodiasporic headwraps as Islamic' and adorning themselves with jewellery shaped in the African continent.

Muneera Williams (left) and Sukina Douglas (right).

Poetic Pilgrimage

After they were inspired by the autobiography of the civil rights activist and Black revolutionary, Malcolm X, Muneera Williams and Sukina Douglas who formed hip-hop duo Poetic Pilgrimage, converted to Islam in 2005 only three weeks after the 7/7 bombings in London. Though they no longer perform together, both Sukina and Muneera continue with their artistry through solo work as playwrights, spoken word poets and other creative projects. The former duo have immortalised their status as hip-hop pioneers who unapologetically articulated the British Muslim and Black British experience through their music.

The influence of their Muslim identity, Caribbean and British heritage spills out from Poetic Pilgrimage's cover of The Abyssinians' 'Satta Massagana' in 'Land Far Away'. It's a reggae and hip-hop fusion which seamlessly melds the curling smoke of burning incense as a shopkeeper with dreadlocks sells his pungent wares, a glimpse of a sepia photo of Sojourner Truth, the African American abolitionist and women's rights activist, Islamic references to Jannatul Firdaus (paradise), the Middle Passage of slavery, and a reference to halal Jamaican patties all in the same breath. To the eyes of a Muslim ignorant of the cultural practices of Afro-diasporic Black Muslims, such music could mistakenly be labelled as 'un-Islamic'. But as Muneera explains, though her race and sex were part of her identity, Islam was her foundation, the lens through which she saw her music:

> Sometimes I feel like people look for codes and conventions. 'Is she wearing the hijab? Does she look Muslim-ish? How does she dress?' I may not mention 'Oh God' or 'Oh the prophet Muhammad peace be upon him'. It's almost as if you don't look a certain way, if you don't dress a certain way then you'll be held up to, 'Is this person even Muslim? Is this person even inspired by faith?' As I look through the lens of faith, I have no choice but to be influenced by my faith. It's just maybe how I express my faith isn't going to necessarily be in codes and conventions people will understand. One of the reasons people are looking for these things is because they want something to hold onto. They want something to make them feel empowered in this time where we can feel so disempowered, when we look at how Muslims are being portrayed in the West and other Muslim countries. People are looking to find themselves.

Islamic references are replete in hip-hop vernacular. Early references allude to the Nation of Islam, Five Percenter philosophy (an offshoot of the Nation of Islam) of men as Gods and women as earths in the lyrics of Busta Rhymes and Erykah Badu. Mos Def, also known as Yasiin Bey, is a well-known example of a male Muslim emcee who merged his Sunni orthodox faith with his music, as can be heard in the opening line of his solo album 'Black on Both Sides': *Bismillah Ar-Rahman Ar-Rahim*, 'In the name of God the most gracious, the most merciful'. Though word through the hip-hop grapevine whispers of her apparent conversion, multi-platinum rap artist Eve thanks Allah, not God, for turning away from her life as a stripper in her debut album. Even hip-hop legend Queen Latifah's Muslim identified stage name nods to the entanglement of Black consciousness, hip-hop, and Islam. However, the relationship between Islam and hip-hop, says Khabeer, isn't that well-known. It has, she says, 'a lot to do with how hip-hop is seen as "Black music" which is configured around pathologies like poverty, criminality and sexuality. Islam and Muslims get pegged around sexuality and being very strict: there's no music, and there's no sex.' Hip-hop is also inextricably bound with Islam because of its Jamaican, African, funk, and jazz roots. '"Knowledge of self", is what Black Muslims gave hip-hop', says Khabeer. 'Although hip-hop has this commercial commodified side, as a genre, it's always had this thread which is inspired by "knowledge of self", of social protest, commentary, critique, of trying to build and imagine something different. Knowledge of self comes from the Black Muslim tradition, particularly the Nation of Islam and the honourable Elijah Muhammad. It's a part of hip-hop music and culture. The "knowledge of self" is an ethical position about knowing your past which is usually hidden because you're from a marginalised community.'

Hip-Hop 'Dawah'

Islam also has a very strong tradition of poetry going back to the classical period. A whole chapter in the Qur'an (Surah Ashu'ara, 26) is dedicated to poets. Historically, poetry was used as a form of dawah to invite non-Muslims to accept Islam. The Prophet Muhammad himself commissioned poetry for Muslim poets to refute verbal challenges to Islam and to inspire

Boshia-Ray Jean, pictured in New Jersey. Credit: Aina J Khan

conviction amongst Muslims. For Oakland-based emcee Alia Sharrief, hip-hop is an inheritance of this poetic mantle, such that the question of whether hip-hop is permissible or *haram* was obsolete. 'Hip-hop is rooted in Islam. It's poetry slam. When the prophet Muhammad (peace be upon him) was delivering the message, they called him a poet. His time was the time of poetry, where people were basically rap battling'.

Model, writer, and Afrofuturist, Boshia Rae-Jean concurs. The New Jersey based emcee converted to Islam in 2015. Her debut song, 'Q Knowledge', begins with *Bismillah hirahman nirahim*, a nod to Mos Def's opening to 'Black on Both Sides'. Though there are no other explicit Islamic references (the music video expresses her passion for Afrofuturism and is set in a space-ship), Jean said the song was about reviving tradition of female scholarship with the chorus line, 'Where you gonna get that knowledge?'. My music, she says, is about Muslim women seeking scholarship, defending their rights, not being afraid to say that's not right. Think about all the prophets that women birthed, all of the leaders. The womb was a source of divine decree. Aisha, the wife of prophet Muhammad, narrated so many hadith. With that, she was able to teach more men scholars than a lot of men did at the time. We have to understand the power of a woman's knowledge and her connection to Allah, really honour knowledge so you can utilise that to make new stories, utilise who you are as a woman to effect change.

Islam has a long, rich tradition of female Muslim intellectuals. The Oxford-based scholar Sheikh Akram Nadwi produced a forty-volume biography of more than 9,000 Muslim women who had narrated hadith, the traditions of the prophet Muhammad, taught in mosques, and issued fatwas over the centuries, just in the field of hadith alone. Some of the most notable intellectuals such as Al Ghazali and the imams of the four major schools of thought within Sunni Islam, attended the classes of Muslim women from Jerusalem, Syria, and Arabia. As Jean rightly points out, Aisha, the wife of the prophet Muhammad was a formidable scholar herself. Muslim women like Nana Asma'u (1793–1864), the Hausa-Fulani poetess, Islamic scholar and revivalist from northern Nigeria continued this tradition well into the nineteenth century. In the present day, the Egyptian songstress Umm Kulthum whose father was an Islamic scholar, began performing as a *qariah*, a female Qur'an reciter. The indomitable Pakistani singer, Abida Parveen, comes from a distinguished family of scholars and qawwali singers.

Carrying the mantle of the great female Muslim scholars and artists who came before her, Jean considers her role as a Muslimah emcee being a way of manifesting a different space for thinking, moving from traditional expectations around gender which dictate how women should behave both within and beyond the Muslim community. She sees Islam as struggle against injustice:

We grow up in families that say, 'Oh, you shouldn't speak too loud' or 'You're a woman, you should do this'. But hip-hop says 'no'. Hip-hop says fight for your rights. Don't sit there and be meek. Islam teaches us that as well, to fight for justice. Don't sit there and let it continue, because then you're oppressing yourself, your community. That's the foundation of hip-hop. Islam is literally in hip-hop.

Ain't Afraid

The identical twins and hip-hop duo, Ain't Afraid, who go by the stage names Straingth and Wizdumb, were home schooled. They had to help support their younger siblings and their mother, a single parent who worked long hours. During those days, music was their catharsis and escapism. Their mother, Umm Ain't Afraid, a former rapper herself, injected optimism into their musical diet from a young age with Michael Jackson and Whitney Houston, a buoyancy, which diffused into the twins' own creativity. 'As the oldest siblings', says Straingth, 'we had to take a lot of responsibility. Taking care of the kids, the household while our mother worked. In that time, we used music and dance routines to cope through the misery: feeling alone, times we used to feel trapped from all the things we were going through. Music was a sweet space. We felt peace and freedom'. At their high school in Dearborn, Michigan, they were given the title, 'The Twinsz'. Though they are now known as Muslimah emcees, they sang, recited poetry and performed in class, school halls and talent shows. Their prolific grassroots activism and advocacy on runaway and homeless youth, gentrification, and Black Lives Matter cemented their

Ain't Afraid, Dearborn, Michigan. Credit: Aina J Khan

status in the community not just as performers but as young, socially engaged leaders. A year after they left high school, The Twinsz became more serious about their faith. They began listening to lectures from Muslim scholars such as Mufti Ismail Menk, Imam Bilal Phillips, spoken-word poetry by Boona Mohammad, and acoustic nasheeds by the well-known three-man band, Native Deen. All the people we came across, says Wizdumb, were 'men, men, men. On top of that, if they were artists, they were still men. We didn't really know about women artists'.

As young, Black Muslim women themselves, they found that not only were Muslim women not given a visible platform for other young women to aspire to, but that many of their peers were struggling to reconcile their Muslimness and Americanness. Using the lyrical sails of their mother who helped orchestrate the synergy between their faith and their music, they set out to create a narrative by and for Muslim women, to instil unapologetic pride that embraced their Muslimness, their Blackness, and their American identity. And so when hip-hop became a part of their musical vocabulary in 2018, Ain't Afraid, which stands for 'Ain't Another Faith Rapping As Islam Does', was finally born; and a form of hip-hop dawah. Wizdumb says:

> We were Straingth and Wizdumb before we were Ain't Afraid. It embodies everything we are: being unapologetic and comfortable. Ain't Afraid is a little contradictory. We're not absence of fear, we have fear. It's about courage. It means when you're being challenged, to challenge back. It's about braving the fear and not being afraid of who we are. We realised young Muslims, especially sisters, needed to see you can live a dope life and still value your religion. That it is possible. So many young sisters ask us, 'How are you guys so cool, and still so Muslim?' For us, that was our life. Our mother brought us up on that.

With a following of over 113,000 on Instagram, their music, explicitly Islamic in its lyrical content, is rooted in the remembrance of Allah. With synchronised recitations and brightly coloured hijabs, they address the 'Muslim baes' of Instagram, summarising uplifting narrations from the prophet Muhammad, exploring the 99 names of Allah, directly addressing the Christchurch massacre victims, and creating Islamic renditions of nursery rhymes such as 'Row, Row, Row Your Boat' which they reprised as 'Ra, Ra, Ramadan'. Their first song 'Take Me To Makkah' is about performing the *hajj* and seeing the Kabah for the first time. Through their music, Ain't Afraid display not just a commitment to their religious beliefs as Muslims, but also social advocacy and politics. 'We need to be talking about things other people are afraid to talk about', says Straingth. 'Racial issues effect your Muslim brothers and sisters, so you should be concerned about that. Housing displacement affects Muslim brothers and sisters. War. Immigration'. In response to Donald Trump's racist tweets last year that 'The Squad' – congresswomen Rashida Talib, Ayana Presley, Ilhan Omar and Alexandria Ocasio-Cortez, all women of colour – should 'go back' to other countries, they penned 'Trumped'. With the star-spangled banner of the American flag draped on the back of their mother's car seat, they plunge into an immaculate rap about the Middle Passage, slavery, and Melania Trump's own immigrant status:

Once they began building a following on Instagram, the duo had also built a growing non-Muslim audience. What started out as primarily Islamic hip-hop for a Muslim audience created an opportunity for Ain't Afraid to educate non-Muslims about Islam and universalise the Muslim experience through the language of rap. 'The prophet Muhammad', says Straingth, 'was an advocate for all people. Allah sent the prophet SAW as a mercy to mankind, not just as a mercy to this Ummah, to just Muslims. As Muslims, we need to embody that message as well. The prophet came for that purpose, and we're supposed to carry out what he came for. So we (Ain't Afraid) advocate for all people.'

There is a lot of 'unsettledness' around the question of religious authority in America and who is the rightful arbiter of knowledge. But the music of Ain't Afraid and indeed other Muslimah emcees is resonating with the Muslim diaspora around the world, both in its Islamic and cultural significance. It is for this reason hip-hop remains the genre of Ain't Afraid's generation of emcees, who use hip-hop as a musical baton to demand social justice refracted through the lens of their faith. Khabeer notes:

> Young Muslims are engaging with hip-hop music and culture because they're finding Islam in it. They're also finding a way to be Muslim that is really engaging in activism and challenging with inequality. It's not surprising that people

who are the intersection of multiple oppressions, religious, gender, race class, would be drawn to or attracted to a music that comes from their own community and experiences, as a way to respond, express and intervene. With a conscious hip-hop, they are interpreting the world, diagnosing it, and providing the remedies, that's what their music is trying to do.

The Legacy of Lauryn Hill

In 1998, the masculinist hip-hop landscape changed irrevocably with the release of 'The Miseducation of Lauryn Hill'. Lauryn Hill eloquently sermonised with her music on how to reconcile love in all its iterations: love of self, unrequited love, navigating heartbreak with Ex-Factor, and the unconditional love of motherhood. The post-civil rights, post-third-wave feminism milieu her music emerged from was the catalyst that begat what hip-hop journalist and author, Joan Morgan, dubbed as 'hip-hop feminism'. From Hill's razor-sharp lyricism and velvety alto voice, a prophetess of tenderness and rage was born offering a liberation theology of the heart for Black women. A morally conscious, empowering hip-hop was resurrected by a single woman's voice. The opening lyrics of her 'Doo-Wop (That Thing)', the first number one single by a female hip-hop artist in history, begins with a well-known Islamic phrase Muslims utter every day whilst performing their five daily prayers.

Hill's invocation of *Siraat Al-Mustaqim*, a phrase, referenced thirty-three times in the Qur'an, was more than just a cocktail of intelligent punchlines mixed with spirituality. She dipped her lyrical pen into hip-hop vernacular that had been in dialogue with Islam since the genre's inception on the streets of South Bronx, New York City in the 1970's. For Miss Undastood, this unlikely marriage between hip-hop and spirituality passed on the baton to Muslim emcees like her, opening the lyrical floodgates to merge the two and create a genre that not only appealed to the Islamic ethos and practices of Muslims but was also culturally relevant. Lauryn, she says, was infusing spirituality into music. 'That is what I really connected with. She was putting some scriptures here and there and dropping some Islamic words. It was hip-hop and spirituality together, which is what I'm doing: Infusing hip-hop along with Islamic messages.'

From the beginning, Miss Undastood's lyrics have fearlessly prodded at taboo social issues within the Muslim community. If there was an elephant in the room, Miss Undastood was the verbal assassin who fearlessly pursued it:

> I'm always speaking about topics that people don't want to talk about, like domestic violence. People want to pretend it don't exist; they sweep it under the rug. I'm probably the only one who has no trouble talking about my experience after 9/11, dealing with discrimination, trying to get jobs. I'm the one whose gonna talk about sexism, gender bias, racism, polygamy, about child support. I'm the one choosing to speak on so many issues where people are like, 'Hush! Hush! Hush!'

Instagram has become the newest medium to share her freestyles, Islamic covers of popular songs about her battles to secure child support and raise her daughter as a single mother against the backing track of Lauryn Hill's 'Lost Ones', amongst other themes. The ricochet lyricism of 'Queen's Best Kept Secret' is unrivalled as she raps in one of her freestyles donning a butter-yellow silk hijab.

For Alia Sharrief, Hill's music planted a seed that helped her cultivate her own musical journey and empowered her to narrate the story of her Black and Muslim womanhood:

> What Lauryn offered was so real. She offered so many jewels to the next generation to do better in a music industry where sex sells. Fast forward to the future, have we ever seen another Lauryn Hill? It's so hard to be a righteous woman in the music industry, trying to deliver a message that uplifts women. When I met Lauryn, I told her, 'I feel like I'm your daughter. Everything I'm doing is because I had someone like you to listen to when I was a little girl'. She grabbed my hand and said, 'Hopefully I planted the seed for you to grow'.

Change Gonna Come

Almost a year after it was announced that a police officer who, on 9 August 2014, fatally shot the eighteen-year-old Black teenager Mike Brown in Ferguson, Missouri, would not face federal charges, it was Alia Sharrief's wedding day. Ferguson became a seismic moment which cast a searching international spotlight on police accountability, and yet another post-mortem of race relations in the United States. Inspired partly by Ferguson, Sharrief's song 'Black Heroes', which she performed with Aminah Bel, saluted the long history of Black radicalism and Black excellence. Ferguson for Sharrief was a harrowing reminder that her music was a weapon to 'fight the power' as the infamous Public Enemy chorus-line goes. 'Mike Brown reminded us of Oscar Grant who was killed here in Oakland, at Fruitvale Bart Station', she says. 'It happened so many years ago, but it will always stay with us. I believe in that hadith, that if you see anything wrong you've got three things to stop it with: Your tongue, your hands, and your heart. I wanna be good on the day of judgement, so I gotta speak the truth.'

Alia Sharrief (left) and Lauryn Hill (right). Credit: Alia Sharrief.

For Sukina, hip-hop whether British or American in its articulation, was not just embedded within the context of the African-American tradition. She saw Poetic Pilgrimage's music as part of the African diasporic, post-slave communities that flowed across the Black Atlantic, utilising music as a weapon with a political undercurrent whether in its jovial and light-hearted forms as in subversively powerful Caribbean calypso music which originated in the struggle for emancipation from slavery, or its more sombre articulation as in Billie Holiday's 'Strange Fruit', or in popular reggae music as in Bob Marley's 'Redemption Song' where he quotes Marcus Garvey. 'Even though hip-hop coagulated in America, its pieces came from the Afro-Caribbean tradition, the Afro-Jamaican tradition, the Afro-Latino tradition, and the African American tradition in that melting pot in New York at the time. It would be unjust to look at it in the context of just the American tradition. A lot of forefathers of hip-hop were also Afro-Caribbean. I don't see myself as being less a part of the conversation on hip-hop', she says.

Though Muneera also saw her music as a continuation of hip-hop's legacy of protest, dissent and demands for social justice, simply viewing her music through a lens of resistance and a singular narrative that captured only the Black British Muslim experience would obscure the heart she poured into her art that gave voice to one story in the taxonomy of human experience.

'Being black in this era', Sukina says, 'you are forced to see things through a lens. I wasn't trying to make protest songs, I wasn't trying to be empowering or talk about social justice and inequality. I was speaking from my heart about what I was witnessing. When you see what people around you are going through, is it some kind of social or political theory that we're trying to put out there, or is it that we just care? Do I think what I do is from a legacy of protest and dissent? Truth to power and truth to the people? Yeah, I think it's all of these different things. But we're living in a world which wants us to have dominant narratives. And when you come with something different to that, you're not trying to speak the truth. You're just telling your story.'

From the slave plantation songs in the Deep South to the streets of New York's South Bronx, Black American expressive culture in music has maintained a position of resistance for centuries. Hip-hop endures as the musical arsenal of choice for a new generation of Muslimah emcees who are building online and real-life communities with their music. Their very existence is a form of resistance that transcends centuries of victimhood of racial oppression. They are nurturing and utilising a potent vehicle of expression, power and catharsis not just for themselves, but for the future generations of Muslimah emcees to come.

AMERICAN GRIOT

Extract from a play by
Reginald Edmund and *Ronnie Malley*

Characters
Mamadou
Robert Johnson
Abiodun
Castor
Lily
Awa
Laila (Mamadou's Mother)
Mr Tanner
Mr Daniel Smith
Mrs Clara Smith
Mrs Emma Taylor
Ibrahim (Awa's Father)
Ali (Awa's Betrothed)
Gaolo Moussa Kouyate
Sailor
Buddy Guy
Auctioneer

Setting
Mid–late eighteenth century/early twentieth century
Mali/Guinea Region, Africa
Natchez, Mississippi, North America

Synopsis
Mamadou, a learned griot from Futa Jallon, Guinea/Mali region of Africa, is enslaved and taken to America in the late eighteenth century. His

enslavement was a consequence of being in love with Awa, a woman betrothed to another. His story is one of heritage, dignity, and the power of music. The story is set to the backdrop of Mamadou's Africa and slavery in Mississippi from the perspective of an African who was one of many with Muslim backgrounds.

The narrative weaves in elements that formed the roots of what we came to call the blues. The call and response of verse, musical instruments, and soulful expression are a continuation of musical culture from Africa, which is influenced by spiritual beliefs including Islam and traditional African faiths. Throughout the narration of Mamadou's story, anecdotes become apparent highlighting the relationship between instruments, song styles, rhythms, and melodic approaches found in early African American music, and later the blues.

<u>ACT 1</u>

SCENE 1 – Robert Meets Scratch

Darkness.

<Live Instruments: Guitar & Diddley Bow>

A singular guitar chord strikes out and light rise on a lone man wandering down a road. Travel-wearied. He drops to his knees, takes his guitar and begins to pluck a guitar. His name is Robert. He waits quietly.
Nothing. Silence.

He plucks at the guitar again. In the distance, he hears the same tune played in response. It hangs in the wind.

Robert
Hello.
                    Silence.

He plays the tune again.
Again it is heard in response. This time closer, there's a complexity to it this time.

Robert
Hello… Who out there?
> *Silence. Lonely silence.*

He plays again.
The response is closer, in the opposite direction heard last time.

Robert
Who out there? I'm serious now. Who out there? Come on out!

A man appears from out of the darkness sitting playing a one-stringed instrument (*diddley bow), he uses a knife as a slide for the instrument.

He appears from the shadow.

Mamadou
Do you know why you play those five notes?

Robert
What?

Mamadou
Those notes that you're playin', do you know why you play them, child?

Robert
Who are you?

Mamadou
Name doesn't matter,
What does though is the music.
That's what brought you to these crossroads.
Isn't it?

Robert
Heard if I stood here I'd meet a man named Scratch and he'd give me the answers I was looking for?
You him ain't ya?

Mamadou

Scratch? You mean the devil? Ain't no devil here. Just me...In order for a man to give the answer, he's got to know the question.
What is it that you are looking for child?

Robert

I want to be the greatest musician alive. Only the devil can give me that?

Mamadou

Can't.

Robert

Can't or won't...

Mamadou

Can't help to make you the greatest if you don't have a know-how of where it came from, now can I?

Robert

I travelled miles, hopped trains, slept in the heat and the damn cold. Journeyed til my boots worn down, and my feet turn raw and bled, walked til I reach the furthest crossroad so I could come to find you. And now you standin' here telling me you ain't going to help me?

Mamadou

Not sayin' I won't... just asking if you can help yourself.

Robert

Help myself out how?

Mamadou

Look child, in order to know where you going you got to know where you've been. There's an order to every story a beginning and an end. Even before your story began. Stories before your story... Now there was a man... maybe this is my story, maybe it's not. You'll do well to listen. There was once a griot, a musician storyteller from a long line of griots, and a Muslim from Futa Jallon in West Africa.

Robert
What does this have to do with playin' the guitar?

Mamadou
History. Child, History… all things are created by history. Listen…

Mamadou strums the diddley bow and the world starts to melt away. As the world melts into another time and place so does his age, his attire. He's younger. The Griot Song begins.

SCENE 2 – Awa and Laila

It is early evening and we are in a public space somewhere in Futa Jallon. As people gather and bustle, Mamadou sings of his ancestry in griot fashion accompanied by two musicians and others who join the chorus.

Mamadou (as Griot) / Chorus Ensemble

<u>Griot Song</u>

Gaolo, Gaolo, Djeli, Djeli

I am a griot, Gaolo, Gaewal, Djeli
Gaolo Mamadou Abdel Rahman is my name
In tradition with my father Ibn Said,
A student of Islam in Timbuktu, Mali,
Where ruled the Keita African dynasty
Descendants of Bilal, the first muezzin of Islam

History can hold no mystery for the Gaolo
We are the memory of mankind
Vessels of culture, languages, and time
Of our people and our religions
Fula, Songhai, Mandé, Arabic

In hard times, we must still know ourselves
And know the hardest life lived is without love *(gestures to Awa)*

Awa enters singing part of the chorus from the song. Crowd begins to disperse. Awa makes her way home.

SCENE 3 – Awa and Mamadou

Mamadou serenades Awa under her balcony with poetry, and musical interlude (n'goni)

Mamadou *(recites the poetry of Antar Ibn Shaddad)*
Like a straight leafy branch
A lover can only feast his eyes
On such beauty, (but not touch)
I am ever anxious to see my love
That is why I so often stop by her camp,
Water my camel then depart
After being so close to her
I can never content myself
With only a word about her

Awa enters she carries with her an ordinate lantern, she looks around to see if anyone sees them and then embraces him.

Awa
Oh, Modou, what are you doing here? Father will have you killed if he sees you here.

Mamadou
I don't fear your father and I don't fear death.
Awa
I'm promised to another.

Mamadou
And I don't care. Let's leave this place.

Awa
And go where?

Mamadou
Anywhere our hearts desire.
Just me and you off on a great adventure. Travelling the unknown together.
I am your Antar Ibn Sheddad and you are my Abla. Picture it, my love.

Awa pulls away

Awa
I can't. I'd shame my family, your position as a scholar would be
compromised…we'd be outcasts… what would the people say?

Mamadou
Do you love me?

Awa
You know I do.

Mamadou
Then come away with me.

Awa
You are speaking fitnah (temptation). This is not the way of the Koran…
you learned in Timbuktu and are a man of faith. You know this.

Mamadou
Awa, I love you. Always have, since the first time I ever laid eyes upon you.
I had prayed to Allah to guide me and grant me happiness. I had prayed for
him to bring me a wife. And there you were… at your sister's wedding,
singing waka.

Awa
I was so nervous, I had never performed for anyone outside of my family
before. My hands were shaking. I was hiding in the garden trying to calm

myself. Your mother was encouraging me to sing when you approached me and said…

Awa / Mamadou
Music is Allah's greatest gift. Just like love.

Awa
I treasure those words.

SCENE 4 – Awa Is Discovered

Awa is packing a bag. Her father watches discreetly and confronts her as she is about to leave.

Ibrahim (Awa's Father)
Awa, where are you going? You're carrying a lot of things with you for an early morning walk.

Awa
Nowhere Baba *(anxiously surprised)*! I…uh…was just taking some things to give away now that I'm to be married and have no use for them.

Awa's father sees that she's packed in her bag some jewellery from her dowry.

Ibrahim
Why are you taking your jewellery with you?!

Awa
I don't know how that got in there.

Ibrahim
Don't lie to me! You were going to meet the griot boy, weren't you! Well, you can keep your meeting… only you will have me and Ali, your rightfully

betrothed, with you. It's only fitting to meet the boy who thinks he will take you from both of us.

SCENE 5 — Mamadou, Father, Betrothed Confrontation

Mamadou awaits Awa, when a short fight erupts. They take Mamadou's knife and hold him down. An elder man appears, picks up the knife, and holds it against his throat.

Ibrahim
Are you trying to shame me? Did you try to steal my daughter away from me?!!

Mamadou winces in pain.

Ali
So what do we do with him? He must be punished.

Ibrahim
Well then, we must let your bride decide his fate.

Awa
No father. Don't ask me to do this.

Ibrahim
Pick one: his hands, his tongue, or his freedom.

Awa
Please father no!

Ibrahim
Decide child.
Silence

Ali
Since he's a thief, let it be his hands then!

They grab Mamadou and position him to lose his hands

Awa
His freedom! Take his freedom.
Take his freedom so that he never sees my face again.

Mamadou
Awa? What did you do?!! What did you do?!!!

Awa
I'm sorry. I'm so sorry.

(Across the Atlantic)

SCENE 10 – The Walk Home

Mamadou *(To Robert)*
They sold me. I looked to the heavy metal shackles that bonded me, and felt my heart shatter like glass. I thought the horror of the slave ship was the end of me but, no… this was… this sealed my fate.
I, once a great judge of men and descendant of kings was now nothing more than a slave.
Slave.
That word cut me.
Cut me deeper than the loss of my love.
It further confirmed that all that I once held dear was gone from me.
I was sold to a married couple named the Smiths.

Mrs Smith
You paid how much for this one dear?

Mr Smith
They say he's a smart one and can speak a multitude of languages dear.

Mrs Smith
You can teach a parrot to speak French, doesn't mean it's worth $800.

Mamadou *(To Robert)*
I, tied and still shackled, walked behind them.
Walked behind them for miles upon miles.
And when they finally reached their home.
A great house supported by pillars and arches.
My feet were blistered and bloodied.
Sweat dripped down my brow.
Chains bit into my flesh.

SCENE 17 – Mamadou / Mr Smith's Office

Mr Smith
Sit... please... I said, SIT! Well now, you've been a great asset to my family and to my business. I don't believe I've told you that. You have a knack for cultivating the fields. Is that something you did back from where you came from?

Mamadou
Yes, Mr Smith

Mr Smith
I also saw you teaching the others how to properly tend the herd. Indeed, you have a multitude of skills, even with languages, is this true?

Mamadou
Mr Smith?

Mr Smith
The world is filled with infinite possibilities. That is if the decisions you make bring you on the right side of matters. You have very nice teeth by the way... very nice teeth. Where was I?

Mamadou
I believe something regarding being on the right side.

Mr Smith

Ah yes. You also seem to have a skill in keeping your fellow slaves in line. Now, these nightly gatherings I hear about are dangerous. Stirring up trouble all across these lands. I need to ensure that they come to a close.

Mamadou

Is that not the purpose of Mr Tanner?

Mr Smith

Mr Tanner can only see so much, I need a second pair of eyes. Eyes that I can depend on and trust… can I trust you? Can you be those eyes for me?

Mr Smith

Another thing… I had a slave tell me that you were once a musician in your native lands.

Mr Smith

I have two tasks for you. One, I have distinguished guests coming in a few weeks' time. I'd like for you to learn some civilised music and perform it for our guests.

Mamadou

Gladly. May I have some of the others accompany me? We'll make sure it's an affair to remember.

Mr Smith

I suppose if you think it'll make it better, but no funny business boy. Only two others, and none of that drumming mess.

Mamadou

Might we have some instruments? I mean, we'd need to practise to make it the best event we can.

Mr Smith

I'll think on it. I'm puttin' trust in you, against the usual better judgement of my wife. Don't disappoint me, it could mean your life.

Mr Smith
And oh yes, the second task. It's really regarding the simple matter of keeping an eye on my property and informing me of any mischief there might be. And perhaps in return I will ensure that you are well taken care of… better yet, I'll make sure that you get to keep all of your teeth. And they are very nice teeth.

Silence
> *Cold silence.*

Mr Smith (cont'd.)
I knew you'd see reason.

SCENE 20 – Mamadou's Entrancement

Mamadou wakes up in his bed and finds a banjo sitting there waiting for him. He picks it up and starts to pluck it.

Mamadou
N'goni, xalam, akonting
Our instruments are as colourful as our cultures
The string and skin give voice to the sacred
The sounds that move us cause our words to move people
Our history is in our blood, we are keepers of time and culture
…
Could I betray them for a kinder servitude?
For my own survival could I leave the rest to suffer?
Destroy that which was sacred?
Take away the only reminder for these people bound and chained that their souls are free?
I asked what kind of man I was
In this moment as I sit running my hands upon these strings, I play,
These words I offered up over and over again.

Allah ya rahman (God, oh merciful one)
His prayer turns into a camp holler. It roars out.

ACT 2

SCENE 8 – The Dinner Performance

Mr Smith
Ladies and gentlemen, honoured guests, I thank you for joining me at my beautiful home. Now I have a fantastic evening in store for you. I've recently acquired a talented slave who has an aptitude for music. I understand he's been learning some of our civilised songs. Please enjoy the music as you mingle.

<Music scene and the big get away>

Mamadou and group begin playing. The first piece is a simple instrumental. The second is a traditional dance piece for the guests. The third piece is the field holler cue to escape.

Mamadou and musicians

<u>Field Holler Song 1</u>

I be so glad when the sun goes down
There's a rainbow on my shoulder ain't gonna rain on me

Modou addresses the audience.
Mamadou *(disrupts a mingling crowd)*
Good evenin' ladies and gentlemen,
Bonsoir mesdames et messieurs
I'd like to start by thanking our gracious hosts Mr and Mrs Smith for giving me the chance to attempt to be… civilised.

I am Mamadou Abdel Rahman Ibn Said
I am Muslim, griot, gaolo, djeli

A vessel of culture, languages, and time
Griots preserve the history of mankind
My people come from a long line

Of kings and queens and the dawn of civilisation

Here we stand before you,
Barely human in your eyes
On land stolen from others
As you have stolen our lives

There will one day come a reckoning
You wait and see
One day soon
My people will be free

*Mr and Mrs Smith are livid. The guests are in shock and mostly speechless. The third
piece begins and slaves escape in the distance.*

SCENE 10 – Robert's Role

Robert
Woo, I bet that man was roarin' mad.

Mamadou
Oh, he was. Believe me, he was.
But we played that night as our brothers and sisters escaped into the
darkness. No one had heard that kind of sound before. I had given them
what they had wanted. The sound of this place called America. Little did
they know that sound was African.

After we played, they pulled us from the stage, bound our hands, brought
us to a tree that stood before them. And then hung us til' we died. They
believed that if they destroyed the things that gave us beauty, that gave us
hope, that liberated us, that it would destroy us. How wrong they were.

The people who we freed spread that sound wherever they journeyed.
Passed it onto their brothers and sisters. Passed it on one generation to the
next. Though our bodies were broken, we found that our spirits lived on
in the music.

The next sequence can be done through Mamadou narration and projection or sound.

Mamadou (cont'd.)
From the griot tradition <*play griot praise tune*>,
to the blues <*crossfade to blues tune*>,
to jazz <*crossfade to jazz tune*>,
to something that you, Robert, will inspire called rock and roll <*crossfade to rock tune*>.

Eventually, the voices of our people will be heard the world around. But it'll all find its way back home to our motherland <*crossfade to Ali Farka Touré style or similar*>.

Some things just can't be separated from the soul.

Robert
So you ain't no devil…you the spirit of the American griot.

Mamadou
Yes. And now I'm handing this role to you. When the time comes, you shall stand at the crossroads spreading the gift to those that seek it, a vessel of our culture and history through song and time.

SEVEN WAYS TO BREAK A FAST

Sameer Rahim

Shawkat found it impossible to balance all four drinks; instead, he manacled two pints of cold beer before depositing them with a manly nod in front of Dominic and Charlie.

'Nice one, Shortcut,' said Dominic, gulping his new pint. There was no story behind the nickname; it was pure euphony.

'Where's Caz's?' demanded Charlie.

Quickly, Shawkat retrieved her white wine and his own yellow-green orange juice packed with ghostly ice cubes. Glancing at the mini-grandfather clock hanging between the spirit bottles, he noted that iftar was still 34 minutes away.

He watched Caz's grey eyes shift between Dominic and Charlie as they swapped stag-do stories. Every so often, she reset the silver band corralling her wavy light-brown hair, or anxiously smoothed out her creased mauve dress. For the past fortnight, she had been interning at his Westminster office and today, Thursday, was her last before going to France with her parents. As the youngest on the team, Shawkat had been tasked with showing her the ropes – how to unblock the photocopier and refill the coffee machine, that kind of thing. Dominic and Charlie had noticed his solicitous behaviour, and so while interns were usually seen off with exaggerated praise and a cheap chocolate cake, for Caz they suggested a farewell drink. Shawkat felt awkward going to the pub in Ramzan, but figured it would be rude not to.

Sitting beside Caz on an uncomfortably narrow wooden bench, Shawkat kept his distance. He hadn't consumed anything – no food, no water – since before daybreak, and his dry mouth was incubating an unpleasant smell. At the mosque they quoted the Prophet's saying that a faster's breath was sweeter than musk; but down the pub it would be nothing more than an unsociable stink. Unwilling to risk speaking, he sat in silence as Dominic and Charlie turned their attention on Caz.

'You've enjoyed working with Shortcut, I take it?' asked Charlie.

'Hope he behaved himself,' Dominic followed up. Shawkat pulled a face.

'Actually, I thought there might be more to do,' said Caz. 'I did a lot of photocopying, which I should expect but…' Shawkat made a sympathetic 'mmm' noise.

'It's nice we're so near St James's Park,' she said more brightly. She came in from Basingstoke every morning and seemed excited to be in the capital. After searching her Instagram, Shawkat had seen she had posted artful selfies with the pelicans. In one you could glimpse a bearded man and his niqabi wife pushing their daughter in a pink pram. That reminded him: he needed to Google what time Friday prayers began the next day, so he could avoid the interminable khutbah. He looked at his watch: twenty minutes to go.

The guys muttered something about train times and wives and short leashes. Putting on his jacket, Dominic cocked his eyebrow; Charlie blew three pouty kisses.

Caz had finished her wine but seemed in no mood to end the evening.

'Let me get this one,' she said. Shawkat assumed an expression of mock outrage, almost snatching her wine glass. From the safety of the bar, he called out to ask if she wanted some snacks. She gave a double thumbs-up. His hunger, having pinched and abated throughout the day, was putting on a dramatic performance. Back at the table, he tore open two packets of roasted peanuts and salted crisps, displaying their contents like spoils of war. She grabbed a handful of nuts, not appearing to notice that he wasn't eating – nor that his orange juice remained untouched.

At her parents' flat in Toulouse, Caz would be seeing her sister for the first time in six months. They had quarrelled after she had missed Caz's birthday party in Basingstoke because she wanted to stay in Madrid with her gap-year boyfriend. Or was it that Caz had missed her sister's birthday party in Madrid because she was in Basingstoke? Dizzy and fatigued, Shawkat couldn't keep track of her cosmopolitan travels.

Day three was always the hardest. By now you had used up your pre-Ramzan calorie reserves but your body still demanded tea and biscuits at the prescribed English times. To keep his concentration, Shawkat focused on Caz's eyes – nodding when she needed assent, tutting when she had been wronged. As she finished one emphatic point – something to do with younger sisters always getting away with murder – he completed her rhetorical flourish with a knuckled drumroll.

'Aw,' she said fuzzily, 'most guys aren't such good listeners.' She cupped her cheeks, elbows on the table, wrists kissing. 'Tell *me* something about yourself.'

Outside the blueish dusk lingered. The clock behind the bar read 8.20, four minutes to go; but his watch said 8.24. Shawkat went with his watch, crunching down some nuts and gulping his now watery juice. Palpably, he felt his sugar and salt levels rebalancing.

'Oh no Caz,' he said, leaning over to adjust her silver hair band. 'You carry on.'

II

Amina was very mature for her age, thank you very much. Now she was nine years old, she folded her hijab into a perfect triangle over her school shirt, and woke up for Fajr at the weekends. Today she was helping to make iftar for everyone and also sehri, which she was allowed to stay up for. Mummy even said that because this year she was fasting the whole month, she could make her own meat pies.

The pies were cooling on a metal rack in the kitchen. They had come out flaky and golden brown and smelt delicious. Having finished the cooking, Mummy was resting upstairs in her bedroom and no one was allowed to disturb her. She had warned Amina not to touch the pies before sunset. Her tummy gurgled loudly and she clenched to make it stop. Through the window the sun was setting over the pear trees. Amina tried to watch it move but it went too slowly.

After school, Mummy had called her straight into the kitchen, and she didn't even have time to take off her hijab. Mummy rolled out a rectangle of cold dough. Amina knew it was cold because, while Mummy was sieving the rice and stirring the mince and onion in the small saucepan, she stuck her fingers in the dough before quickly trying to comb it smooth again.

Mummy saw her finger marks and got angry.

'What's the matter with you?' she demanded, waving her dusty rolling pin. 'Do you like making work for me?'

'I'm sorry,' said Amina, but not like she *really* meant it. Mummy had been boiling rice in the big saucepan and her face was wet, like when she put on creams at night. She re-rolled the dough, then sliced it sideways (once) and up and down (twice) to make six rectangles. The last rectangle she cut in half to make two smaller ones. These would be Amina's pies.

'Now watch me, properly.' Mummy took a spoonful of mince-and-onion filling and put it on the big dough rectangles, dabbing the edges from a glass of cloudy water. Then she rolled up each one like a Swiss roll, except instead of red jam inside it was the mince and onion cooked together. She flattened out the top and bottom of the pies so they looked like the flared end of a school skirt. The sharp knife made three slits in their fat bellies.

'Your turn,' said Mummy.

Amina cracked her knuckles like Mummy did before driving. Slowly, she spooned the filling on to her small rectangles, sticking her tongue out for balance. Were they full enough? She *was* really hungry. She took a second spoonful for each mini pie. But when she tried to roll one up, the filling spilled out from the sides. And when she tried to seal it, the thin dough laddered like tights in winter.

'Kutti!' shouted Mummy, whacking Amina on the back of her legs with the rolling pin. 'I have to start from scratch now!' She threw the forlorn pies in the bin. Right then, Amina, wiping the flour off the back of her skirt, hated her mother. She hadn't done it on purpose, like the time Salman wrote his name in lipstick on the wall, and got deservedly slapped. Her art teacher would always be nice when she made a mistake; Miss Formby would say 'just do better next time.' But Mummy always got angry in Ramzan. She felt a tear tickling her cheek, just out of reach of her tongue. She watched helplessly as Mummy rolled out a small rectangle of dough, and then filled, sealed and pricked two mini pies.

'You do the basting,' she said, in a softer voice. Amina dipped the brown brush into the egg yolk, painting the pies with sunshine.

Now the light had nearly faded and the cooked pies gleamed under the kitchen lights. Amina touched the pies – they were cool and hard. She used the sharp knife to prise them from the silver foil and presented them nicely on the blue serving dish. She put the two small ones on her Little Mermaid plate. Again her tummy grumbled and this time, instead of ignoring it, Amina felt like spoiling her fast – she didn't care what Mummy wanted. But instead of eating one of her mini pies, she would be really clever and take one of the big ones right from the bottom. She devoured the whole thing in ten seconds, munching faster and faster, furiously wiping the stray pastry flakes sticking to her clothes. As she wiped her mouth with the end of her hijab, she looked up and saw in the dark window Daddy's reflection standing in the doorway. He put his fingers to his lips and, in reply, so did she.

III

Jennifer checked her equipment: tubes, needles, swabs, tourniquets, blood bags, all in place. She adjusted the chair's height and noted the time on the digital watch hanging from her top pocket. The headscarfed lady had told her to set up here in the annexe hut; the women, she assured her, would arrive after sunset. Jennifer had volunteered for the Ethnic Minority Phlebotomy Programme – her badge read EMPPact – because it was a good cause, and the overtime was handy. So far she had been to a black church in Wembley, a Gurdwara in Southall and now a mosque in Watford. Not that she had ever noticed, driving past on the way to the hospital, that it *was* a mosque: there weren't minarets or a dome or anything like that. Instead, it was a collection of green corrugated iron huts shaped like long, semi-circular cakes, apparently left over from the war. The annexe hut was crowded with stacked blue chairs, shelves of Arabic books and wicker baskets filled with dark red rosary beads. To Jennifer, whose mum volunteered at St Thomas More's in Pinner, it felt strangely familiar.

The Arabic singing ended and the next door huts creaked with collective movement. Jennifer was about to sip her cooling creamy tea when a middle-aged woman in an orange sari bounded up the steps while smoothing down her felt-tip-black hair. She introduced herself as Kaneez, and inquired if she was the first.

'You are,' said Jennifer in her reassuring nurse's manner.

'I wanted to make sure you hadn't gone,' said Kaneez, pulling her sparkly *dupatta* to reveal a chubby arm. Jennifer inwardly prepared herself for a troublesome vein.

'Have you donated before?'

'Oh many times. You know my blood type? *O+*.' She proclaimed proudly. 'That's very good, isn't it?'

'Yes,' she said, happy to humour the lady. 'It's very good.' She ushered her into the chair and helped her complete the health-check form. It wasn't ideal she had been fasting, she told her, but a carton of sugary water would make everything right. Kaneez drank it down in a few gulps.

'Jen-*ni*-fer,' Kaneez read slowly from the name-badge pinned to her blue scrubs, 'Jennifer, you're a doctor?'

'Nurse.'

'Married?' Pricking her donor's thumb, she shook her head.

'We don't need men, do we?'

'Just checking your haemoglobin. Might take a minute.' She dropped the blood into a testing kit and measured the results on her app. Kaneez whistled as she waited. 'All good to go,' said Jennifer, 'left arm or right?'

'Right,' she said certainly. 'I started writing with my left but my teacher in Dubai, he trained me the right way.'

'So we'll take the blood from your left?'

'No: my right is strong.' Jennifer wanted to avoid the palaver of explaining her mistake; part of her thought it might be vaguely racist to do so.

'How's the fasting?' she asked, pressing for a vein.

'Early days. Ask me in two weeks and I'll be collapsing.' Jennifer didn't need to prompt her to talk while she pushed in the needle. She learnt about Kaneez's nephew who worked somewhere in central London; he would be joining them all for late-night *sehri*.

'Oh really?' said Jennifer, easing the blood into the thirsty tube. Kaneez shot a glance at the thick, bubbling liquid.

'Oh no, I can't look.' As the blood bag filled up silently, she shielded her eyes as though from a horror movie.

'All done,' said Jennifer cheerfully, smartly taping a ball of cotton wool over the pinprick wound.

'*Alhamdulliah*,' said Kaneez, who began explaining that bloodletting originated with the Prophet, peace be upon him. 'Even Olympic athletes are doing *Hijama* now.' She threw her *dupatta* over her taped cotton ball, shaped like the sign for omega Jennifer always thought.

'Where does all the blood go?' asked Kaneez.

'Hospitals use it for transfusions, during operations usually. We're always keen to get more BME donors.'

'Maulana says we must give blood only to Muslims, but I'm sorry to say that's nonsense.'

'Really?' said Jennifer, pleased somehow that Kaneez had been so dismissive of the cleric.

'If we give non-Muslims just one pint of our blood, they will have a bit of Islam in them!'

'We don't actually label the blood Muslim and non-Muslim…'

'I know that,' she replied sharply, making Jennifer regret her tone. 'But Allah, He knows.'

Kaneez stood up awkwardly, using her good left hand for support, and rearranged her orange sari. Jennifer thanked her formally for the donation; it was so generous of her.

'My good deed for the month,' she replied, with a wink. 'Now, where are those chai girls?'

IV

'White girls are trash.'

'Trash.'

'You seen what Hazel's posted? With her arm round Tim?'

'That's *so* wrong. Where is that?'

'Paradise. Between the station and Kebab World. It's where they go on Thursdays.'

'You think Tina's seen it?'

'She doesn't follow her.'

'That *is* mental.'

'Come down here. Auntie Kaneez on the prowl.'

'Why isn't she praying with everyone else?'

'She's a bit of a weird one.'

'My grandparents died before they could find her a match even though dad and Auntie Rubina tried. She stayed with us when I was a baby but mum said she always argued.'

'I heard that's a wig...'

'...'

'Don't cough like that!'

'Sorry, sorry... this ciggie is really doing my throat in.'

'Just give it a *taste*.'

'My dad smoked a pipe. I'd sit on his knee, and he'd blow smoke in my face for a laugh. You'd get taken away for that now. Child abuse or something.'

'Yeah.'

'Wouldn't be that bad. At least I'd escape mum.'

'Just write a story about Syria. Teachers would have to report you.'

'I always liked the smell of tobacco.'

'Don't hog it all for yourself.'

'You go for it. I'm on my Airwaves.'

'Clever girl, mum will never know.'

'It's extra-strength. Gives you a real hit up your nose.'

'Alright, druggie.'

'Whatever.'

'Tina tried some real stuff with Tim once, just before they did it.'

'What?'

'Tina's as easy as GCSE RE.'

'She's *your* friend!'

'Who goes round telling everyone the morning after?'

'Well, now Hazel's after him.'

'*You* told me Tim was buff.'

'*No*. I said, *if* you like that kind of guy...'

'...buff white boy...'

'...who looks at us like we're aliens anyway.'

'I might take off my hijab at uni. Mum said she wouldn't mind. Dad wouldn't even notice.'

'Really? My parents would go ape. Just don't end up dressing like Hazel.'

'Yeah, look what she's wearing in the photo.'

'"Showing her gully," that's what my nan says.'

'I might message Tina. She does have the right to know.'

'Really!'

'They have their own hashtag – #TeamTima – even if no one uses it except her.'

'I don't know. Hazel could be stirring.'

'What would Tina say if she knew I knew Hazel had posted that photo, and I said nothing? It would be like the end of our friendship.'

'Forward the photo. Message her now.'

'But what if it's nothing, and I've gone and put a spanner in it with Tim, and she thinks it's because I'm jealous, and she never speaks to me again…'

'…and then I'm the victim because, be honest, Tina only knows I exist because you're mates.'

'And then who would you have to copy your bracelets?'

'I *told* you we saw the same advert.'

'Actually, I like it on you. Let me look at it again. Yellow band could almost be gold.'

'Aw, thank you.'

'I'm messaging her: "Probably nothing, but thought you should see this… X." What do you think?'

'Just one X?'

'Too many and she'll think I'm in sympathy mode. Keep it neutral.'

'Oooh, smart.'

'Okay. My finger's on the trigger…'

'Go on, just send it!'

'…'

'Has it gone yet?'

'Two ticks! She's online now. Must be messaging Tim.'

'I reckon she's ringing. This is a definite pick-up-your-phone-and-say-my-name-type situation.'

'*Say my name, say my name…*'

'…*Say my name, say my name…*'

'Shh. They've just finishing *namaaz*. Take the samosa basket, I'll bring the water jug. Make sure you serve the old ladies first but mind they don't take any extra home. Otherwise not everyone gets one. And only take one when everyone's eaten. Then we come back for the tea kettles.'

'Yes, *bwana*.'

'…'

'Do you have the jug?'

'Have a quick sip. Then we need to get on.'

V

Sophia turned her phone shyly towards her husband. Her ovulation app had come alive with a beating red heart. Ali Reza caressed his wife's shoulders. First, he told her, they should say their evening prayers and complete their Qur'an; they were behind schedule for the month.

'I'll bring up one of your cup-a-soups,' he said.

'Will your mum be okay?' The meat pie aroma had spread to their bedroom, and she didn't want her mother-in-law to feel snubbed.

'It's fine,' he said, pulling on his blue shorts, 'we'll go down for sehri.' He turned the brass door handle which, a few moments after he left the room, popped open leaving the door ajar. We need a proper lock, thought Sophia, retying her long black hair into a tight oval bun.

Since arriving from Orlando, Sophia had spent the year repeating her training as a primary school teacher. Life had been pretty stressful. After a tough day dealing with English kids who pretended not to understand her US accent, she would return home to help with the chores. She unloaded and loaded the dishwasher with her mother-in-law, always addressing her as *Sasuji* – a quaint term resurrected by Indian soaps. On Sunday mornings, she would mop the bathroom floors and every other weekend help Ali Reza and little Amina deep clean the fridge. She had hoped she would be able to practise her cooking but – apart from Thanksgiving, when she had insisted on preparing the halal turkey sourced from a Muslim farm near Oxford – the kitchen was out-of-bounds. 'Oh no,' Ali Reza's mother would reply to her requests to relieve her of dinner-duty, 'you must be *so* tired from those naughty kids.' Sophia's aspirational recipe books lay piled under her bed, the pages edged a grimy black.

She went to her clothes drawer to find something nice for Ali Reza. Putting aside the baby doll nightie his mother had given her for their wedding night – that was weird – she sorted through the sets of blue, grey and red underwear. Nothing inspired her. She flopped back on the bed. Looking down at the Minnie Mouse t-shirt she was wearing, the one her parents had bought for her at Disney, she felt homesick. The colours had faded in the wash: Minnie's red-and-white polka-dot hair bow was now a light pink. She needed to ration how many times she wore it.

Ali Reza pushed open the door with his foot, balancing in his hands a plate of toast – white bread, burned black, just as his family liked it – on a bowl of soup wrapped in a blue tea towel.

'Is it time?' she asked.

'It's time,' he said. She aligned two hardback recipe books on the bed, on which she balanced the watery soup and sooty toast.

After eating, Sophia put on her white *namaaz-e-chador* and Ali Reza his clean black trousers. He led her in prayer and then put the Qur'an on YouTube. As she listened to Sura al-Imran, her mind wandered, as it usually did when Qur'an was playing, to feelings she otherwise tried to supress. When it had finished, she asked her husband directly: 'Does your mom like me?'

'Why wouldn't she?'

'Sometimes I think she's only nice because you're the son who can do no wrong.' Her voice got more Floridian when she was upset.

'That's not fair. I think my mum is pretty easy to get along with.'

'Does she mind that I work?'

'She always lays into girls who don't have careers – ladies of leisure, she calls them.' They were by now lying side by side, and Ali Reza had re-started his caressing routine.

'Shut the door properly,' she insisted. He did as he was told and came back to bed, but the brass handle soon betrayed him again.

'Can't you get that old thing fixed?' She started to lose her composure. 'Please!'

'Alright, I just haven't had time,' said Ali Reza, surprised by her vehemence.

'There's no privacy here,' she cried out, pouring into this small but legitimate complaint a thousand buried slights. Smartly, he looked for something to block the door: the unwashed bowl and plate were the nearest heavy objects. After arranging them, he cautiously returned to bed.

'I like that t-shirt,' he said. 'It's your signal to me – Minnie Mouse is ready.' She giggled, though she wasn't quite ready to give up her annoyance.

'I spend hundreds of dollars on fancy bras, and all you like is this crappy t-shirt.'

'You know what I'll do,' he said, softly kissing her fingertips, 'I'll message the handyman and get the handle replaced.'

'Really?' she said, physically relaxing at his reassurance.

'And I'll bring your recipe books down to the kitchen.'

'I'm so glad I married you,' she said, with the same brilliant smile she had given him on their wedding night.

VI

Salman pushed through the green tarpaulin separating the living room from the incomplete extension. The newly-concreted floor breathed a hard coldness through his socks; a shivery wind rushed through the glassless patio doors. Salman pulled his school blazer tight, carefully fastening the single button hanging limply on strands of black thread. *Dad said he wanted everything done by Ramzan, but the builders have been so slow.* In the first week, the men had efficiently churned up half the garden, including a couple of the pear trees and the pond with the massive goldfish. *Has anyone told Amina what we did with the goldfish?* But after the first month their cheery English-speaking overseer Witold – who came in each morning with a new red-top paper that he would read slowly with his sandwiches—was around less often, and the pace of work slowed.

All the painting paraphernalia – the pots, brushes, rollers and palettes, all encrusted with magnolia drippings – was stashed in the corner. Nearby was a scrappy pile of Witold's red-tops. Salman picked one up with an air of innocent curiosity. The lead story was about a German teacher seducing a schoolboy – *Top Marks For Oral!* There was a picture of the teacher at a party, *probably taken from her Facebook*, cocktail in hand, her plump face tracked with glitter. *Who was that?* It was just his mother, going upstairs for her pre-*iftar* nap. *She would never come to this building site anyway – especially near Maghreb time. Jinn might be lurking!* The pear trees rustled in the evening wind.

Salman's conscience twinged. *Surely I should take these dirty newspapers and throw them in the bin. Such things shouldn't be in the house during Ramzan… But they belong to Witold. Maybe just leave them.* Even as his surface thoughts tripped over each other, though, a more cunning and forceful part of himself – the part that had *come sniffing* for exactly what he had found – compelled him to lick a finger and turn to page three.

Angelika, twenty-one, was a student from Austria. *She came here to learn English and find some hunky guys.* She was wearing blue eyeshadow and a slightly crooked smile. Her blonde hair cascaded *like, like a waterfall* over her breasts, which were wrapped in a specially made bikini top printed with the Union Jack (left side) and the Austrian (right side) — thereby signalling to the red-top's readers that Angelika was a *homely girl who never forgot to ring her mum,* but also *welcomed any English lads wanting to try it on.*

Salman glanced through to the garden where the sun was retreating inexorably. The other day, flicking through the ayatollah's rulings on his father's shelf, he had found that aside from eating, drinking, bloodletting, smoking and vomiting, another physical activity that would break your fast was ejaculating. This he found reassuring. *Fasting means not doing normal things, and so self-pollution, as the ayatollah called it, was probably okay after dark.*

Of course, Salman was no brute. He required the enthusiastic consent of the woman about whom he was fantasising. Angelika he imagined as his German teacher — so unlike his dumpy real one — who kept him after class for extra lessons. *Fraulein Angelika, wir haben eine Katze und einen Hund. Der Hund frisst Brot. Die Katze trinkt milch.* Impressed, she removed her blouse to reveal her bra with the two flags. Salman felt a riot starting in his head (it always began in his head), as he pulled out two handkerchiefs from his pocket.

Then he noticed the story on page two.

Muslims Demand Ritual Slaughter
By Paul Gallagher

Muslim parents in Manchester are demanding children be given burgers made with ritually slaughtered halal meat.

Burnt Edge Academy, which has seen a recent influx of refugees, has just announced the change in policy.

Said one parent, 'What's wrong with English burgers? Why don't their kids eat our meat?'

In 2017, Manchester was the scene of a sickening Islamic suicide bomb attack on a show by Ariana Grande (right) that killed 22 innocents.

The city has also seen more Muslim butchers on the high street, while traditional English meat-sellers close down.

A school spokeswoman said it was 'normal' for halal meat to be served at lunchtimes.

As he finished reading, Salman felt the pages become incredibly hot in his hands. Not stopping to even glance at Angelika, he closed the paper and put it exactly where he had found it. *Feels like kryptonite.* Right then he realised how dark it had become. Wiping his sweaty hands with his handkerchiefs, he tiptoed back to the carpeted living room from where he could see the lights from the kitchen blazing.

VII

Good job Faz sent me the link, beard feels well lush. You see guys with these beautiful long beards and you think it's dead easy. But it's hard, man. Doesn't always come out straight and smooth. It's curly and scratchy, like pubes on your chin. That was Faz's. Always chatting shit, even though he's done proper *fusha*, knows *maghazi* back to front. Few drops of zaytoun oil, Asda own brand, mix with hot water. Dip, squeeze, drip. Dip and squeeze and drip. Like stroking a sleeping cat. Cut a piece out of his mantle not to wake her. Prophet's law. Lore. Keeping up appearances. Musk and miswak. Turn to eleven o'clock. White guy, red tie. What's he looking at? Bare chinny. Like he doesn't even need to shave. I was the first in my class. Wore tracksuit bottoms in PE to cover my hairy legs. All dad said? Now your sins count, my boy. Kiraman Katibayn, the honourable recorders, weighing on my shoulders. Don't avoid eye-contact man, that's rude. I can read your thoughts. Big beard, black t-shirt, combats. Flicker of fear. Faz's essay, *The Other Boot.* Repeating history repeating. See the patterns. Taraf al-Gharb. Square's packed. Big screen. *Tosca.* Sounds like an Italian salad. Dudes in deckchairs, wrapped in silk, champagne from rainbow cups. Could not make this shit up. Why not incest? Search horny sister. Ah, here's my guy? Grey plinth. Swipe to camera. General Sir Charles James Napier. Shiny fucker. Long hair. Massive sword. Google his best quotes. Slowly: *The human mind is never better disposed to gratitude and attachment than when softened by fear. Clever guy. I have Sindh.* Funny, too. Butchered and raped with a smile on his face. The jolly crusaders. Probably a pub name. Learn from the worst. Not fanatics. Like Tony Soprano says: soldiers don't go to Hell. Big Ben tolls for thee. Mother of all parliaments. Mother of all. His last speech was shared again on Telegram. Bad-ass Saddam. First name only. Like Stalin or Beyoncé. Or Clive. Loot's an Urdu word, did you know? A Wikipedia away. Lootis? Bum-bandits. Can't even speak your own language, says Faz. Look what they did to you. Still do. Will. Peek behind the black door where it all went down. Durand, Sykes-Picot, weapons of mass. See those sleeping babies? Sweet but dead. Assad's gas. No one gives a. Moves a man to tears. Wets my beard. Deleted the video but Faz keeps sending it. Nightmare before *Fajr*. Hey, was he at Cromwell Grammar? Shabs? Something Sh. Handling a white girl. Fit as. Fit ass. Go on my son. After dark it all comes out. Especially this month. Doesn't clock me with the beard. Sixth form? Yeah, it's him. Deputy head boy. Giving head boy. On stage he was singing hymns. *Onward Christian Soldiers*. Scraps from the feast. *Rule Britannia*. Where's that coming? *Britannia rules the*. Lads on tour. *Bri-tain, never never shall be*. Sure about that? Miss a fast and free one. Easy as. Read hadith. Possessed by my right hand. Make me toast and suck my. Winston! The big man. The daddy. Face like an arse. *Our empire beyond the seas will carry on the struggle*. Pity Bengalis are starving. Empty pot-bellies. Selfie with the fat bastard? Smile, Winnie. Flash it a bit. Just a glint. And there – posted. This had better be my most liked. Faz won't. Like but not *like*. Analogue Avenger. Never sends emails. Shared account, save it in drafts. Knows his stuff. Dr Ghuraba. Desert life. Milk and dates. Mosque serves Jordan Valley for *iftar*. Ignorance is bris. Must remember to tweet that. Over there. Policeman's giving me evils. Black guy. House slave doing his master's bidding. His master's tools. Kill Bill? Chasing in the final over. No reviews. Umpire's decision is final. Finger of *tawheed*. Remember Banu Qurayza. The poet's mockery. *Fucked men of Malik and Nabit, You obey a stranger*. Yeah, but blessed are the strangers. And you're about to get fucked.

Just jogging. Innocent jogger. Knifed up. Asda, £14.99 for five. No, I don't have a loyalty card.

Look at me bare-chin. Make your tie proper bloody red. Boom! 'Tis but a flesh wound. Tourists typing. Hope they settle on a hashtag.

Keep walking. Nah, nah, nah Shabs, run away. No brown on brown. *Salaam-aleikum.*

I said salaam.

Won't you salaam a fellow Cromwell boy? Stop shouting mate, I can't hear you. Don't have time for a stop and chat. Curb your.

Call that a… This is a…

Wa-aleikum. On your way. Keyser Söze spared one to tell the tale.

Clear black light. Return of the Salaf. Badr's 313.

What you chatting, bruv?

Stupid question.

Ramzan's more blessed, innit.

***

The table was laid; the rice reheated; the curry on the cooker steamed alongside the masala chai. All Rubina had left to do was wait.

'Where are they?' she asked, as her husband Saif laid the table.

'Patience,' he said. 'In this month of all months.' He enjoyed playing the benevolent patriarch.

'For iftar, you go where you want,' she said, addressing her absent children, 'but we must all be here for sehri.'

Sophia and Ali Reza came down in their pyjamas. Rubina kissed her daughter-in-law on both cheeks. She had just been boasting to her sister Kaneez, who had come round after mosque, that she was very American in her politeness. Yes, Kaneez had replied, much better than the girls born here, breaking their fasts with cigarettes. Still, Rubina replied, she wished Sophia would rinse the plates properly before loading the dishwasher.

Amina ran straight into the kitchen and into her father's arms.

'Sweetie, would you like some toast?' Rubina asked. Her daughter ignored her. 'Or one of your special pies?' But Amina had moved on to Sophia, who began re-plaiting her hair.

Ali Reza was scrolling through the news. 'Someone's gone on a stabbing spree,' he said.

'Where?' asked Rubina instantly.

'Westminster.'

'Call your brother now,' she ordered, at the same time picking up her phone.

'Only one of us should call,' he said. She threw the phone down and switched on the television; but there was nothing on Sky.

'It's all over Twitter,' said Ali Reza, 'but sometimes people lie, for kicks.'

'I'm sure it's nothing,' said Saif.

'I'm allowed to panic!' asserted Rubina, as Kaneez took her hand in solidarity. Ali Reza put his phone on speaker, and they all heard it reach

Shawkat's impersonal voicemail. Collectively they sent WhatsApp messages, plastered his Facebook, rang his work – but still there was no answer. Sheepishly, Salman crept into the kitchen and pawed a cold meat pie. His mother knocked it from his hand: didn't he know his brother was missing?

'How would I know?' he said, feeling an obscure dread that this was all his fault.

Right then, Shawkat's key rasped in the lock; before he had even stepped in from the dark, though, he faced a barrage of angry, relieved questions. Rubina led him to the head of the table, motioning to Kaneez to bring chai. Shawkat spoke slowly. 'I'm fine. The guy let me go. He said he knew me, but I don't think so.' No, the police hadn't been in touch.

'Let them call you,' said his father. 'We don't want complications.' Shawkat told them he hadn't answered his phone because he had been looking after his friend – a colleague – who had been with him. 'She's our intern. I felt responsible.'

'Family comes first,' chided Saif.

'Don't tell him off now,' said Rubina, instinctively checking his chest and arms for damage.

So far the news had spoken only of injuries, not deaths. The attacker had been shot by police and was now under the surgeon's knife. Kaneez wondered what his blood type was.

'Why are people so angry in Ramzan?' asked Amina, looking sadly at her mother.

'Turn it off,' said Rubina, regaining her composure. 'We'll need our strength tomorrow.' One by one the family sat down together, and they ate and drank until the white thread of dawn became distinct from the black.

A DEATH SWEETER THAN HONEY

Tamim Sadikali

At last, water. One plastic cup, three-quarters full. He hands it over and a tremor assaults me, causing the surface to ripple. Instinctively my grip tightens and the plastic crinkles, the water rising to the lip. Snatching a breath I loosen my hold, my eyes locked on the cup - the roll and break, miniature waves crashing. I try to steady myself with a deep breath...but some water spills. He then smacks my hand with his baton and the cup falls.

He stares at me, the silence between us thumping in my ears. I avoid eye contact and look down, the tip of his baton on the cup, crushing it. Sweat drips into my eyes and I feel unsteady. Outside, beyond these four walls, dogs bark...and a man screams.

I force a smile, still trying to play the game. 'Your friends are having more fun than you, huh?'

'You want me to take you to them?'

Feeling light-headed I close my eyes, his words dislocated, disembodied, bouncing around my empty head. Drunk with fatigue, I laugh, 'You know you can't do that.' I mop my brow, sufficient sense returning to feel him bristle. With a rare point scored my laugh deepens before he whacks me on the knee.

I crumple, cradle myself. 'Don't get too comfortable,' he states, standing astride me. 'There's plenty I *can* do.'

I gulp for air in between waves of tropic heat. Holding my knee with both hands, sweat once again runs freely down my face.

'For you, time is running out. My bosses will soon expect answers. And if they aren't happy, we hand you over.' He stays standing over me, a bag of bones on the floor.

'So that's easy for you, then. Wash your hands of me...give your Sponsors what they want.'

'To hell with what they want. Is that what you want?'

His faux concern throws me; an unexpected move in this game. I try to process, digest his words, but that lost cup of water is now haunting me. When I make to speak, my tongue feels like sandpaper in my mouth.

'Why do you care?'

He raises his baton to strike me once more, his eyes furious.

Unable to rise, I hold up a hand. 'Stop...*please.*'

He hesitates, adjusts, then rams the butt into my stomach. Bent double I wretch, but there is nothing to expel.

'I don't care for our Sponsors...it's our country that matters,' he yells. Pain, thirst and the blast of noise crash inside my head. I keel over. He steps toward me, the cap of one boot nuzzling my body. Curled up at his feet, I can only play dead. 'And my guess is, you feel the same way. Am I right, 'Bro'?' Sniggering at his own joke he nudges me with his boot, like one might do with roadkill.

That entitlement...the surety of the well-fed lackey. It burns me now as it did as a kid, as an urchin, as a nobody. Before 'The Movement' began – all those years ago. "If you cared for our country, you'd be with us. Not propping up our enemies for thirty pieces of silver."

He withdraws his boot and meets my eyes, holding his downward gaze. I look away, readying myself for the end.

'You should know that your recipe is already cooked. For our Sponsors, you are...how do they say it...the "*main man*" '. And for a moment he is elsewhere, tickled by foreign words. The spell breaks when he catches me observing him. He expels phlegm, the glob of sputum missing my face, though mist from his spittle sprays me. 'If they weren't so interested in you, I'd have fed you to the dogs.'

'Go ahead,' I say, swallowing a mortal dread. 'You'll only strengthen The Movement.'

'And what is The Movement for? What are you fighting for?'

'Freedom. From you, your bosses and your Sponsors.'

'And what will you do with your freedom?'

'It doesn't matter. We want to be free...not under the yoke of some foreign power.'

'But I insist, what will you do, once you are free? You must have some plan, no?'

He places a foot on my head. Though he applies no pressure I instantly recoil and try to stand.

'We will build a just society. One that gives pride to the common man!'

His laugh runs deep, is unscripted – not part of this game. When re-composed his eyes seem lighter, his menace lifted, and that hurts more than the baton.

'But we were free before, no? Before the Sponsors came, bearing the gift of democracy. Did the common man have pride then?'

'Our leaders were puppets...have always been puppets.'

'And in your new dawn, they won't be? Who will you raise up? A secularist? Or someone from the clergy?'

'What matters right now, is gaining freedom.'

'But don't you get it? We've failed at freedom. We're too fucking stupid to be free. At least under a foreign yoke, we have someone to blame.'

'Enough! Just hand me over!'

Again a baritone laugh, filling these four walls. 'As you well know, our beloved nation gives few things to the world. But we excel in laying a man's soul bare. And you, my friend, have been loaned to us. To me.'

I'm on all fours, still willing my body to stand. He puts a foot on my shoulder and applies just enough pressure so I again topple.

Face up, I lay splayed out before him. 'Please, I need water.'

And for the first time, he looks unsure. 'If it was up to me, I'd kill you now.'

He blinks out of stasis and moves away, swiftly leaving the room. When he returns he holds another plastic cup, re-triggering my spasmodic response. I try again to stand, at least regulate my breathing, but nothing is within my gift. And these four walls, my torturer, The Movement – at this moment, none of it matters. I want for nothing but control over this spastic body.

He stands askance, a curious onlooker – observing my dance. He's still holding the cup and the thought of further reprisal, of him throwing it down, only heightens my body's rebellion. Placing his baton on the ground he grabs my jaw and holds the cup to my mouth. He tips it gently and I gulp, gulp and gulp again, my mind vacant, merely a valve, releasing the body's craving. He keeps tipping the cup until upside down, my tongue searching for the last drop.

I rock back, panting.

'Do you want more?'

With wide eyes I search for the terror that must surely be coming, but that I cannot yet see.

'I said, do you want more water?'

He stands still, an outstretched hand holding the empty cup. His baton remains on the floor.

'For the last time…'

'Yes…yes, please.'

He again walks out and for the first time in years, I beg for God's mercy. I look around these four walls, where I have been held. I rest up against a bathtub from which no water runs, but to which I am often chained. A slop bucket and a threadbare mattress are the only other furnishings. We are less than an hour from civilisation, but I know not where. Strobe lighting never gets switched off. I touch my shrunken face, buried under unkempt hair. Morbid thoughts threaten to take shape but quickly dissolve, the urge to sleep overwhelming me.

'Water', he states simply. Slowly, I open my eyes. Seconds pass before the full weight of my situation re-crystalises. I make to stand but again fail. He squats down in front of me, a full cup outstretched. I don't meet his eyes but, like the coward I now am, I take the cup. I drink, more slowly this time, losing myself in sensation – of ice-cold water on a burning tongue.

'Thank you', I say, placing the empty cup down. And a dread which I cannot suppress finds expression: 'so what now?'

'Well, here's what we think – you are smart. People like you; follow you. The Movement, the losses dealt to our Sponsors – you are behind it.'

My thirst somewhat abated, hunger now shreds my thoughts. I try to rise above it, as I have since my capture.

'Well?'

'It's true. All of it.'

He sits down on the floor, opposite me. 'So, what is it that you want?'

'Something to eat would be nice.'

He smiles, relaxing into his victory. 'No, what I mean is, what is The Movement really hoping to achieve?'

'I told you already – total, unqualified freedom.'

'But you must know that's impossible.'

'Then we die trying.'

'Except you, it seems. A day's thirst was enough to melt your resolve.' I look away, ashamed, and he does not hide his victory. 'Death is easier in the abstract, wouldn't you say?'

He slaps me on the knee, playfully, like he's already missing the game.

I absorb it, silently, my mind wandering. 'Have you heard the story of this King, a good King of old, ambushed by a rival in the desert?'

Rolling his eyes he puts his baton aside, decides to humour me.

'Cut off from reinforcements, the King and his small band were heavily outnumbered. For his enemy, this was the chance to end their bitter stalemate. But were the King to have submitted, sworn allegiance to his rival, he could have walked away - his life, his freedom and wealth intact. But days passed and the King did not acquiesce - he stuck to what he believed was right.'

'So, what happened next?'

'To force his hand, his access to the nearby river was cut-off, leaving him and his company without even a drop of water, under the burning sun.'

'And did it work?'

'After three days in the desert without food or water, and the King still holding firm, they were slaughtered. Starting with the King's companions, then his family, before the King himself was beheaded with a blunted knife.'

'Nice.'

'When facing certain death, the King asked one of his company, a young man, about dying — dying for his cause. And the youth answered, "Oh, King! Death like this is sweeter than honey." '

'That's a lovely story.' He faux gushes, openly mocking me. 'Shame you're no comic book hero, eh?'

'No, it really happened.'

'I'm sure it did.' Standing up he reaches for his baton and folds it under his arm. 'I'll let my bosses know you're co-operating. You can expect a meal tonight.'

'The Movement will go on. I did my best for them.'

'Well don't beat yourself up', he says, patting me on the cheek before walking to the door. 'Leave that to the experts.'

The door shuts and I hang on to his footsteps, terrified of the silence filling the space he has left.

THREE POEMS

Mosab Abu Toha

Yaffa in Winter

In the old Arab neighbourhood of Yaffa,
the hens wander along dirty streets.
A rooster cries at dawn.

Worn-out houses, naked forever,
Sag, trying to survive
like wounded men on crutches.

Electric, phone and TV cables
mingle and merge like a sprawling spider web,
unnerving migrating birds.

Outdoor drainage pipes pose
as traffic lights for stray cats and dogs,
unable to resist sniffing the ground
inhaling the stink from the gutters.

A car parks on the sidewalk
of a narrow street.
An angry teen throws a stone and cracks
his neighbour's frail A/C,
then runs away.

Yaffa's clock tower chimes ten at night.
Rimmed with fatigue, the neighbourhood
finally goes to sleep.

Waves hit pebbles on the beach
wishing the neighbourhood good dreams.

Layla saeeda. Good night. Layla saeeda.

Gazan Pigeon

My small bird sits on my left thigh,
listens to music with me on YouTube.
It tries to sing but remains mute—
numb tongue and featherless wings.

In the street,
my neighbour's child waited for
his dad many days.
He searched for him
in photo albums in months gone by.

The boy, having trained his small
carrier pigeon,
now ties his handwritten notes
to the bird's little feet
to fly and visit his father
in Negev Prison—
far away.

Palestinian Streets

My city's streets are nameless.
If a Palestinian gets killed by a sniper or a drone,
we name the street after them.

Children learn their numbers best
when they can count how many homes or schools
were destroyed, how many mothers and fathers
were wounded or thrown into jail.

Grownups in Palestine use their IDs only
so as not to forget
who they are.

WINTER ELECTION

Naomi Foyle

A grey day, bone-cold. In black coats,
red scarves, we snuffle and shift
on a pavement in suburban North London –
some brown, most white, some young,
the rest of us grizzled and lined,
a pack of aging hounds, scenting,
at last, that wild creature: hope.

As light drains from the sky
we embark on the hunt, fan out
through a tired council estate,
rattle gates, ring bells, knock on doors,
meet Jane, who 'isn't political';
Rajiv, who has views, but is
'not able to discuss them';
Dawn, who wants to know why
she's worked hard all her life
and doesn't have any money;
the Singhs, who, yes please,
take a leaflet and poster;
Hamid, who asks 'how many
MPs do I have?', and doesn't know
the one he has is the Prime Minister.

The sky spits in my face, but refrains
from sleeting contempt.
Are we hot on the tail of history,
or drag hunting fake stink?
High above, a red kite, fork-tailed,

surveys the cul-de-sac
for kitchen scrapings,
rats, mice and voles.

for Ali Milani
whose day will come

REVIEWS

BITTER AYRAN

Emre Kazim

On the right-side of my sight, at arm's distance, a restless text sits upon my bed. It agitates in a place of rest and rejuvenation, indeed a domain of solace; it disturbs me by the conjugation of the words 'Islam' 'Authoritarianism' and 'Underdevelopment'. It challenges me, my intellectual honesty and integrity, indeed by filial piety and communal loyalty. Might anything other than a polemic reveal latent doubt, even subversion, to the collective, to one's ancestry and the very real struggles of today – both political and spiritual? Better take up arms and pontificate with a rhetoric that constructs an ignorant supercilious enemy of nefarious intent. And yet, to construct is to project an image of 'self' – the true self? Such enemies would only be those that reside within me, where might I hide from them?

I am of the fortunate, insofar as in my formative years I was imbued with a deep warmth and loving faith, one potent with the demand to seek truth and realise compassion in the world around me. My suspicion is that this is the overwhelming experience of people of faith; one that reflects the love one develops towards one's parents and that which is most closely associated with them. In this vein we can think of the judgement one has towards one's tradition, where tradition is simply the world one was born into and the cultural framework of values and references cultivated within us by that very world, as simply a reflection of the experience one has with one's parents.

This experience, so emphasised by the psychoanalytic traditions, is formative and goes beyond 'good' and 'bad'. For the notions of good and bad are themselves often products of these experiences, rather than objective categories through which judgement is being made. In elementary textbooks on logic we are taught that logic is thought thinking about itself, and yet what is it to think about thought thinking about itself? To evaluate the values that are oh so arbitrary and dependent on the culmination of the forces of formation is to attempt, in the proverbial sense, to take God's eye. An eye constitutionally denied to us. As such, given that beliefs are readily explained simply by an investigation into the origins of the believer, the question posed is 'is truth possible?' A question the great al-Ghazali asked himself when in existential doubt – himself reflecting on the fact that the children of the Christians are Christian, and the children of the Muslims are Muslims. I, a Muslim, am indeed the child of Muslims. My romantic faith a reflection of the romance of those dear parents.

Ahmet Kuru, *Islam, Authoritarianism and Underdevelopment*, Cambridge University Press, 2019.

This majestic love for Islam, the source of meaning with iridescent sheen, is precisely a love with a face of my mother on it. A defence of it filial love ... Islam, was deemed a matter of honour. And yet, in this understanding there is revelation. Where the world itself is transformed in the very moment of this understanding. The universal is in the particular, insofar as our particularity, the world we were born into and the forces of our formation, is universally experienced as a rule in that all others are as accidental as we are. To understand the other, as such, is to understand that they too are a construct whose only difference is in the expression of the world of formation and forces in their existence. As such, whereas I conjugate Islam with a deep romanticism, I respect and embrace Ahmet Kuru's conjugation of Islam with authoritarianism and underdevelopment. Indeed, his brief autobiographical notes and dedication to his family, make it clear that the text comes from warmth, as dear a love as can be. It is with this that I disabuse my reactionary Self and it is also because of this that I despair at the inability of many of my co-religionists to take seriously the relationship between Islam and the depressing state of politics in the Islamicate world.

Indeed, although the non-equivalence of causation with correlation is basic, it is at the very least worthy of serious thought as to why democratic systems have not emerged in the Muslim world in more pluralistic and institutionally respected forms. His argument, as I understand it, is that through a series of historical events, the traditional thinking class, the Ulema, and the militaristic state has entered a symbiotic/co-dependent alliance. That it is this alliance that retards the emergence of a middle class, defined in terms of intellectualism, creativity and economic productivity. And that this continues till today.

The book is divided into two parts, Part I, Present, I read in terms of a conceptual framework and methodology; the second and lengthier Part II, History, I read in terms of the historical narrative. Two questions immediately arise. First: is the historical deliberately woven in order to explain the present in terms of the role of Islam, or whether Kuru came to his understanding of the present through his historical investigations? Second: why isn't this a book about Turkish Islam, exploring the understanding of Islam as it has come about through the Turkish experience? In fact, it is my contention that the book renders itself liable to broad stroke critiques by maintaining the precarious assumption that the 'Islamic world' exists.

Though, at an abstracted level, the category 'Islamic world' may have some utility, in the case of supporting an argument though a granular historical narrative, as is exhibited in Part II, the category becomes cumbersome and liable to simple, albeit effective, critique. For one, we can point to examples of scholarly communities and militaristic states aligning in the historical experience of nations that Kuru rightfully refers to as developed. A clear example of this is Aquinas, exemplified in *Summa contra Gentiles*, who birthed a Thomasitic tradition crucial to Iberian development and colonialism, that is, the alliance of scholarship with power does not straightforwardly lead to authoritarianism and underdevelopment. Second, with respect to authoritarianism the context with which Kuru is using the term is one of political power rather than authoritarianism of personality or paternalistic cultures.

This creates a greater tension with the notion of the 'Islamic world', when there is substantive and lengthy experience of Muslims living in context where they do not have 'power' with which authoritarianism can be meaningfully realised. Indeed, in the last two centuries, it is perhaps the exception (Turkey and possibly Iran) and not the rule given the history of colonialism, to speak of meaningful Muslim expression of power in the form of state structure. Furthermore, consider my position as a Muslim who is from, and writes in the context of, a majority non-Muslim nation. What is the relationship between our Islam – Muslims in non-Muslim majority states – and the question of Islam and authoritarianism and underdevelopment? Indeed, Muslims in these contexts often suffer from non-Muslim majority authoritarianism.

If we streamline Kuru's arguments as Turkish specific, the question remains as to whether Islam is fundamental to authoritarianism and underdevelopment. At this point, a tension emerges between Islam-in-essence and Islam-in-existence, where the former relates to 'true' Islam, whatever that may be, and the latter to the describable way in which people understand and practice Islam. This distinction allows us to pose more precise questions, namely, is there a negative relationship between Islam-in-essence and authoritarianism/underdevelopment? And, is there a negative relationship between Islam-in-existence and authoritarianism/underdevelopment? Whereas the former question is speculative, fortunately for me (and Kuru) the operative question is the latter, and to this question, surely the answer is wholeheartedly 'yes'. Indeed, ironically, both those who are motivated by a desire to disabuse Islam/faith from society, let's call this militant secularism, and those who are motivated by a desire to bring about an 'enlightened' faith, within which development is fostered and democratic pluralism flourishes, there is the shared assumption that Islam-in-existence-in-contemporary-Turkey is regressive. Ergo something needs to be done about the understanding of Islam. Importantly, this allows us to remain agnostic with respect to the essential truth of Islam. Instead the shared premise is that a toxic matrix exists of the current understanding of Islam-in-existence and authoritarianism/underdevelopment and so we ask ourselves whether this is a description and factual claim about the world as it is.

By construing the core intuition in this way as an observation that something needs to be done about a regressive state of affairs, a number of interventions are possible. Kuru's intervention is to say that Islam in its current existence is the problem and the medicine is implied in the diagnosis, that is, tear the alliance between the religious thinking class and state/political regimes. The historiographic form of his argument I read as underpinned by a desire to emancipate - genealogy as revealing that the current state is contingent and historical, rather than necessary and metaphysical. More explicit it is a position that Islam is not necessarily allied with authoritarianism.

This intervention is explicitly a political act – Kuru speaks from the subjectivity of a nation where historical truth is the battle field that confers legitimacy. In this sense, it is myth-making and note that I use this term in a neutral non-pejorative sense, with the purpose of affecting the world of 'meaning'. By meaning I am referring to the value system of people. If Kuru is effective, by altering this meaning a new reality will come about, a reality conducive to his emancipatory and pluralistic vision for society. While it would be beyond the remit of this review to survey theories of social causation, Kuru's arguments lean heavily on the notion that meaning, read as ideas, beliefs, values, is the centre of social agency. In other words, that a change in the value system (bought about by cleaving the Ulema-State nexus) will be reflected in a (positive) change in state structure and development. The principal contention is that the cause-effect here of regressive Islam (cause) – authoritarianism/underdevelopment (effect) can readily be inverted, showing regressive Islam as an effect of authoritarianism/underdevelopment.

Because of this, from a methodological perspective, should it be the case that Kuru is committed to a straightforward view that meaning is the agency of social causation, then I would read Kuru's work as a polemic. Indeed, a principle reason why the text is so difficult to satisfactorily critique is because there is a tension between Kuru the academic (the historiographer, Part II) and Kuru the activist (Part I). Kuru the academic is scholastic, tempered, and precise. Kuru the activist is sweeping, polemic and rhetorical. This is a precarious position rendering the text unstable, however, it is also the reason why the text challenges the community of scholars (get out of the academy!) and the community of activists (be diligent in your historical knowledge and claims!) so much. It is also why the polemic is forgivable – leveraging his academic credibility, his own subjectivity, and the current reality of politics in his home nation, I read Kuru as focusing our attention on the structures of thought itself.

At this point, it is necessary to address the elephant in the room – the book is a political commentary on the situation in Turkey as it stands. Indeed, strong reactions to this text are almost certain because they have been read precisely in this vein. Not only a commentary but a call for change. Only Kuru can explicitly state this, however, allowing myself the liberty of reading the text in his vein, I enthusiastically celebrate Kuru's intervention.

HER STORY

Samia Rahman

When I picked up Hossein Kamaly's beautifully bound *A History of Islam in 21 Women*, my subconscious mind attempted to dismiss the title as a potential foray into harem politics. Such thoughts are borne out of a, possibly unjustified, weariness of the endless hand-wringing over the 'woman question' in Islam. Fetishised, pitied, prized and always needing to be delivered from the clutches of someone or other's oppression, Muslim women are endlessly reduced to caricatures. Their victim status has become a cloak for the dagger of neo-colonial interventions in the Muslim world under the guise of 'saving' exotic damsels in distress. The men from whom said Muslim woman must be saved are demonised while the project to bring her to salvation is an assertion of the supposed moral superiority of liberal western values that seem to so narrowly define that very construct we label 'freedom'. With this in mind, I wondered how, in the context of history, contested female bodies would fare in this book. Would their stories be mere appendages to the postulating male characters who have, since time immemorial, monopolised Islamic discourse? Or will these women be given a voice with which to articulate each and every one of their unique and individual lived experiences?

It wasn't long before any such fears were allayed. Upon opening the pages it became clear that, mindful of the way in which the language of power is gendered, Kamaly skilfully and sensitively negotiates the matrix of history, gender and language through the lived realities of 21 remarkable Muslim women. The result is a rich, vibrant and meticulously researched exposition that instinctively unpacks the intersectional context Muslim women have occupied from the sixth century to the present day. Each profile illustrates prestige hierarchy at play, highlighting the importance of the role of female protagonists in Islamic history. Acknowledging that Islamic history has long been marked by gendered and racialised exclusion,

Kamaly makes a concerted effort at redress: 'Legions of male writers of women's biographies, both from within Islamic societies and later the foreign Orientalists gazing from the outside, have shared unexamined, misogynistic, and self-contradictory assumptions about the nature of women. Their tainted premises are intellectually untenable and sometimes psychologically disturbing. For example, dismissing women's agency.'

Hossein Kamaly, *A History of Islam in 21 Women*, OneWorld, London, 2019

Kamaly also steers clear of becoming the kind of champion of Muslim women who denounces the cultures, traditions and beliefs of the Muslim world into which he was born, in a loathsome flourish that would only serve to fuel Islamophobia and do little to inspire introspection. Taking seriously the responsibility that comes with being a male academic writer of women's biographies, Kamaly, who is Associate Professor of Islamic Studies at Hartford Seminary and scholar of the Middle East focusing on the history of ideas, rises to the challenge, alert to the pitfalls he must necessarily avoid.

The premise of the book was borne out of a discussion about women as agents of historical change, during which he was informed of the existence of BBC Radio 4 'Woman's Hour' presenter Jenni Murray's *A History of Britain in 21 Women*. This tome selects the biographies of 21 pioneering women pivotal to our understanding of British history. Why just 21 women? The number is a nod to the 21 centuries of history the Gregorian calendar has allotted global society so far. Any number is arbitrary but this seemed appropriate enough. Recognising that writing about women in Islam, or women and Islam, or Islam's relationship with women, and so forth, was a minefield but also necessary, he set out to conquer the task with a sensitivity, intellectual voracity and enthusiasm that may well have been missing if attempted by a less holistic scholar.

Compelled by an awareness that gendered histories have the consequence of shaping practises we accept today to be irrefutable positions, Kamaly was aware that with any limit on the innumerable women he could choose to profile, there would be omissions. However, he was also careful not to ease into predictability in his choices. The female voice has for too long been obscured by male scholars who continue to dominate Islamic studies, particularly lauded when it comes to Islamic jurisprudence and scholarship from which the sharia is seemingly derived. Yet, as Kamaly illustrates with his work, these fields of study have an increasingly diminishing centrality to our contemporary understanding of Islamic traditions. Reportage, biography and forensic re-appraisal of the tools that have contributed to the construction of history can offer a more relevant insight into the practices of Muslims around the world, in a way that dismantles the choke-hold of patriarchy.

This was also not destined to be a book that lionises Muslim women by measuring their significance in terms of piety. Having said that, of course it is no surprise that the first, longest and most detailed of the biographies is of Khadija, the first wife of the Prophet Muhammad. She was, after all, the first believer after him. Her support of her husband in his anguish at the burden of revelation, along with her influence as she stood by his side as his monogamous wife for 25 years, is indisputable. She is revered as the 'Mother of the Believers', but was also a successful businesswoman in her own right, a widow who by some accounts may even have been 40 years old when she proposed to the 25 year old Muhammad. Kamaly casts doubt on the exact age, but that she was older than her husband is without question. Her inclusion in the series of 21 profiles is not just a re-hash of all that we already know. It re-asserts her agency in the story of Islam and Kamaly shines a spotlight on her singular achievements. As one of the most important women in Islam, revered and adulated, she is emblematic of the way in which women continue to navigate their contexts. Meccan society was riven with contradictions when it came to gender equality, with female infanticide rampant and the prevailing attitude that women were inferior. However, as Kamaly explains:

> more women than men in Mecca could read and write, and, importantly, could own wealth and property as Khadija certainly did. As both her mother and father belonged to influential branches of the Quraysh, Khadija had capital, connections, children and honour. She was strong, wise and independent, and men and women answered to her.

Introducing his collection of biographies with Khadija makes perfect sense, because what Kamaly sets out to do is embark upon a representation of the formation of Islam. And this undoubtedly begins with Khadija. She is not the only member of the Prophet's immediate family to feature. His daughter Fatima and his young wife Aisha, who he married after Khadija's death, are also included. The two women found themselves on differing sides at one of the most critical junctures in Islamic history, the Battle of Camel. The schism that emerged out of the bloody spectacle evolved into the Sunni-Shia divide, which has impacted the Muslim world since.

Aisha, who was educated and intellectually curious, proved a proficient chronicler of the life and times of the Prophet and the immediate aftermath of his death. Her narrations, despite being presented via a patriarchal lens, became authoritative sources for future generations of Muslims. For some believers, she is a contentious figure. Aspersions upon her character and swirling rumours questioning her loyalty characterise the chatter that surrounds her, possibly because she was feisty and strong-willed. Kamaly does not shy away from such controversies. In fact, his choice of 21 biographies includes women who, to my delight, may well raise eyebrows among self-appointed members of the Muslim morality police.

With such an abundance of pioneering Muslim women to choose from, singer Umm Kulthum, who mesmerised audiences with her melodic voice for five decades, soothing a demoralised Arab world after the Six-Day War of 1967, was a pleasant surprise. Trail-blazing architect Zaha Hadid, whose untimely death in 2016 left a gaping void in the field of radical mega architecture, was another genius addition. However, both these women did not base their identities on their Muslim origins. As is the case with many Muslims around the world, their Muslim-ness did not follow a conservative trajectory of outward rituals and pieties. Similarly, the inclusion of Noor Inayat Khan, a spy working for allied forces during the Second World War, brought up in Europe and born to Indian and American parents, is representative of the fragmented identity complexities Muslims negotiate in the increasingly globalised context of the twenty-first century.

It is the manner in which Kamaly utilises his profiles as a means of speaking of wider geopolitical issues that Muslims are confronted with, that is one of the strengths of the book. He has compiled more than a series of nice, neat potted histories of admirable women, but is the author of a coherent narrative of what it means to be a Muslim woman through the shifts of time. The spectre of patriarchy lurks in these lives, indeed in all our lives. This is no better illustrated than in the chapter dedicated to Tajul-Alam Safiatuddin Syah, titled Diamonds Are Not Forever.

Sultana Tajul-Alam Safiatuddin Syah was born in 1612 and succeeded to the throne of Aceh Darussalam at the age of twenty-nine. A widow, her reign was characterised by skilful diplomacy and support of Islamic scholarship. Her negotiations with the West Dutch India Company on settling a debt incurred by her ostentatious and jewel-enamoured late husband proved a deft strategic move. Three consecutive female rulers followed, but eventually the local male elite, the ulema, put an end to female succession by invoking the hadith that 'those who entrust their affairs to a woman will never know prosperity'. Contrast this with the long-time ruler of Yemen, Queen Arwah who was endorsed by the ulema. She founded a number of notable mosques and had the khutbah proclaimed in her name, one of only two female monarchs in the Muslim Arab world to be bestowed such an honour.

Kamaly's biographies are deliberately diverse and non-partisan. Sectarianism, theological judgements or knotty issues of *fiqh* are in the landscape of some of these narratives but are only part of the framework. What these women represent is the course of global Islam, freed from the airbrushing effect of patriarchy. After all, as the book demonstrates, women's history is human history.

ET CETERA

ON 8 MINUTES AND 46 SECONDS

Hassan Mahamdallie

'I can't breathe'.

'Please'.

'Mama'.

'I'm about to die'.

'Please, the knee in my neck, I can't breathe.'

'Mama'.

'Mama'.

'My stomach hurts, my neck hurts, everything hurts'.

'Water'.

'Please, I can't breathe'.

'Don't kill me.'

'Did they fucking kill him?'

2020: The Year That Answered

In the days following the murder of George Floyd, Black Lives Matter protests take place in 2,000 cities and towns in all 50 states of the USA. Protests also occur around the world, in over 60 countries, across every continent except Antarctica. In Nairobi, protesters also demonstrate against extra-judicial killings by Kenyan police. In Lagos, BLM marchers also highlight the murder of a 16-year-old girl, suspected of being killed by Lagos State Police Command officers. In Capetown they also march against the death of a local man at the hands of soldiers. In Tokyo they highlight a beating by police of a Kurdish man living in the city. In Bangkok they hold banners stating 'I can't breathe' and protest the disappearances of Thai anti-regime activists. In Haifa they also march in protest at the death of an Ethiopian-Israeli shot by Israeli police in 2019. Across France BLM marchers highlight the campaign for justice for Adama Traoré, a 24-year-old Malian French man asphyxiated in police custody in 2016. In Reykjavik protestors observe 8'46" of silence against racism in Icelandic society. In Madrid protesters also highlight the death of a local African street vendor after a police raid in 2018. In Kingston, Jamaica people gather outside the US embassy to demand justice for both Floyd and Jamaicans killed by law enforcement. Protests break out in towns and cities across the UK. In Bristol demonstrators pull down the statue of slaver Edward Colston and dump it in the city harbour.

The global waves of anger throw regimes, governments, state and regional institutions, law enforcement agencies, multinational businesses, sporting, cultural and educational organisations on the defensive. 'Virtue signalling' – defined as 'a conspicuous but essentially useless action ostensibly to support a good cause but actually to show off how much more moral you are than everybody' becomes all the rage across government and business, as those in positions of power scramble to appease anger at their complicity in sustaining and perpetuating racial inequalities and discrimination. As Harlem Renaissance luminary Zora Neale Hurston wrote in her 1937 novel *Their Eyes Were Watching God*: 'There are years that ask questions and years that answer.'

London 1993 – 1998. The Years of Questions (but few answers)

On 22nd April 1993 black teenager Stephen Lawrence and his friend Duwayne Brooks were ambushed at a bus stop in Well Hall Road, Eltham, south-east London, by a group of young white racists one of whom shouted 'What, what nigger'. Duwayne managed to escape his attackers, all of whom were local to the area, but Stephen was caught, surrounded and knifed to death.

The failure of the police to catch the killers in the hours and days following the murder is well documented. The killers were allowed to escape to their nearby houses, construct alibis, dispose of the murder weapon (that has never been found), destroy clothing and other evidence and set about intimidating witnesses. Much later it was revealed that the killers had also quite likely colluded through family criminal connections with corrupt police officers in an effort to shield themselves from arrest.

The growing realisation that the police investigation into the murder of Stephen Lawrence was heading for failure, with the fear there would be an escalation of racist attacks and killings in that part of south-east London, catalysed a campaign in support of Stephen Lawrence's parents, Doreen and Neville, and their insistence on justice.

The police reacted precisely as they had done in past similar circumstances – they denied any racial motive in the killing (leading to the dismissal of vital information and intelligence), they planted undercover police spies in the family campaign, and sought to paint anti-racist campaigners as criminals and the 'real problem'.

The scandal of the police racism and corruption that dogged the murder inquiry, would, thanks to the determination of Doreen and Neville, many years later, come back to haunt the Metropolitan Police and provoke a national reckoning on racism in British society and the institutions of the State. But in the immediate years following Stephen's murder, his family faced an uphill, seemingly hopeless, battle for justice.

Shortly after Stephen's murder in 1993, I began work as a journalist on a weekly socialist newspaper. I had for a long time been an anti-racist activist, and so it was logical that one of the areas assigned to me to report on was race – covering Black history and politics, far-right and state racism and campaigns against racial attacks and injustice.

There was plenty to do. The country had been under Tory rule for fourteen long years. During that time there had been a quickening of state racism, set in motion by Margaret Thatcher, who had promised her supporters that she would deal with 'the enemy within', including the trade unions and rebellious Black communities. The police were to be 'Maggie's boot-boys' and let off the leash. In 1984–85 they had been used to beat the coal-mining communities into submission. The riots of 1981 and 1985 showed how the police acted as an army of occupation in the multiracial and multicultural areas of the inner cities, daily dealing brutal racism out to Black people, including indiscriminate stop and search, fitting up Black men for crimes they didn't commit and murdering them in custody. It was the death of Cynthia Jarrett during a police raid on her north London house that sparked the Broadwater Farm uprising in October 1985. The Tory persecution of asylum seekers also climbed through their years in office, eventually building an inhumane edifice of state racism including barbed wire-surrounded detention centres staffed by private security firms, filled by snatching whole families for deportation. (A policy enthusiastically continued by the New Labour government that came to power in 1997).

Violent deaths of Black people and other minorities in police or prison custody were a constant during the Tory years, and very quickly I found myself reporting on one atrocity after another. A recurring feature was the thrusting into the public arena of the grieving family members whose loved ones had been killed in the most horrific circumstances.

I can't pretend to begin to comprehend what these family members went through. But I could (and still can) see the pain and grief, anger and incomprehension, reflected in their eyes and etched on their faces. And then the realisation that their right to know the truth, and to pursue justice, would be denied them at every step. That the British state had rendered the killers of their loved one untouchable, far out of reach of the justice which the rest of us are subject to. And finally, that those with power had decided that the life of their brother or sister, son or daughter, did not matter.

I observed time and again this cruel, arrogant, amoral, relentless process set in motion by the police and the criminal justice system, to continually humiliate and then obliterate the families and so render them without hope. So, it was always a marvel to me, that despite all this, family members fought to preserve their personal integrity, desire for peace, dislike of violence, and conviction that the biblical command 'Do unto others as you would have them do unto you' was for them the very foundation of a civilised existence.

I can vividly recall the goodness that radiated from Myrna Simpson. Her daughter was Joy Gardner (official date of death 1 August 1993) whose shocking death came as the result of an immigration raid on her north London flat by the Metropolitan Police's Aliens Deportation Group. In the presence of her five year-old son, Joy was bound with cuffs and leather straps and gagged with 13-foot length of adhesive tape wrapped around her head. Unable to breath she collapsed, having suffered irreversible brain damage due to asphyxia. Taken to hospital, she was placed on life support but was pronounced dead after a cardiac arrest four days later. In 1995, three of the police officers involved stood trial for Gardner's manslaughter, but all were acquitted. The authorities refused to hold an inquest into Joy's death.

As Benjamin Zephaniah bitterly observed in his poem 'The Death of Joy Gardner':

Let it go down in history
The word is that officially
She died democratically
In 13 feet of tape.

Throughout the years following Joy's death, Myrna, a small, round, big-hearted elder blessed with a Jamaican accent and loud voice, could be relied upon to arrive at every protest and public meeting following the latest death in custody. We would sometimes chat (she would chat to one and all), she would express her outrage and sympathy, talk about Joy, seek out the family involved and give her support. Typically she would have a plastic bag with whatever she needed for the day, including a 13 foot roll of material, that, when asked to speak she would have people unfurl, as a visual symbol of the mediaeval brutality the police had meted out to her daughter. A sweet lady, Myrna had some steel in her, because after having fought and lost a prolonged legal battle for Justice for Joy, she set about raising her daughter's son Graeme, who is now in his thirties.

Just absorb for a second the fact that, despite the hundreds of Black deaths in custody in the UK going back to the 1950s, not one police officer has ever been brought before a British court and successfully prosecuted for manslaughter, let alone murder. This has bred a culture of impunity in the police's ranks.

Going right back to 1970, the two sadistic Leeds police officers who subjected David Oluwale to what has been described as 'the physical and psychological destruction of a homeless, black man', before chasing him towards the River Aire, where his body was found two weeks later, escaped with just minor assault convictions. The trial judge, having described

Oluwale to the court as 'a dirty, filthy, violent vagrant', directed the jury to find them not guilty of the charge of manslaughter.

During my time as a reporter through the 1990s, I came to realise that each violent death in custody, and the political and judicial events it set in motion, tended to follow a similar pattern.

As with David Oluwale, the deadly encounter with the police would tend to happen at night. The victim's family would find out that something serious had occurred, maybe via an eyewitness at the scene, sometimes via the press, or a knock on the door by police officers. Sometimes the family, having found their loved one was missing, would set out to search for them. They would call friends, try to pinpoint where and when they had been seen last, ring hospital accident and emergencies, and finally with dread in their hearts go to the police to ask who was banged up in the cells. This search could take hours or even days.

This was the case with the death of Brian Douglas. One afternoon I received a message from activists in south London, that there would be a demonstration outside Kennington police station in protest at the death in custody of a local African-Caribbean man. When I arrived, there was a line of police guarding the entrance to the station, facing off local people and the family of the dead man. I spotted a young Black man with a beard and green eyes. In soft spoken, and what I can only describe as respectable tones, he was attempting to liaise with the police to prevent the situation escalating. This was Brian's brother Donald. There were a small group supporting a clearly devastated young white woman, Brian's long-term girlfriend Rochelle.

The police guarding the station were hard-faced, cocky and dismissive of the scenes of grief before them. This attitude began to enrage those protesting, but the appearance of a weeping older Jamaican woman on the concrete ramp leading into the police station, stopped everyone in their tracks. It was Jasmin, Brian's mother, who had been in Jamaica when she had received a phone call from her daughter Brenda telling her that something terrible had happened, that 'her baby' Brian was lying in hospital, being kept alive by life support, and that she should come back to London on the next flight before the doctors switched off the equipment. Jasmin, a devout Baptist churchgoer, wholly wedded to religious peace, calmed the crowd, thereby denying the police what they clearly wanted; a punch-up on film and some more Black men in the cells they could point to as violent, dangerous and lawless – just like Brian was.

Except Brian Douglas was the opposite of the racist stereotype thrust upon him by the police in their subsequent efforts to smear him, as a crude justification for his death at their hands. He was a well-liked and well-regarded respectable guy, from an upstanding working-class Jamaican family, who made a living as a boxing promoter. His family described how he loved dressing up, going out and having fun. On 3 May 1995, Brian, after a celebratory night out with a friend, and on his way home, was confronted by two Metropolitan Police officers armed with newly issued 22 inch US-style side-handed batons, of the type that had been used by LAPD officers to beat down Black motorist Rodney King in 1991. (The later acquittal of the LAPD officers involved, despite the incident being filmed, sparked six days of rioting in Los Angeles during which 63 people were killed).

One of the police, PC Mark Tuffey, later testified that he believed Brian was a threat and that he struck him with his baton in self-defence. Tuffey said he had aimed for Brian's upper arm but the baton had (somehow) slipped upwards and hit Brain's neck. This was disputed by eye-witnesses, themselves backed by medical experts, who testified that Tuffey had in fact delivered a downwards blow on the back of Brian's head, fracturing his skull and damaging his brain stem. The force of the blow was later estimated as being the equivalent of Brian being dropped 11 times his height, head first, onto the ground.

Brian was arrested, taken to Kennington Police station, processed as being drunk and drugged, denied medical treatment and thrown in a cell, where he lay alone and untreated for 15 hours, as paralysis from irreversible brain damage spread through his body. Eventually someone must have realised Brian should be taken to hospital, where after drifting in and out of consciousness, and asking his siblings to take him home, he eventually succumbed to his injuries on 8 May 1995. He was 33 years old. He died before his mother Jasmin could get to his bedside.

The police top brass, their lawyers and the Police Federation representing Tuffey and his fellow officer, embarked on a concerted strategy of denial and obstruction from the get-go. Their legal costs, running maybe into millions of pounds, were paid by the state, whereas the family had no recourse to public funds to hire lawyers to represent their interests. The police reluctantly released evidence they had to the family. They also fed disinformation and lies about Brian to friendly journalists who published it in the right-wing newspapers. This was a common technique by police spin-doctors. The aim was to murder Brian's reputation, to soften up public opinion in order to play the law and order card. They declined to take any disciplinary action against the officers, and lined up the Crown Prosecution Service, who announced that no charges would be laid against PC Tuffey and his colleague PC Paul Harrison. The remaining hope for the family was that an inquest jury would deliver a verdict of 'unlawful killing' and open up another path to justice for Brian.

During this time I reported on a number of inquests at Southwark Crown Court, then presided over by the fantastical figure of Sir Montague 'Monty' Levine. By the mid-1990s Monty Levine was in his 70s and in the twilight of his career. Born in Moss Side, Manchester, of poor East European Jewish parentage, he first made a career as an industrial chemist before switching to medicine, working as a General Practitioner and then becoming an eminent surgeon specialising in anatomy. He served as coroner to the Inner South London district from 1987 until 1997, presiding over as many as 500 inquests a year in an area covering the multiracial boroughs of Lewisham, Lambeth and Greenwich. Many cases of violent police deaths in custody were placed at his door.

Levine was known as a liberal by reputation, having once served as private physician to Labour leader Lord Callaghan. He was an eccentric, with his long wavy hair, large handlebar moustache, bushy eyebrows, and flamboyant dress sense featuring a broad-brimmed hat, a fresh flower in his lapel and succession of psychedelic patterned waistcoats. He favoured vintage Jaguar cars and was known to visit the scene of death in the small hours to deduce whatever he could Sherlock Holmes-style. He was courteous in manner, known to buck the process and ask awkward questions in cases involving the police. But what was the Douglas family to make of Levine when they arrived at the coroner's court in August 1996? He must have seemed to be a figure from a very distant past. What would he know of the relations between the police and the local population?

The inquest is a quasi-judicial entity that has its roots in twelfth century English common law. It is convened to investigate sudden, unnatural and unexplained deaths. The coroner has a lot of leeway – for example in cases of unnatural death while in the custody of the state, he can arraign a jury to hear the evidence and help him make judgement. But an inquest is not an adversarial court that determines blame, guilt or innocence – its purpose is only to confirm the identity of the deceased, the place and time of death and how they came by their death. It is not designed to be a vehicle for justice or a democratic holding to account, although the Douglas family and their lawyers were aware that if the inquest returned a verdict of unlawful killing, the Crown Prosecution Service would be forced to reopen the criminal case against the police officers.

I remember sitting in the public area of the coroner's court, watching Sir Monty Levine go about his business. He seemed to want to signal a number of things – that he was empathetic towards the family, that he wanted to be 'fair' to all parties, that he was prepared to somewhat stretch the boundaries of the inquest on occasion, but that ultimately he would rule as he saw fit. Whether he succumbed to pressure from the police, or was simply outflanked by the police lawyers, I do not know. But he made two concessions that tilted the outcome in the police's favour. Firstly he allowed a majority of the jury to be drawn from the citizens of Eltham, the majority white area in outer south-east London known to have a high level of racism and pro-police attitudes. Stephen Lawrence had been murdered in neighbouring Welling. It was a demographic far removed from the multicultural community Brian had been a part of. Secondly, Levine allowed the police lawyers to reveal to the jury a selective account of Brian's past encounters with the law. This was important to the police's argument that the officers had acted purely in self-defence, faced with a 'dangerous' Black man. I remember Brian's family exploding in anger at this dirty move.

If I recall correctly, the police lawyers told the jury that Brian had a record for carrying an offensive weapon. But in a break in the proceedings I found out that not only had the offence taken place in his distant youth, it said much, much, more about the police as a racist institution than it did about Brian's supposed character . The offence has arisen when police had stopped and searched Brian, and found on him a metal afro-comb, popularly used by Black kids at the time as a fashion accessory. This was the 'offensive weapon'. In other words, it demonstrated not that Brian was a criminal, but, as with many of his generation, that he had been criminalised.

Despite the efforts of the Douglas family lawyers, the inquest jury went with the police version of events and concluded that Brian has died as a result of 'misadventure'. The verdict meant that Brian had been legally killed by police going about their lawful business. Yes, something unexpected had gone wrong during the encounter, resulting in Brian being fatally wounded, but the officers could not be held accountable. Levine added a rider to the verdict, that the Met Police should review their baton training. The Met said they would think about it. The Douglas family then publicly demanded the release of Brian's brain, which the Crown Prosecution had been keeping back for 'further investigation'.

When I first saw the video of George Floyd and heard his desperate cry, 'I can't breathe', it triggered a memory in me: 'Let me up, let me up. I can't breathe. You win!'

But this was not Minneapolis 2020, this was south London 1994.

Just nine months before the Douglas inquest, I had reported on another inquiry into a violent death in police custody presided over by Montague Levine. How had Richard O'Brien, a 37-year-old market trader and father of seven, met his end? The details, as they unfolded, shocked me. It was the random, casual nature of the violence he had suffered, that stood out.

It was the evening of Sunday 3 April 1994, and O'Brien was standing quietly outside an Irish community hall in Walworth, south London, waiting for his wife and 14-year-old son to join him, so they could all get a taxi home. A police van pulled up, and three officers, Richard Ilett, Gary Lockwood and James Barber, got out. They had been called to the premises after a report of a fight inside. But this had nothing at all to do with Richard. Yet for some reason the police zeroed in on Richard and set about arresting him. The three pulled him to the ground. They pinned him face down to the pavement, pulled his hands behind his back and cuffed him. PC Illet knelt on Richard's back and kept it there. Richard's son heard his father say, 'Let me up, let me up, I can't breathe. You win.'. One of the officers replied, 'We always win'. Richard's son begged them to check his father, who had gone silent. Within 10 minutes of first contact with the police Richard was dead. The police dragged his limp body to the back of the van and roughly pulled him in. 'We can't get the big fat paddy in' one was heard to complain. For good measure the police then arrested Richard's wife Alison and two of her children, including her 14-year-old son, but not before also giving him a good slapping.

I remember very well Richard's widow Alison, a small woman with close-cut grey hair, who sat quietly, with gathered composure, through the two-week inquest. The police officers attempted to argue that Richard was drunk and disorderly, and that, despite plentiful eyewitness and forensic evidence to the contrary, that they had treated him with nothing but compassion. It seemed to me at the time a lackadaisical defence. Perhaps the police assumed that no-one in the jury would care enough about the life of a lowly Irish market trader enough to find against them.

A special report by human rights organisation Amnesty International later summarised Richard's injuries:

> The pathologist instructed on behalf of the Coroner conducted a post-mortem and found that Richard O'Brien had 31 sites of injury to his body, including cuts and bruises to his face, a dislodged tooth, fractured ribs, and torn muscles. None of the officers involved were able to advance any explanation for the findings of physical injury. The pathologist gave the cause of death as 'postural asphyxia following a struggle against restraint'.

The inquest jury delivered a verdict of unlawful killing. The Crown Prosecution Service then had to explain how was it that they had already decided there was insufficient evidence to bring any charges against the officers responsible for Richard's death. Two years later Dame Barbara Mills, the Director of Public Prosecutions, was forced to concede that her decision not to prosecute in the O'Brien case was unlawful, after she was forced to disclose an internal memorandum which revealed her judgement had been based on the police accounts alone.

The three officers were eventually put on trial in 1999, accused of manslaughter. But they were acquitted after their defence argued that Richard had died because he had an enlarged heart, not because of what the officers had done to him. (The family of George Floyd take note). Eight years after her husband's death, Alison and her children were awarded £340,000 in compensation from the Metropolitan Police. However, the police top brass flat out refused to apologise to her.

In September 1998 a young black man in a jacket and tie stepped forward to address a public meeting against police racism held in south London's Brixton that I was reporting on. The audience had already heard from Myrna Simpson and others. I had not seen this man before. He introduced himself as Kwesi Menson, and proceeded to lay out the truly shocking account of his brother Michael's death and the seemingly unbelievable events that followed. Kwesi spoke in rather posh tones, and I later found that he, his brother Michael and his sister Essie, were the children of a Ghanaian diplomat.

Looking in my reporters' notebook now, I can see how my notes switched from short quotes from previous speakers to long verbatim passages covering five pages. 'I was woken one evening beyond 2 am by some police officers' my notes begin.

Kwesi explained how at 2 am on the morning of the 28 January 1997 he had been woken by the police. Officers told him that his 30-year-old brother Michael, (full name Michael Tachie-Menson) a former musician with once prominent '80s band Double Trouble, had been found by motorists staggering along the North Circular Road, Edmonton, north London, flames leaping from his back. By the time police arrived the horribly injured Michael was almost naked, his clothes leaving a burning trail across the road as they melted and dropped off him. Michael had massive burns to his back, torso and buttocks. Kwesi then told how, when he rushed to see his brother in hospital Michael had been lucid: 'When we saw him he was lying on his back, he was alert and the hospital staff had done a good job minimising the pain and he was able to talk to us'. Michael spoke to his brother, saying that 'four white lads, they set my back on fire-why did they do this to me?' Kwesi recounted how, 'I was shocked and urged them [the police] to come and take statements'. He then explained how the family had 'told everybody' at the hospital what Michael had said and asked why the police had not even taken a statement. Kwesi recalled that, 'one of the sisters said she would be contacting the police and urge them to come down directly. She was shocked and angry'. He explained how subsequently a police officer had come to the hospital, but had 'indicated he wasn't going to ask any questions and he left the room'. Michael slipped into a coma and two weeks later died of what a pathologist would describe at his inquest as 'multi-organ failure as a result of severe burns'. No statement had been taken from the dying, but initially conscious, man.

Of the police Kwesi told the shocked Brixton audience, 'from the outset I asked for a thorough investigation and I was assured that was the case'. Kwesi's Brixton speech came just days before the inquest into his brother's death opened in Hornsey Coroners Court in north London. The questions that would be raised during the inquest were: had Michael Menson been failed by the police because of racist assumptions that officers had made about him from the moment of their first contact with him? Had the officers approached Michael in the same way as the officers involved in the Stephen Lawrence case had done? What if Michael Menson had been white and smartly turned out – would he have been treated differently?

The inquest opened in north London on 7 September 1998. I was there throughout. I didn't honestly know whether Kwesi's insistence that his brother had been set alight by racists was right, but what I did know from previous experience was that what family members said had happened, most often turned out to be the truth. On the first day the national and regional press were all there, but their interest quickly waned. Most assumed the police account was correct, so by the third day there was just me and one or two others in the press seats.

From the outset the police strongly argued that there was no evidence of a crime and therefore no crime scene had been established, and no forensics had taken place, and that Michael Menson, in a mentally-ill state, had most likely set fire to himself in a crazed suicide attempt.

This was the view of WPC Johanna Walsh in her evidence to the inquest. She was on night duty in an unmarked car when she heard the call for an ambulance to attend Michael. When she arrived she found a Black man 'burnt all over his shoulders, down his back, side of the body and the top of his buttocks'. Walsh said that Michael 'behaved as if he were in a trance. When I arrived at the scene I had an open mind' she testified, but then she began to believe he was mentally ill. 'I came to that conclusion', Walshe added, 'I didn't believe at the time he knew what he was saying'.

However, this was not the assumption of others who went to Michael's aid. David James, an off-duty fire-fighter based in the West Midlands, was driving along the North Circular when he spotted flames. He was shocked to see that they were emanating from a man, who, by the time he saw him, was naked apart from his socks. James helped the police who arrived first and assisted the paramedics. James, under questioning from the police legal team, was firm that 'it didn't cross my mind that he [Michael] was mentally ill'.

Then within minutes everything changed. I sat there transfixed as a forensic scientist called to give evidence utterly destroyed the police's chain of assumptions in the course of a few sentences. Kwesi had been right all along. He knew his brother and believed what he had been told. Why would he believe otherwise?

James Munday, a forensics science investigator specialising in fire and explosions, testified that the nature of the spread of the flames consistent with the burns found on Michael meant that 'Michael Menson's jacket was ignited by a naked flame while he was lying down, the fire consuming most of the coat, before walking away... While I can't eliminate Michael Menson lit the back of his own clothes while lying down, that method would have been unique by my experience'.

Michael had been deliberately set on fire by an attacker or attackers. The fictional police narrative, built upon racist assumptions, instantly evaporated. The inquest jury returned a verdict of unlawful killing. The police were forced to belatedly open a high-level murder investigation and in December 1999 three men were found guilty of murder. They had come across Michael, robbed and assaulted him, taunted him, poured an accelerant on the back of his coat and set him on fire. One of the killers, Mario Pereira, on being questioned about the murder had replied 'So what, he was black'.

MALCOLM X STILL SPEAKS: NINE QUOTES

Kayla Renée Wheeler

Fifty-five years ago, Malcolm X, also known as El-Hajj Malik El-Shabazz, was assassinated. He was just 39 years old. In his short life, he inspired urban Black youth to resist the white supremacist structures that kept them oppressed and encouraged them to celebrate their African heritage. His message inspired other Black activists, including Kwame Ture and Maya Angelou, to promote Black empowerment and self-determination.

Towards the end of his life, Malcolm X embraced Sunni Islam, and travelled throughout the African continent, which led him to move away from Black nationalism and to embrace Pan-Africanism. In doing so, he connected the struggles of Black Americans with other Black diasporas and continental Africans. While the contemporary reimagining of Malcolm X's post-hajj life often presents him as post-racial, in truth, as his final days drew closer, Malcolm X continued to refine his analysis against white supremacy. He recognised that racism was a structural issue, rather than an interpersonal issue.

Malcolm X's criticism of white supremacy, his desire for solidarity among all people of colour, and his commitment to seeing marginalisation through a human rights framework rather than a civil rights framework remains relevant today, especially as people in the US and UK witness a rise in Islamophobia, renewed public conversations around anti-Black racism, and a resurgence of the far-right. Below are nine quotes from Malcolm X that still ring true in our contemporary context.

1. 'The press is so powerful in its image-making role, it can make a criminal look like he's the victim and make the victim look like he's the criminal. This is the press, an irresponsible press…If you aren't careful, the newspapers will have you hating the people who are being oppressed and loving the people who are doing the oppressing.'
(Speech at the Audubon Ballroom, December 13, 1964)

2. 'I have these very deep feelings that white people who want to join black organisations are really just taking the escapist way to salve their consciences. By visibly hovering near us, they are 'proving' that they are 'with us.' But the hard truth is this isn't helping to solve America's racist problem. The Negroes aren't the racists. Where the really sincere white people have got to do their 'proving' of themselves is not among the *black victims,* but out on the battle lines of where America's racism really is – and that's in their own home communities; America's racism is among their own whites. That's where the whites who really mean to accomplish something have got to work.'
(*The Autobiography of Malcolm X*, p.384)

3. 'The Muslim world is forced to concern itself, from the moral point of view in its own religious concepts, with the fact that our plight clearly involves the violation of our human rights. The Koran compels the Muslim world to take a stand on the side of those whose human rights are being violated, no matter what the religious persuasion of the victims is. Islam is a religion which concerns itself with the human rights of all mankind, despite race, colour, or creed.'
(Letter from Lagos, Nigeria, May 10, 1964)

4. You 'can't separate peace from freedom because no one can be at peace unless he has his freedom.'
(Prospects for Freedom in 1965, January 7, 1965)

5. 'We want freedom by any means necessary. We want justice by any means necessary. We want equality by any means necessary. We don't feel that in 1964, living in a country that is supposedly based upon freedom, and supposedly the leader of the free world, we don't think that we should

have to sit around and wait for some segregationist congressmen and senators and a President from Texas in Washington, D.C., to make up their minds that our people are due now some degree of civil rights.' (Organization for Afro-American Unity Rally, June 28, 1964)

6. 'I said that physically we Afro-Americans might remain in America, fighting for our Constitutional rights, but that philosophically and culturally we Afro-Americans badly needed to "return" to Africa—and to develop a working unity in the framework of Pan-Africanism.' (*The Autobiography of Malcolm X*, p.357)

7. 'The cords of bigotry and prejudice here can be cut with the same blade [on the African continent]. We have to keep that blade sharp and share it with one another.' (Interview with Gordon Parks, February 19, 1965)

8. 'It is impossible for capitalism to survive, primarily because the system of capitalism needs some blood to suck.... As the nations of the world free themselves, then capitalism has less victims, less to suck, and it becomes weaker and weaker. It's only a matter of time in my opinion before it will collapse completely.' (Interview with the *Young Socialist*, January 18, 1965)

9. The 'only real power a poor man in this country has is the power of the ballot.' (Interview with the *Young Socialist*, January 18, 1965)

CITATIONS

Introduction: What is the Muslim Atlantic? By Daniel Nilsson DeHanas and Peter Mandaville

The works mentioned include: Paul Gilroy, *The Black Atlantic: Modernity and Double Consciousness* (Verso, London, 1993); Hisham Aidi, *Rebel Music: Race, Empire, and the New Muslim Youth Culture* (Vintage, New York, 2014); Sohail Daulatzai, *Black Star, Crescent Moon: The Muslim International and Black Freedom Beyond America* (University of Minnesota Press, Minneapolis, 2012); and Patrick Bowen, *A History of Conversion to Islam in the United States, Volume 2: The African American Islamic Renaissance, 1920-1975* (Brill, Leiden, 2017). AbdoolKarim Vakil's 'British Values and the British Muslims', 2014 Keynote address to the Muslim Council of Britain, is republished on *OpenDemocracy*: https://www.opendemocracy.net/en/opendemocracyuk/british-values-and-british-muslims/

See also: Jason Idriss Sparkes, Challenging Global Coloniality from a Sufi Perspective', in Mohammad H. Faghfoory and Golan Dastagir, editors, *Sufism and Social Integration: Connecting Hearts, Crossing Boundaries* (Kazi Publications, Chicago, 2015).

Realising a Muslim Atlantic by Aisha Khan

Afroz, Sultana, 2003. 'Invisible Yet Invincible: The Muslim Ummah in Jamaica,' *Journal of Muslim Minority Affairs* 23(1): 211-222

Afroz, Sultana, 2007. '*As-Salaamu-Alaikum*: The Invincibility of Islam in Jamaican Heritage,' *Wadabagei* 10(2): 5-39.

Aidi, Hisham, and Manning Marable, 2009. 'Introduction: The Early Muslim Presence and its Significance,' in *Black Routes to Islam*, edited by Manning Marable and Hisham Aidi. pp. 1–14. New York: Palgrave Macmillan.

Austin, Allan D., 1997. *African Muslims in Antebellum America: Transatlantic Stories and Spiritual Struggles*. New York: Routledge.

Bilby, Kenneth, 2006. *True-born Maroons*. Kingston, Jamaica: Ian Randle.

Bilby, Kenneth, 2012. 'An (Un)natural Mystic in the Air: Images of Obeah in Caribbean Song.' In *Obeah and Other Powers: The Politics of Caribbean Religion and Healing*, edited by Diana Paton and Maarit Forde. pp. 45-79. Durham: Duke University Press.

Buck-Morss, Susan, 2009. *Hegel, Haiti, and Universal History*. Pittsburgh, PA: University of Pittsburgh Press.

Campbell, Carl 1974. Jonas Mohammed Bath and the Free Mandingos in Trinidad: The Question of their Repatriation to Africa 1831-1838. *Pan-African Journal* 7(2): 129-52.

Diouf, Sylviane, 2013. *Servants of Allah: African Muslims Enslaved in the Americas*. New York: New York University Press.

Geertz, Clifford, 1973. Religion as a Cultural System. In *The Interpretation of Cultures*. pp. 87-125. New York: Basic Books.

Gilroy, Paul, 1993. *The Black Atlantic: Modernity and Double Consciousness*. Cambridge: Harvard University Press.

Gilsenan, Michael, 1982. *Recognizing Islam: An Anthropologist's Introduction*. London: Croom Helm.

Grandin, Greg, 2014. *The Empire of Necessity: Slavery, Freedom, and Deception in the New World*. New York: Metropolitan Books.

Karam, John Tofiq, 2015. 'African Rebellion and Refuge on the Edge of Empire,' in *Crescent Over Another Horizon: Islam in Latin America, the Caribbean, and Latino USA*. María del Mar Logroño Narbona, Paulo Gabriel Hilu da Rocha Pinto, and John Tofik Karam, editors. pp. 46-62. Austin: University of Texas Press.

Khan, Aisha, 2015. 'Contours: Approaching Islam, Comparatively Speaking,' in *Islam and the Americas*, edited by Aisha Khan. pp. 23-45. Gainesville: University Press of Florida.

Khan, Aisha, 2012. 'Islam, Vodou, and the Making of the Afro-Atlantic,' *Nieuwe West Indian Gids/New West Indian Guide* 86 (1-2): 29-54.

Khan, Aisha, 2004. *Callaloo Nation: Metaphors of Race and Religious Identity among South Asians in Trinidad*. Durham: Duke University Press.

Khan, Aisha, 1997. 'Migration Narratives and Moral Imperatives: Local and Global in the Muslim Caribbean.' *Comparative Studies of South Asia, Africa, and the Middle East* 17(1): 127-144.

Khan, Aisha, 1995. 'Homeland, Motherland: Authenticity, Legitimacy, and Ideologies of Place among Muslims in Trinidad.' In *Nation and Migration: The Politics of Space in the South Asian Diaspora*. Peter van der Veer, editor. pp.93-131. Philadelphia: University of Pennsylvania Press.

Linebaugh, Peter, 1982, "All the Atlantic Mountains Shook'," *Labour/Le Travailleur* 10: 87-121.

Mazrui, Ali, 1990. 'Religious Alternatives in the Black Diaspora: From Malcolm X to the Rastafari,' *Caribbean Affairs* 3(1): 157-160.

Mintz, Sidney and Richard Price, 1992. *The Birth of African American Culture: An Anthropological Perspective*. Boston: Beacon.

Ouzgane, Lahoucine, 2006. *Islamic Masculinities*. London: Zed.

Reis, Joso Jose, 2001. Quilombos and Rebellions in Brazil. In *African Roots/American Cultures: Africa in the Creation of the Americas*. Sheila S. Walker, editor. pp. 301-313. Lanham, MA: Rowman and Littlefield.

Samaroo, Brinsley 1988. Early African and East Indian Muslims in Trinidad and Tobago. Paper presented at Conference on Indo-Caribbean History and Culture, May 9-11, Centre for Caribbean Studies, University of Warwick, Coventry, England.

Shivley, Kim, 2006. Looking for Identity in the Muslim World. *American Anthropologist* 108(3): 537-542.

Smith, Jane I., 2010. Islam in America. In *Muslims in the West After 9/11: Religion, Politics, and Law*. Jocelyne Cesari, editor. pp. 28-42. London: Routledge.

Toner, Jerry, 2013. *Homer's Turk: How Classics Shaped Ideas of the East*. Cambridge, MA: Harvard University Press.

Return to Almadies by Amandla Thomas-Johnson

For more on the colonial-era France CFA currencies used by fourteen African countries, see Fanny Pigeaud, 'And now get lost, France!', *Le Monde Diplomatique*, April 2020 and Ndongo Samba Sylla and Fanny Pigeaud, *Last Colonial Currency: The CFA Franc Story* (Pluto, London, 2020). There is an ongoing debate about the relative importance of Goree island to the slave trade overall, see Max Fisher, 'What Obama really saw at the "Door of No Return," a disputed memorial to the slave trade', *Washington Post*, 28 June 2013, https://www.washingtonpost.com/news/

worldviews/wp/2013/06/28/what-obama-really-saw-at-the-door-of-no-return-a-debunked-memorial-to-the-slave-trade/

For more on the debates around Pan-Africanism among African nations in the early 1960s see Immanuel Wallerstein, *Africa: The Politics of Independence and Unity* (University of Nebraska Press, Lincoln, 2005); on the young radical Omar Blondin Diop, see Florian Bobin, Omar Blondin Diop: 'Seeking Revolution in Senegal', *Review of African Political Economy* website, 18 March 2020; and Zachary Wright, 'Islam and Decolonization in Africa: The Political Engagement of a West Africa Muslim Community', *International Journal of African Historical Studies*, January 2013

For more on the legacy of Cheikh Anta Diop, see Boubacar Boris Diop, 'What African writers can learn from Cheikh Anta Diop', *Chimurenga Chronic*, 23 April 2019, https://chimurengachronic.co.za/what-african-writers-can-learn-from-cheikh-anta-diop/ and on Frantz Fanon's views on Senghor see Katie Kilroy-Marac, 'A Letter Unanswered', Africa is a country, 2 April 2020 https://africasacountry. com/2020/04/a-letter-unanswered; and on Senghor's cultural policies see Amandla Thomas-Johnson, 'Museum of Black Civilisations aims to "decolonise knowledge"', 5 December 2018 https://www.aljazeera. com/indepth/features/museum-black-civilisations-aims-decolonise-knowledge-181204221519936.html

For more on Malcolm X's "anti-plantation" politics see Hannibal Abdul-Shakur, Tanzeen R. Doha, and Isra Ibrahim, 'The Wolf and The Fox: Message from the Grassroots on American-Muslim Leadership', *Milestones Journal*, 23 July 2019 https://www.milestonesjournal.net/articles-homepage; and on his views towards the end of his life see Malcolm X and Alex Haley, *The Autobiography of Malcolm X* (Penguin, London, 2007); Manning Marable, *Malcolm X: A Life of Reinvention* (Allen Lane, London, 2011) and Maytha Alhassen, 'The "Three Circles" Construction Reading Black Atlantic Islam through Malcolm X's Words and Friendships', *Journal of Africana Religions*, Vol. 3, No. 1 http://www.jstor.org/stable/10.5325/jafrireli.3.1.0001

For more on the impact of Schedule 7 airport stop and search powers on the Muslim community, see Dan Sabbagh 'Detention of Muslims at UK ports and airports 'structural Islamophobia', *The Guardian*, 20 August, 2019, https://www.theguardian.com/news/2019/aug/20/detention-of-muslims -at-uk-ports-and-airports-structural-islamophobia

Closed Minds by Ahmed Younis

Timothy Winter's videos are available on YouTube; the 'The Salafi Fallacy' can be accessed here: https://www.youtube.com/watch?v=1MRXs5fqlXQ (April 21, 2012).

Imam Zaid Shakir's, 'New Islamic Directions' Facebook post on 'ISIS sex slaves and Islam' can be accessed at:
https://www.facebook.com/imamzaidshakir/posts/isis-sex-slaves-and-islamas-salaamu-alaikumtodays-new-york-times-nyt-article-hig/10153073698933359/

The quotes from Ibn Rajab al Hanbali, *Refutation of those who do not follow the four schools*, translated by Musa Furber Abu (Dhabi: Islamosaic 2016) is from p.4; from Maher Hathout, *In Pursuit of Justice* (Los Angeles: Muslim Public Affairs Council, 2006), p115; and Peter Pomerantsev, *This is not propaganda* (New York: Public Affairs books 2019), p. 130.

See also: Muhammad Al-Yacoubi, *Refuting ISIS*, (Herndon: Sacred Knowledge, 2006); Paulo Freire. *Pedagogy of the oppressed* (New York: Bloomsbury 1970); and Ahmed S. Younis, 'Muslim American Conscientizacao', in *Culturally Responsive Methodologies*, eds. Berryman, SooHoo & Nexin (London: Emerald: 2016), 127-142.

The Muslim International: Sohail Daulatzai in conversation with Peter Mandaville

For more on The Muslim Atlantic project, visit muslimatlantic.com. Lupe Fiasco's song, 'The Show Goes On' is available on YouTube. Sohail Daulatzai's *Black Star, Crescent Moon: The Muslim International and Black*

Freedom Beyond America is published by University of Minnesota Press (2012). See also: Michael Hardt and Antonio Negri, *Empire* (Harvard University Press, 2001).

Terrorism by Tahir Abbas

Abbas, Tahir (2011) *Islamic Radicalism and Multicultural Politics: The British Experience*, London: Routledge.

Abbas, Tahir (2019) *Islamophobia and Radicalisation: A Vicious Cycle*, London: Hurst

Dorling, Danny and Tomlinson, Sally (2019) *Rule Britannia: Brexit and the End of Empire*, London: Biteback.

Ebner, Julia (2017) *The Rage: The Vicious Circle of Islamist and Far-Right Extremism*, London: IB Tauris.

Elshimi, Mohammed S. (2017) *De-Radicalisation in the UK Prevent Strategy: Security, Identity and Religion*, London: Routledge.

Kimmel, Michael (2013) *Angry White Men: American Masculinity at the End of an Era*, New York: Bold Type.

Kundnani, Arun (2014) *The Muslims are Coming!: Islamophobia, Extremism, and the Domestic War on Terror*, London: Verso.

Leiken, Robert S. (2012) *Europe's Angry Muslims: The Revolt of The Second Generation*, New York: Oxford University Press

Rattansi, Ali (2007), *Racism: A Very Short Introduction*, Oxford: Oxford University Press.

Rex, John (1988) *The Ghetto and the Underclass*, Aldershot: Gower.

Traveller by Zahrah Nesbitt-Ahmed

For more on world music, see Mark Slobin, *Global Soundtracks: Worlds of Film Music,* Wesleyan University Press, 2008; Janet Sturman, editor, *The SAGE International Encyclopedia of Music and Culture*, Sage, London, 2019. On the genre of Hausa Music and the different categories of Hausa music and musicians, see Tara F. Deubel, Scott M. Youngstedt, Hélène Tissière, editors, *Saharan Crossroads: Exploring Historical, Cultural, and Artistic Linkages,* Cambridge Scholars Publishing, 2014, and Brian Larkin, *Signal and Noise: Media, Infrastructure, and Urban Culture in Nigeria*, Duke University Press,

2008. And on Caribbean music, see *Music in Latin America and the Caribbean: An Encyclopedic History* REANNOUNCE / F05: Volume 2: Performing the Caribbean Experience edited by Kuss, Malena University of Texas Press.

See also: G Nisbett, 'Calypso Music in St Kitts', https://www.sknvibes.com/islandfacts/sitepage.cfm?p=165
'Do the limbo! How the Windrush brought a dance revolution to Britain' https://www.theguardian.com/culture/2002/jun/28/nottinghillcarnival2002.nottinghillcarnival

White Muslims, Black Muslims by Juliette Galonnier

The data for this article comes from two different yet interrelated research projects: my ethnographic and interview study on conversions to Islam (*Choosing Faith and Facing Race: Converting to Islam in France and the United States*, PhD dissertation, Sciences Po and North-Western University, 2017); and a research project on Muslims of Sub-Saharan and Comorian descent in France and the way they position themselves in the French Islamic landscape conducted by me and Mahamet Timéra (*Les musulmans d'origine subsaharienne et comorienne dans le paysage islamique français,* Bureau Central des Cultes du Ministère de l'Intérieur, Paris, 2020).
The quote from Malcom X is from *The Autobiography of Malcolm X* (Penguin, London, 1999, pp 346-347, original 1964).
Other sources include: Babgy Ihsan, *The American Mosque 2011: Basic Characteristics of the American Mosque, Attitudes of Mosque Leaders* (Washington, CAIR, 2012).
Diallo Rokhaya, "Il y a une vraie invisibilité des musulmans non arabes en France'", *Saphir News*, April 18th 2011, https://www.saphirnews.com/Rokhaya-Diallo-Il-y-a-une-vraie-invisibilite-des-musulmans-non-arabes-en-France_a12458.html
Diouf Sylviane, "Invisible Muslims: the Sahelians in France", in *Muslim Minorities in the West: Visible and Invisible*, eds Yvonne Yazbeck Haddad and Jane I. Smith (Walnut Creek, Altamira Press, 2002), 145-160.
Gallup Coexist Foundation, *Muslim Americans: A National Portrait* (Washington, Gallup Consulting University Press, 2009).

Garner Steve and Selod Saher, "The Racialization of Muslims: Empirical Studies of Islamophobia", *Critical Sociology* 41, 1 (2015): 9-19.

Grandhomme Hélène, "Connaissance de l'islam et pouvoir colonial : l'exemple de la France au Sénégal 1936-1957", *French Colonial History*, 10 (2009) : 171-188.

Grewal Zareena, *Islam is a Foreign Country: American Muslims and the Global Crisis of Authority* (New York, New York University Press, 2013).

Jackson Sherman, *Islam and the Blackamerican: Looking Toward the Third Resurrection* (Oxford, Oxford University Press, 2005).

Laurence Jonathan and Vaïsse Justin, *Intégrer l'islam. La France et ses musulmans : enjeux et réussites* (Paris, Odile Jacob, 2007).

Malcolm X and Haley Alex, *The Autobiography of Malcolm X* (New York, Ballantine Books, 1999 [1964]).

Meer Nasar, "Racialization and Religion: Race, Culture and Difference in the Study of Antisemitism and Islamophobia", *Ethnic and Racial Studies* 36, 3 (2013): 385-398.

Mohammed Marwan and Hajjat Abdellali, *Islamophobie: Comment les élites françaises fabriquent le 'problème' musulman* (Paris, La Découverte, 2013).

Pew Research Center, "Five Facts about the Muslim Population in Europe" (Washington, Pew Research Center, 2016).

Pew Research Center, *A New Estimate of the U.S. Muslim Population* (Washington, Pew Research Center, 2016).

Robinson David, *Paths of Accommodation: Muslim Societies and French Colonial Authorities in Senegal and Mauritania, 1880-1920* (Athens, Ohio University Press, 2000).

Sambe Bakary, "Musulmans d'origine 'subsaharienne' dans l'islam de France : contre un paternalisme d'un nouveau genre", *Saphir News*, June 10th, 2011 (https://www.saphirnews.com/Musulmans-d-origine-subsaharienne-dans-l-islam-de-France-contre-un-paternalisme-d-un-nouveau-genre_a12731.html

Triaud Jean-Louis, "L'islam au sud du Sahara. Une saison orientaliste en Afrique occidentale. Constitution d'un champ scientifique, héritages et transmissions", *Cahiers d'études africaines* 2/3/4, n°198/199/200 (2010) : 907-950.

Dangerous Ideas by Abdul-Rehman Malik

The work of scholars mentioned in the article include: Paul Gilroy, *Black Atlantic: Modernity and Double Consciousness* (Verso, London, 1993), the quotes are from p19 and p4 respectively; Sylviane A. Diouf, *Servants of Allah: African Muslims Enslaved in the Americas* (New York University Press, 1998); Hisham Adid, *Rebel Music: Race, Empire, and the New Muslim Youth Culture* (Vintage, London, 2014); Jeff Chang, *Cant' Stop Won't Stop: A History of Hip Hop Generations* (St Martin's Press, New York, 2005); Walter Rodney, *The Groundings With My Brother* (Verso, London, 2019); and Salman Rushdie, *Imaginary Homelands* (Granta, London, 1992). Su'ad Abdul Khabeer, *Muslim Cool: Race, Religion and Hip Hop in the United States* (NYU Press, New York, 2016); Sylvia Chan-Malik, *Being Muslim: A Cultural History of Women of Color in American Islam* (NYU Press, New York, 2018); Sohail Daulatzai, *Black Star, Crescent Moon: The Muslim International and Black Freedom Beyond America* (University of Minnesota Press, Minneapolis, 2012). Amir Sulaiman's poem 'Danger' can be heard on YouTube. The work of Asad Ali Jafri can be found at www.asadalijafri.com.

Black Radicalism by Rasul Miller

The remarks in this essay were originally delivered as an oral address during a workshop titled 'Race and Securitization in the Muslim Atlantic' as part of the fifth annual British Islam conference held in London, UK on February 22-23 February 2020. It has been edited here for greater clarity. On Moorish Science Temple of America, see Tauheedah Najee-Ullah El, editor and complier, *Califa Uhuru: A Compilation of Literature from the Moorish Science Temple of America* (Moorish Science Temple of America, 2014); On Marcus Garvey, see Amy Jacques Garvey, *The Philosophy and Opinions of Marcus Garvey* (Routledge, London, 1977); and on the Nation of Islam, see Ammar Abduh Aqeeli, *The Nation of Islam and Black Consciousness* (Peter Lang, New York, 2019); and Dawn-Marie Gibson and Jamillah Karim, *Women of the Nation: Between Black Protest and Sunni Islam* (New York University Press, 2014). Some background on Muhammad Ezaldeen is provided on the blog by El Aemer El Mujaddid, 'Ezaldeen,

Muhammad a.k.a. Lomax Bey Founder Of The Addeynu Allahe Universal Arabic Association' at: https://murakushsociety.org/ezaldeen-muhammad-a-k-a-lomax-bey-founder-of-the-addeynu-allahe-universal-arabic-association/

See also: H. Rap Brown, *Die Nigger Die: A Political Autobiography* (Chicago Press Review, 2002); Jules Archer, *The Had a Dream: The Civil Rights Struggle from Frederick Douglas to Marcus Garvey to Martin Luther King and Malcolm X* (Puffin, London, 1996); and Sherrow O Pinder, *Black Political Thought* (Cambridge University Press, 2019)

Security by Shirin Khan

The interactive map detailing anti-Muslim activities in the US can be examined at: https://www.newamerica.org/in-depth/anti-muslim-activity
The report form Hope Not Hate can be found at: https://www.hopenothate.org.uk/wp-content/uploads/2019/02/state-of-hate-2019-final-1.pdf

Echoes Across the Pond by C Scott Jordan

To learn more about the London Mayoral Election that didn't happen see Maire Rose Connor, 'Everything you need to know about the London Mayoral Elections,' *Londonist*. 5 February, 2020. https://londonist.com/london/politics/everything-you-need-to-know-about-the-2020-london-mayoral-election; For more on Obama's war against the Alt-Right, see 'Frontline: America's Great Divide (Part 1 and 2),' *PBS*. Premiered 14 January, 2020; also see Ta-Nehisi Coates, *We Were Eight Years in Power: An American Tragedy* (One World, London, 2017); For more on Malcolm X and his Hajj Realisation, see Malcolm X and Alex Haley, *The Autobiography of Malcolm X* (Grove Press, New York, 1965).

Black Female Muslim Emcees by Aina Khan

Su'ad Abdul Khabeer's *Muslim Cool: Race, Religion and Hip Hop in the United States* is published by New York University Press (2016). See also her article, 'Rep that Islam: The Rhyme and Reason of American Islamic Hip-Hop' *The Muslim World* 97 125-141 (2007)

On Lauryn Hill, see Joan Morgan, *She Begat This: 20 Years of Miseducation of Lauryn Hill* (Atria Books, 2018). See also: Carolyn Moxley Rouse, *Engaged Surrender: African American Women and Islam* (University of California Press, 2004) and Anaya McMuray, 'Hotep and Hip-Hop: Can Black Muslim Women Be Doum with Hip-Hop?' *Meridians* 8 (1) 74-82 2008.

To listen to the music of the artists discussed in this article, see:
Trumped by Ain't Afraid,
https://m.youtube.com/watch?v=XuyiXQrliM8
Black Heroes by Alia Sharrief and Aminah Bell,
https://m.youtube.com/watch?v=QZJub-2fYho
Land Far Away by Poetic Pilgrimage,
https://m.youtube.com/watch?v=-mdLvy8o1cU
QKnowledge by Boshia Rae Jean,
https://m.youtube.com/watch?v=G41IAlPgV2M

CONTRIBUTORS

Tahir Abbas is Assistant Professor, Leiden University in The Hague ●
Sohail Daulatzai explores the after-lives of empire across theory, history,
film, sound, and the curatorial. He teaches at the University of California,
Irvine and lives in Los Angeles ● **Daniel Nilsson DeHanas** is Senior
Lecturer in Political Science and Religion at King's College London ●
Reginald Edmund is Managing Curating Producer at Black Lives, Black
Words International Project, Chicago, Illinois ● **Naomi Foyle** is a well-
known science fiction writer ● **Juliette Galonnier** is Assistant Professor at
CERI, Sciences Po, Paris ● **C Scott Jordan**, philosopher and futurist, is
Deputy Editor of *Critical Muslim* ● **Emre Kazim** is a digital ethicist based in
the department of Computer Science, University College London ● **Aina
Khan**, journalist and playwright, showcased her first play *Pashto Thriller* at
Bradford Literature Festival in 2018 ● **Aisha Khan** is Associate Professor at
New York University ● **Shirin Khan** is an independent contractor and
security expert ● **Hassan Mahamdallie**, Arts Consultant and Theatre
Creative, is a senior editor of *Critical Muslim* ● **Abdul-Rehman Malik** is a
Lecturer at Yale University School of Divinity and Founding Program Manager
of Radical Middle Way ● **Ronnie Malley**, multi-instrumentalist musician,
theatrical performer, producer, and educator, is a faculty member at the
Chicago Academy for the Arts ● **Peter Mandaville** is Professor of
Government and Politics in the Schar School of Policy and Government at
George Mason University, Virginia ● **Rasul Miller** is a William Fontaine
fellow of Africana Studies and History at the University of Pennsylvania ●
Zahrah Nesbitt-Ahmed is a Gender & Development Research Manager
currently based in Florence, Italy ● **Sameer Rahim**, Managing Editor (Arts
& Books) at *Prospect* Magazine, is the author of the novel *Asghar and Zahra* ●
Samia Rahman is the Director of the Muslim Institute ● **Tamim Sadikali**
is a reviewer and author of the novel *Dear Infidel* ● **Amandla Thomas-
Johnson** is a Senegal-based journalist who covers West Africa for Aljazeera
English and Middle East Eye ● **Mosab Abu Toha**, a poet and writer from
Palestine, currently a Fellow at Harvard, founded the Edward Said Library,
Gaza's first English-language library ● **Kayla Renée Wheeler** is Assistant
Professor of Area & Global Studies and Digital Studies at Grand Valley State
University ●**Tanya Muneera Williams** is one half of the hip-hop duo Poetic
Pilgrimage ● **Ahmed Younis** is Assistant Professor at Attallah College of
Education, Chapman University and Former Principal Deputy Assistant
Secretary of State, Department of State, US.

CRITICAL MUSLIM 35, SUMMER 2020